Advance Praise

"Kitchi Feenix writes, poignantly, of life — her life — her *prevailing* life. With words she breathes tender care, honesty, and reclamation into *her* story. The following pages are her testament to the power of unearthing one's truth; a resonance, ceaselessly pulsating through time and space to reach listener and non-listener alike, never to be buried nor discarded."

—Madison McMillion

"Rarely do we hear a true depiction of the untold stories of women that served in combat. Women are unfortunately subjected to those like Kitchi's journey. *Discarded* goes into details of incidents on how "entrusted" therapists have little clue of where one comes from and what we have been through. Those who join the military have been abused, and some abuse while on duty. A hidden truth. A must read! Therapeutic."

—Rosa-La Pastora, U.S. Army (ret.)
female combat veteran, BS, MS

"A traumatic yet powerful page turning read. These vulnerable experiences are a brave reminder of how important it is to find your "why" to heal and hold everyone's presence as sacred and safe. When reading the series of events hopping through her life, the traumatic and painful stories make the happy and empowering moments all the more sweet.

Every therapist should read this powerful read for immersion into lived experience of the challenges one faces as an orphan, a woman in the military to veteran coping with post traumatic effects of sexual assault and violence, and a single mother breaking the cycle—and in Kitchi's case, all of the above. The flickering sweet moments, witty sarcasm, very real telling of difficult life stories and the need to find how she survives in her next chapter of life are what keeps you turning the pages."

—M.L., BS, CTRS

Discarded

Discarded

A True Account of How Abandonment, Abuse, and Control Became a Journey of Finding Purpose

Kitchi Feenix

Published
by Do Good Get Good Publishing

DO GOOD GET GOOD
PUBLISHING

Discarded: A True Account of How Abandonment, Abuse, and Control Became a Journey of Finding Purpose
Published by Do Good Get Good Publishing
San Diego, California, U.S.A.

FEENIX, KITCHI, Author
DISCARDED
KITCHI FEENIX

Library of Congress Control Number: 2024905631

ISBN: 979-8-9902973-0-2, 979-8-9902973-2-6 (paperback)
ISBN: 979-8-9902973-3-3 (hardcover)
ISBN: 979-8-9902973-1-9 (digital)

PSYCHOLOGY / Psychopathology / Post-Traumatic Stress Disorder (PTSD)
BIOGRAPHY & AUTOBIOGRAPHY / Military
HEALTH & FITNESS / Work-Related Health
FAMILY & RELATIONSHIPS / Dysfunctional Families

Editing: Lisa Shrewsberry (getfinelines.weebly.com)
Interior & eBook Design: Amit Dey (amitdey2528@gmail.com)
Publishing Management: Susie Schaefer (finishthebookpublishing.com)

Dedication

My heart, my loves, my girls.

Table of Contents

Foreword

In the traumatic landscape of military service, there exists an often unspoken and invisible challenge—military sexual trauma (MST) and post-traumatic stress disorder (PTSD). As a society, we owe a debt of gratitude to those who have bravely served our country, and it is our responsibility to address and support the unique burdens carried by those who have experienced this form of trauma. The journey through trauma and the challenges it presents can often be a lonely, confusing experience.

This book stands as an encouragement of validation, unity, and understanding, providing a voice to those whose stories may have gone unheard for too long. These pages aim to foster empathy, educate, and advocate for those who have been impacted by military sexual trauma (MST) and Post-Traumatic Stress disorder (PTSD).

As a mental health professional, I have borne witness to the resilience and profound strength of those who have survived such unimaginable experiences, and to the impact of PTSD and MST on individuals and their loved ones. It is with unwavering dedication that I lend my voice to this crucial conversation, with the hope that this book provides comfort, validation, and actionable support to survivors and their allies.

It is my sincere wish that as a society, we no longer turn a blind eye to the enduring impact of MST and PTSD and female veterans in general. May this book serve as a compound for change—a tangible symbol of our collective commitment to understanding, intervention, and support of those who have carried the weight of such trauma. Within these pages, you will find insights that shed light on the far-reaching effects of trauma. More importantly, you will discover a story of resilience, recovery, and the human spirit's capacity to heal.

My hope is that this book will serve as a source of comfort and knowledge, fostering a sense of community and understanding but also providing female veterans with validation and companionship they once lost due to the aftermath of trauma. It is a testament to the strength of the human soul and how difficult it can be to reach out for help and gain the appropriate services deserved without being further traumatized. This book is a collective journey through trauma and gives you a feeling that none of us are truly alone.

Kitchi's story is raw and real and shows the struggles of a female veteran, including those experiences they may have carried within themselves since birth; her narrative is a true example of resilience. It is not only a good read for veterans but for those who work with veterans or have veterans in their lives. If one has not been through these struggles or served in the military, one can never fully understand, but reading this book can offer a piece of understanding of what someone suffering with PTSD and MST encounters. It is also important to recognize that we, as professionals, can cause more harm than good, and it's important to recognize what Kitchi went through in trying to find the help she deserved. There are very few books written by and for female veterans to help them throughout service and after transitioning into civilian life with these traumas.

Writing is a therapeutic way to put thoughts and stories down on paper and I recommend everyone to write their story down to "get it out" for therapeutic purposes, but also to help others. Writing a life story can be a powerful way to explore your past, understand your present, and shape your future. It offers time for self-reflection, emotional release, a sense of accomplishment, and shared wisdom— all of which can lead to personal growth and leave a meaningful legacy for future generations. We all have a story to tell, and each one is important.

I end this foreword offering a message of hope and support for those who have experienced trauma. I express gratitude for the courage and sacrifices made by military personal and their families. As you turn the pages within *Discarded*, may you remember that seeking help is a sign of strength, not weakness and that your feelings are valid. To all those who have carried the burden of military trauma or childhood trauma, may this book serve as a testament to your courage, and a beacon of hope for a brighter, healthier future. Thank you all for your service and sacrifice. My hope to all is that you never feel *Discarded* again.

—Sydney Shrewsberry, MSW, LGSW

Introduction

*Y*ou are about to dive into a collection of thoughts and memories from my past. Warning—there are triggers scattered throughout. I did not have any control over this—it is my life. I wish I were exaggerating or forming the skeleton for a screenplay in a Lifetime movie. This is my unscripted reality show. Scattered optimism with self-care avenues which took years to find and appreciate. Finding what puzzle piece gently fits into place. This will be ongoing and revolving, and I am trying my best to be open to work and to "feel". After twenty years of my trauma from the military and a lifetime of feeling discarded, it is time, my time, to be open and discuss my story. It has been freeing to write. These funny little letters swirling in the universe have brought me into a better place. Together, these letters that fell into the right place made it possible for me to tell my truth, be honest, and work through the footsteps of my past. I am tired of being hushed, degraded, pushed away—a constant in my life: discarded (definition: to get rid of someone or something as no longer useful or desirable). I'm exhausted from apologizing for my story. The road has been long. By no means is this a step-by-step or self-help instruction. Or a guide to follow. I wish I had the answers to the age-old questions of the meaning of life and the one thing that will help all mankind. For me it has been self-discovery, a long path of trying new things, being open to trying, and having the mindfulness to stay safely in the moment. Feeling the discomfort and calming my survival mode of flight. My life unravels not so politely and is written to unload the strings and weights that have been attached since birth. Questions I have... they may never be answered. For example: can I truly accept that this is what was given to me? Is this a curse? Why did the obstacles come to me? What was their purpose? Is there a purpose?

I am writing to free my overloaded mind and release these events that I have felt for decades. Hoping to unwind the tangles. Unfolding the deepest, darkest thoughts. Put the trauma in a box, duct tape any chance of release, and bury it deep in the Earth. It will always be there, but at least it won't be the most primary emotions I feel. I want to find my smile again.

CHAPTER 1

a moment of thoughts

Quotes from my youth that I remember, revealing that words do hurt:

"At least my mom wanted me..." - *from an elementary classmate*

"I never wanted you..." - *adoptive "mom"*

"She is dirty, she doesn't shower..." - *from an elementary classmate who thought because my skin is brown, I was dirty? Sigh. The glorious 1980s.*

"Shut up bean burrito..." - *teased an elementary classmate.*

"What are you black or brown?" - *ignorance from a group of students on a school bus when I was in elementary school.*

"Bastard..." - *adoptive "mom"*

"Take her back..." - *adoptive "mom"*

"Your (real) mom was a whore..." - *adoptive "mom"*

"I know these girls are different..." - *2nd grade teacher while I stood in front of class with another student of color after being teased.*

"I'm going to kill you nigger..." - *grown white males yelling at me, three males swerving into my lane, red truck, making me go to the side of the road as I was driving in my car (1999).*

"I don't care if you get shot in the face, you signed up..." - *adoptive "mom" (referring to a dinner where I gave my will and power of attorney to my adoptive parents, who took care of my one-year-old daughter while I was deployed for Operation Iraqi Freedom).*

*M*ost days, I struggle to not remember these statements, to not repeat them. The emotions bubble up as I speak. My voice pauses and I stammer over words that refuse to be spoken. At times, it's a quiet moment of letting the horror settle in and the listeners try not to get melancholy by the incidents of my life, or at times, tearing up when I am done sharing a snippet of my story. I'm grateful to be at this point, though, where now my story can be told. There isn't the stuck-in-the-throat emotion anymore. It's me, it's mine. I don't know any other story. The therapeutic feeling after writing has been my savior. I can liquefy the keys on the computer, tapping, being in tune with each press, releasing the emotional valve. Not avoiding my pain but tapping into the freedom to let out these events without interruption or judgment. Through the unfortunate outcome of events, the trauma, over time the constant beating of negativity grew—low self-esteem and dark thoughts. These ugly souls who themselves are deeply hurting, rooted their negativity elsewhere. I just wish I wasn't the casualty of their faults.

It has also been over twenty years since I took the oath for this country I love. Signing a contract to serve in the military. Fourteen years and counting since I honored my full enlistment and was honorably discharged. Now, my resume of adjectives consists of being a combat veteran, a sergeant, logistics specialist, certified combat lifesaver, deployed for Operation Iraqi Freedom, college graduate, mother of two daughters. But with these qualifications came sacrifice. My life has been summed up in a whirlwind of anger, alcohol, drugs in my youth, depression, anxiety, suicidal thoughts multiple times a day, multiple mild TBIs (which translates in my body's response as daily headaches, migraines, and nausea), short-term memory loss, OCD (obsessive compulsive disorder), service-connected PTSD (post-traumatic stress disorder), MST (military sexual trauma) and unfortunately, so on. It has only been a few years since I finally was seen at the VA—over twelve years after I was out of the military—not knowing the rules of being a female veteran and who was able to be seen. I thought I had to have a limb amputated to be able to receive treatment; I did not know my invisible wounds were also a priority. I wish I knew so that the previous decades would not have been so spiraling.

This journey of my patriotic duty left me depleted. I'm discovering my own process of healing now. I reached out to a variety of veteran organizations, trying to be social; I tried weekly chats with my therapist, en route to learning how to use coping mechanisms other than locking myself within my four walls, letting life pass me by. My battled mind constantly falls back, whirling those negative thoughts and giving isolation and avoidance their voices. It's then that I take a few steps backwards and regain a small momentum forward at the slow-crawl pace.

Though I have struggled through the years, I can have a conversation with a veteran of any branch and quickly develop a foul-mouthed roster of funny stories involving horrific scenes sarcastically recalled. Humor and crude behavior: it is the best for coping. There is an understanding of brotherhood and sisterhood that will never be taken away. Talking shit and making it fun. If there is someone who just doesn't get the humor or is completely astonished by how many F-bombs come out of a greeting, we will not be able to relate. I would never want it to change. Our military bond is a "drop the mic" motion. I will never have the word "veteran" taken from me. I proudly served. I was honored to serve.

CHAPTER 2

what is it about me?

Quick, heavy anxiety. My chest gets tight, I start to sweat, get hot, the feeling of being quickly overwhelmed and breathing is difficult. It happens at a moment's notice. Not a scheduled or welcomed feeling. Sitting down, eating at my dining table, lying on my bed; even when there is peace, my anxiety will envelop me. Then the fast, dark thoughts of *I'm going to faint or die or need to go somewhere, anywhere* spreads through my veins. Unable to sit. Pacing around my home. Feeling like I need to run, but my legs can't move. Trying not to hyperventilate. Remembering in the past there is no coming back from spots of black and white that will devour my vision—fainting is the final step. Most days are spent trying to calm restless thoughts. Reminders of my military service. Reaching out for help has been a journey by itself. I think of an incident from a pamphlet that I picked up at the local VA (Veterans Affairs) clinic and scanned the schedule for different classes on a variety of triggers. Looked for a drop-in class to attend. These groups can give some relief and do not need weeks of prior approval. I have noticed a few VAs are set up the same; as you walk in the building, a couple of volunteers will scan you over and say hello. I really don't want to talk to anyone and give a short, quick grin. Just to make it through the awkward stares. So that step is done. I continue the walk of shame directly to the first office lobby with a huge sign and reminder of what's wrong with me: MENTAL HEALTH. Not a welcoming sign. A civilian marketing team should sweep through the VA and collectively agree to make this experience not seem so dire. An idea of names— Mental Spa, Brain Retreat, or Relaxation Resort— come to mind. Inside my local VA it is gloomy with outdated maroon décor filled with wooden, lightly padded chairs surrounding the walls. A small display, almost empty, racks of pamphlets and flyers of services given. One reception desk that rarely has any correct information.

"Last name and last four, please. Thank you. Take a seat."

This group I made it to was for healing and a workshop with a curriculum. I really needed something to focus on and make healing the forefront. I thought I would be welcomed. Of course, there are some obstacles to joining some classes. Most VA classes, you need a psychologist to make the recommendation. The only problem is that these needed classes should be given if a veteran walks into the office. Period. We are there for a reason. I don't have a PTSD schedule and cannot pre-plan my episodes.

As I sat in this lobby and looked at other faces consumed with suicidal thoughts, addiction, depression, self-harm scars, and a long list of the effects of our military service, the feeling of "we are not in Kansas anymore, Toto" is evident. A scattered collection of veterans can be seen figuratively "peacocking" their service ribbons and unit names by their mere presence and lip smacking while looking at each other. Making others think about their time in service was not as important. Like clockwork, there is consistently someone arguing at the check-in about a cancellation or there is some PTSD-infused interaction. It is cringy to witness the rage and, often, strange chuckling from the madness that is happening. Then when the tables are turned, I know for a fact when I am in that state, look out! My "sergeant" tone of confidence will make things happen. And the cycle continues. The chaos of service-connected pain keeps on.

One-by-one we filed back into the windowless room. We all sat down in a small circle. Six males, and then me. The VA representative was an older woman with a hippie-inspired shoulder wrap, old thick black leather strapped sandals, with socks and loads of clinging bracelets that rattled as she wrote her name on the dry erase board. The sound of bracelets like hers annoy me to this day. She asked us to introduce ourselves and describe some effects of our service. There was one highly overactive male who could not sit still in his chair. He eagerly went first with name, branch, depression, anxiety. The same happened around the circle. Everyone introduced themselves. Told their diagnosis. Then, it was my turn. Name, branch, and my list. This highly overactive veteran screamed out, "Why is the Army here?" The overly excited male was a former Marine whose loud mouth suggested the Army is somehow weaker, lower. This assumption is very common when joking within the branches. Most times, it is a funny back-and-forth, witty or sarcastic exchange. The Marines can be called dumb, asked not to eat crayons, or dished out USMC (Uncle Sam's Misguided Children) comments. It is a common, innocent rivalry within the branches to make fun of each other. The uniform differences alone can start a long conversation. Sometimes the Army is described as an acronym: A.R.M.Y. (Ain't Ready to be a Marine Yet), or U.S. Army (Uncle Sam Ain't Released Me Yet). Always ridiculed for the patches we wear with pride. This banter has been going on since the infancy of the branches. Pride in one's branch will always be defended. At the end of the bickering, generally, common ground can be found. We all served, took the oath to defend our country. Brothers and sisters in arms.

Unfortunately, this particular male didn't get the memo on how to not be a total asshole. He took it to the extreme, delivered his venom not in a flirtatious manner nor with a laugh, but with a locked, on-target, direct stare. He seemed to take no notice that this was a mental health group for combat veterans and not a bar. We all had the same qualifications to be in this group. I looked in horror and scanned the room to see if anyone else would speak up. Not a soul. All quickly just glanced down at the floor or ignored the hurtful outburst. Just a few quick side looks, but everyone sat still, arms crossed. I raised my hand, looking dead into his eyes, and told him specifically that I also had anger issues and told him to "shut the fuck up." I got out of my chair, pushing the door angrily, with intention, and ran out of the room. I cried as soon as I got in my car. This representative said nothing and did nothing. Her job was to keep the group in a safe environment, techniques should have been enforced to de-escalate the negative and volatile situation. It took a lot for me to join this group and get out of my small bubble of safety. She failed me.

Discarded. Not welcome. What is it about me?

What I did not know is this representative called the local police department on me for leaving the group. It was within an hour of leaving, and I was trying to forget the complete disaster of group therapy. I needed the help and had reached out trying to learn new coping skills. At the time, I was pulling into my driveway with both of my daughters. I couldn't believe it. Right behind me in my driveway, a tiny cul-de-sac. Neighbors' eyes on me. A cop car and the lights fully glowing in my rearview mirrors. I drove into my garage and told the girls to go inside. The officers got out and simultaneously shut their doors with cautious eyes and gentle steps towards me, walking cautiously, which only got me irritated. They asked, "Is your name Kitchi Feenix?" I responded affirmatively, annoyed. They went on to give me a series of questions asking if I was sad and or if "I had a plan to kill myself," all while grabbing onto their belt at-the-ready. This wasn't a robbery or hostage negotiation. They needed to relax. I explained the incident from the VA group. They asked again "if I had a plan to hurt myself"; I said "no." Again, I told them I left the group because of a male who yelled at me like an asshole. I didn't want to be there and left. All the while this VA representative did nothing. The officers left.

This incident would not be the last incident with this unfortunate VA representative. I needed help with the triggers of PTSD. I also needed these drop-in group sessions…

Months later, after convincing myself I needed to go back, I tried it again. I signed up for another group for combat veterans learning ways to restore mental health and wellness. Hoping this time, it would be a safe, supportive environment. As I scanned the description for the class:

Combat stress: sleep problems, lack of energy, poor concentration, jumpy, anxiety, withdrawn. Yes, that's me...checklist done.

I was there to learn. Same bland waiting room, side-eyes, and scoping out the other veterans in this group. Luckily, that former Marine was not there. I told myself if I saw him, I'd just leave. But my soul wanted to beat the shit out of him. Again, all called back, single file, walking on the right side of the hallway. Just as the military ingrained in us. Some faults that may never leave include the way we walk, never walking on the grass, always using the pathway. Don't put your hands in your pockets. If you did so, boot camp drill sergeants would run up to you, tell you to "drop" for pushups or yell into your face and ask, "Hey pri (private)! Do you think you're back on the block, smoking and joking?" Translation: You aren't back home and doing what you want; you're mine now. All with punishment. So, over twenty years later, just the casual nuance of walking down a hallway can bring back some memories. We filed back. Another institutional-like room. This one surrounded by one wall of ceiling-to-floor wooden lockers and a group of chairs. A group of eight males and me. Not very good odds, again. The VA representative was the same unfortunate one I had before! Shit. Stay calm. Will she apologize for calling the cops for a 5150 (the welfare and institutions code which allows an adult who is experiencing mental crisis to be detained for a 72-hour psychiatric hospitalization) call? For her not paying attention to the group and letting it be like a scene from the movie *The Purge*—complete anarchy and verbal attacks on an individual? I almost walked out immediately. But my stubbornness kept me in. This group sat patiently to have a chance to be in a safe environment, to share struggles. I, on the other hand, sat with anger fuming throughout my body. Couldn't wait to see how she took control of this group! I sat down. She would occasionally glance at me. There were those bracelets again; the count had to be doubled and now on both arms, this time to almost mid-arm. The clanging as she wrote her name falling up and down. Did she remember me? Or was she confused as to why there was a female there?

In my mind...a dark, sinister voice. It went a little like: "Hey you, remember me? You called the cops on me. You better fucking pay attention to everyone in the group. I didn't do shit and was bullied and if I hear those fucking bracelets keep jingling, I will leap over the chairs and strangle you with that oversized scarf."

But I digress. Was anger a qualifying factor for this group? It sure as hell was.

We all sat and gave slow, smirking side smiles looking at each other. This lady sat down with a packet of papers and looked at me again. She spoke to the group while only looking at me.

"I want to remind you all that this class is only for combat veterans, not for MST." Military sexual trauma refers to sexual assault or sexual harassment experienced during military service. MST includes any sexual activity during military service in which you are involved against your will or when unable to say no. Being pressured or coerced, being overpowered, being touched, grabbed, comments on your body, hazing experiences, unwanted and threatening advances. MST applies to all genders.

Okay, really? Why do you have to stare at me? Make me not feel comfortable in a group that I belong in? Can you move on, lady? My blood was boiling at that time. Waiting for her to speak again, not wanting me to be in this group. She did not bother to look at anyone else while she pointed me out. She would have never given that ignorant speech if the class was only male.

Again, before the class started, she looked at me.

Repeated her statement, glancing at me, again.

I couldn't believe it! Why do I have to carry my VA list of qualifications wherever I go? I'm here for help. I am a combat veteran with service-connected PTSD and a slew of its effects along with suffering from MST, but I was there for my combat PTSD. She only sees that I am a female and was not considered a combat veteran in her ignorant and biased eyes. Does this VA representative know that females are in the military and are actively deployed in combat zones? This was frustrating. After multiple times of just staring at me, I could just half-smile, eyebrows lifted slightly, lips tightly shut giving her a nod of "move on." My heart started to race; the heat of my body made me sweat. I tried to get comfortable, but I was shifting in my seat uncomfortably. The pain, again, of not feeling welcome and totally disregarded was extremely hurtful. I was there as a female, with qualifications like those of any of the other males there. But I was the one getting pointed out. This lady needed to go.

I stayed due to my stubbornness, not wanting her to win again and walk out. I belong. I belong in this group, I knew it, she couldn't handle that. I sat there in a deep emotional rift. I wanted to take all those bracelets and shove them down her throat. My mind wandered in a one-sided conversation on how I could get rid of this lady. This group lasted an hour, and I felt so unwelcome. I did not pay attention to anything she said. I sat fuming with anger. I came for help, and she did not accept me. After class, the representative made a small speech and dismissed us. I walked out of the room and out of the lobby, reached my car, and sat in the driver's seat, crying. I felt so much anger. I wondered—do I leave pissed or go back and complain? This can't be happening. Is it just me?

As I locked my car and made the journey back into the mental health department, my anxiety was leaping out of my body. I walked back into the office and asked to speak to anyone in management. There was one friendly female in the office who knew me from past visits. This particular lady was the kind smile behind the big computer. She knew most of the veteran's names by sight. I felt comfortable talking with her. She knew I had just left and immediately knew something was wrong at a glance with my eyes filled with tears about to flow. She ushered me in the back hallway and told me, "Go into the back office." In the past, I had been escorted to that very back room for anxiety attacks that came. She asked, "What's wrong, Hun?" I told her about my experience in the combat group class. She shook her head in disbelief. "Oh honey, I'm sorry, I can call our supervisor, would you like to talk with him?" I was a bit hesitant and finally responded, "Yes?" She called someone in the chain of command on the phone. "He's on the phone honey, I will give you some privacy, but just let him know everything that happened today, we are here for you." I felt reassured. The male who oversaw the mental health offices at this outpatient VA clinic was in disbelief over what happened, and he apologized multiple times. I started off with a clear explanation of how this lady, on multiple occasions, had completely dismissed me. But as the story went on, the tears flowed, and my throat got stuck. I did my best to translate my pain to this supervisor. I repeated that my qualifications are not less, but the same as anyone who was in these groups. I should not have been pointed out in such a personal attack. To openly say "this group is not for MST" was clearly not anyone else's business. He agreed with me and apologized again. He reassured me that he was going to talk with this employee. I hung up the phone. I felt I did what I needed to do. I wiped my eyes and sat for a moment. The kind lady checked in on me. She asked if I was feeling any better. I nodded and she apologized, telling me that she hoped I would come back for more groups. I sighed and walked out of the building.

This cycle of trying new VA approved groups has been rough. I tried again; the cycle of bad juju continued. I tried another VA group hosted by a representative with an overly eager environment emphasizing her pushed etiquette. She insisted an ethical and moral code of a Sunday church group. The disapproval from this other female employee ended very high. It was a drop-in class, dealing with combat stress and coping mechanisms. She was very religious and insisted we all become believers in the group. I sat in this group for the first time and thought we would be able to openly communicate and share. As an adult, not a child in Sunday school. One veteran shared about his new job, and we were all very happy for him. Another veteran told of a grievance about his marriage. An overwhelming tone set over the group and a "mmmmm" was spread around. The instructor brought up God and how each veteran is loved, and Jesus loves them. Insert, the sound of a record scratching. I started to mindfully step back. What is going on? I am not religious nor share these particular thoughts in my life. I was a bit uncomfortable. I was then asked to share and introduce myself. "Hi, everyone. I am Kitchi and I have been having a fuck—"

"Excuse me, Kitchi," the instructor said, interrupting me, "we don't use that language in this group." Right then I was over it, having just gotten scolded like a child. I am a grown ass adult. Nope, not today. I responded with a smirk, "Yea...whatever...this fucking week has been hell." Instructor blurted in a *tsk, tsk* sound and told me to stop. She again reminded me of how that language was inappropriate and was not allowed. She went into an all-holy mode and pushed her religious status and looked at me with disgust. I had not been in a group without this kind of language being the dialect. It is a form to accurately share true feelings. Example: this shit fucking sucks vs. I do not like this. It doesn't have the same je ne sais quoi. I looked at her, stood up, and while walking out of the room said, "fuck this." I heard a few chuckles while the door shut.

Many of these unfortunate situations arise throughout the "healing" process. At that point, not a lot was happening in the healing realm. So let me be me. I gotta express my true feelings. The religious push was not my cup of tea.

PTSD can come in at any moment, anxiety-filled. It doesn't have to happen in front of anyone or a group. Physical aspects affecting my body take a huge toll. Hot weather can be a huge trigger, and my body reacts as if I were back on deployment. Long days of convoys spent in heat, high alert, full gear. When the right recipe is collected—lack of sleep, recent triggers, being jumpy, depressed, and high-anxiety—it will only take small disturbances to have flashbacks and for my body to fully react. Recently, it was during a planned self-care "relaxing" bubble bath. A movie set up, popcorn, water—all the elements for a night of relaxation. But my body felt a bit off. It was the hot water triggering me, and I had to get cool quickly. This has happened dozens of times over the years. This time, my body began going into shock. Taking a few minutes, I slowly and painfully pushed myself to try and move to drain the tub. I managed to grip my towel and cover myself, as I called for my oldest daughter. She is a certified medical personnel and privy to my PTSD. She ran and got a fan, took my pulse and blood pressure. I thought I was acting nonchalant to not scare her, but I was extremely weak, barely able to describe how I was feeling, my skin clammy and white. I couldn't lift my legs or arms. It took over twenty minutes to be able to get assisted out of the tub. She told me I was tachycardiac—fast heartbeat, fast breathing, and my blood pressure dropped below 50. She took care of me and watched over me until I was back on my feet. I'm grateful for my daughter and her unpaid caregiving job for her mom.

Years later, and I'm still seeking out more opportunities to feel a part of society. Various veteran groups. Giving it another try. To get out of my bubble. Be social. Trying not to isolate. This has been an absolute struggle due to the trauma I have received and me being a natural intro-vert. Seeking out these groups has been very painful, and deciding to go often leads to a panic-induced feeling. There are plenty of art therapy, water therapy, hiking, storytelling, and writing workshops, comedy classes, trauma-based yoga, equine therapy, PTSD groups, individual therapy, hiking, peer groups, etc. It is exhausting to find "our" purpose—that welcoming feeling of being in a supportive environment. To find meaning in "our" lives. I want to find MY purpose.

I tried my hand at the oldest veteran community in the United States. It quickly turned into an unwelcomed "why is she here?" feeling. This chapter was in my hometown, and, like all the other members, I qualified to be a part of the group. Before my first official meeting, the members started a coffee and chat morning group. I showed up, never having met anyone in the group before. I was already out of my comfort zone. I noticed the table was almost full and introduced myself. There was confusion and half smiles. After the introductions no one opened a spot for me to sit but waved their hands to their wives who were sitting across the room. They told me I could sit with them...the female, non-military dependents. I sat there a bit angry as to why I couldn't sit with the members and thought, "Why do they think this is ok?" I chatted with the wives, and we had nothing in common. I tried the following week and did the same thing: sat with the wives.

"what is it about me?"

So, my last try was to bring a friend of mine—a male, retired, former Marine, Purple Heart recipient, and on and on in terms of esteemed accolades. They would have to let me sit at *the table*. We both walked in, and I introduced him to the group. A couple of the men stood up and shook his hand with: "Hey buddy, you can sit right here, OORAH!" We looked at each other and he walked with me over to the *wife's table*. I told him, "See what I mean?" He responded, "Ouch. I wasn't going to leave you and let you sit here alone. That was interesting." So, I was done with those coffee groups. I was hoping these incidences were isolated and my treatment at the member meetings would be better and inclusive. I was happily motivated to buy a shirt and get a cap. I was officially sworn in and felt some pride. Some members were welcoming, some stayed their distance. It was vocalized to start thinking of events and fundraisers to raise money. I was on it and quickly got the creative juices flowing and had pages of events to share. Not only did I share, but received some positive head nods. The path to make any of it happen was stopped by the money overseer of the group. It was a fight for $5 for supplies. There were angry emails calling me an idiot and saying no one was interested; that he, the overseer, would not be doing a thing to help or participate. A bit discouraging. I didn't need to stay in a toxic environment. I have since joined another town's membership. Unfortunately, I now have such a poor taste in my mouth, I just sit quietly. Observing—not participating.

Then there are some groups that want to support the veteran community. But often, some of these groups are not equipped to identify or help alleviate symptoms of PTSD. Recently there was an incident at a six-week course writing workshop I signed up for. It was months in advance and I was really excited to go. I was only hesitant due to it being another new group, in an unfamiliar town, inside a new building, and in this particular location the noise level was extremely high due to an airport and planes flying overhead every few minutes. I was a bit late, lost, and in a state of panic. Then I had to walk past everyone in the group. I sat down with some eyes passing my way. No, "Hi!" or, "How are you?" The silence made me feel instantly uncomfortable. I knew it wasn't a good recipe. Then it started—my body got warm, I had to breathe in and out in longer breaths, then the sweat, which started to leak through my pores and make me fidgety. Hello, anxiety. The instructor asked if there was anything she could do to get everyone comfy. I asked, "Can you please open a window?" I said "*a window*" and she reluctantly got up from her chair and slowly opened all four very tall windows that spanned the entire side of the classroom. Ok? A few attendees started to put on their sweatshirts and glanced at me with side eyes. At that point I felt so claustrophobic that I could not concentrate on the introduction question. I left the room for a minute to go into the bathroom and cry. This was not going too well. I walked back and I wrote quickly and just waited in my enveloping swarm of anxiety. My body wanted to yell and run out. I stayed. The group shared their answers and the teacher noticed that I did not answer, for a reason. My anxiety was screaming. She looked at me and her gaze was trying to tell me that I needed to read. All eyes were on me at this time; I immediately began to cry and covered my face with a hand and finally read one sentence. The entire time the instructor could not identify a student whose panic was obvious, with fidgety movements. I obviously was not doing well, and she pushed me to share when I was not ready. I packed up my things and left. I cried in panic all the way to my car. I called my daughter who calmed me down and stayed on the phone until I went through a few breathing exercises. I had to walk around for over twenty minutes to calm my body and be able to drive home. The instructor was very oblivious and not considerate to recognize and respond to anxiety. She was not capable of being in that situation. If she was paying attention at all, she could have taken a break, talked to me outside, let me know that she knew being in a new environment can be challenging. Anything. I cannot control the overwhelming moments of anxiety that I regularly experience. I felt no one cared in this particular group. And I never went back. My daughter, who felt awful about my experience, emailed the instructor about how badly she handled the incident and thus, it was forwarded it to the owner. I received a PC voicemail, saying she hoped I would come back. Ah, nah—thank you.

I had all the hopes in the beginning to try and push me out of my bubble or comfort zone, but it takes a toll on my body, physically and mentally. Some programs are unfortunately limited, and it is said they'll be funded for a selective number of times or another increment of limited sessions. Once I got a grip, felt bonded or developed trust, it was taken away. Then, the journey of finding another approved experience to help me thread through the dark struggles. Writing has been that constant for me. I can do it in pajamas sipping on my coffee in the safety of my home. Listening to background TV noise, moving around to jingle any new ideas from inside. Writing has been my constant happy place.

CHAPTER 3

"is this your baby?"

I'm one of a kind
No one can find
anyone exactly like me

*T*his was a framed quote in my room growing up. It was in a red frame, white background, red print, pictures of teddy bears with sweaters on surrounding the poem. This was the dark and mocking poem of my life. Words that were sent into the universe to become true. It was hung right next to my bedroom door. I looked at it every day. It was not encouraging to me. It amplified my being different. This poem seemed to be an imprint of my trauma; theme of being discarded, abandoned in infancy. Where do I come from, where are my roots? Any cultural identity? Will someone love me?

I was not born in a hospital. I was left on a dirt floor. It was a one room building in a very small town near Tijuana, Mexico. A border town. No record of my birth in any court paperwork. I have never existed in that country. I was told when I was found, I was wrapped in multiple blankets. My umbilical cord was sheared long and taped around my belly, and I was left in the corner of a room. That's it. My beginning.

I can't write about my first few moments of life. I do not have the opportunity to ask my biological mother about my birth. How did she feel when she saw me for the first time? I cannot run to her and wrap my arms around her, share funny moments and enjoy long talks. I only have questions. Obviously, I was a mistake. This is a thing you should know, biological mom: you set me up for a lifetime of not knowing how to trust. You sent me into a life of abandonment issues. My genetic code is imprinted with being always left alone and never lovingly held. After you left me, was I crying, screaming, hungry? Did I know to stay quiet or just exhaust my lungs and fall asleep? Left.

I'm one of a kind
No one can find
anyone exactly like me

Later, time unknown, American strangers walked me across the border as if I was their own biological child. Then, I was adopted by these strangers, who did not know how to love. I was told that these strangers got a call from clients of my adoptive dad. These clients knew of the struggle they had with having their own kids. My adoptive dad expressed a desire and asked the clients that if they knew anyone who couldn't keep a baby, to let them know. And then there was me. Just my luck.

These strangers, my adoptive parents, were trying to have kids for many years with no success. They had already adopted a boy a few years earlier who became the prized possession of the family. Noah was born in the States with no biological connection to me. So, our bond had always been a bit awkward, and we were more like people just passing each other in the hallway. I played the role of the typical, annoying younger sister to him. Getting him in trouble and catching lies he told. This golden child had a secret, though, one only I knew. I was young and idolized my brother. He was beloved by all his classmates and friends—a super athlete who always excelled in all sports. It seemed his charm was untouchable. The girls adored him, and he had no problem with the dating scene.

This was all very annoying because if a friend of mine came over, they would flirt with my brother. I was an extremely shy girl, quiet, and didn't feel comfortable getting attention. It was only with my close friends that I could be myself and be carefree. The idolization of my brother came to a screeching halt one dreadful and confusing night.

One time, while having a sleepover, during which I'd always be on the top bunk, happily spending time with my big brother on the bunk below, he exposed himself while calling my name to look. I bent over the rail and in the gleaming of the moonlight there it was. I had no idea what the heck I was looking at and I felt confused about why he wanted me to look at it. He pulled his waistband up and told me not to tell. This should not have happened. I enjoyed our sleepovers. But that unfortunate night, Noah thought it would be okay to do something inappropriate to his sister. I just pushed myself back from leaning over the guard rail and fell asleep. It was never mentioned again. Until over thirty-five years later— an early, dark family secret. Unfortunately, it was a foreshadowing of what was to come for me.

When Noah was adopted, his biological parents were teens and were too young to keep a baby. Decades later, Noah in his young adulthood was sought out by his biological dad who always wondered about his first-born son. The young teenage parents ended up marrying each other and having another son that had no knowledge of an older brother. His biological parents throughout the years had thought about the first boy they gave up. Of course, how could they not think of my brother? He was the chosen one. After finding Noah, his brother met him for the first time. Noah told me that there was some anger from his brother towards his parents about not knowing that they gave a boy up for adoption. To be honest, most of the story I blocked or heard as though the Charlie Brown teacher told it to me. Muffled to keep my sanity. I was happy for him, but also steaming inside. I didn't want to hear about this rekindled family due to all the pain of the family I was stuck in. His parents had sought him out. I found out this information after the fact, years later. This brother who I had trusted and then who exposed himself to me. It was very confusing to live with knowledge of this highly regarded person's secret inappropriate side.

Noah always had the love of our adoptive parents. Now, another set of parents needed him and would love him. They found him. The one part of the conversation that hurt me was when Noah asked me to meet his biological brother. What? I screamed in my head, "I am your sister! I'm the only one." That stung in my being. Abandonment is my imprint. Soaked into my DNA. I thought the despising of me, and of me being me, was the only vibe that existed because it was all I picked up as a child. No, I don't want to meet him. End of conversation. This subject will never be brought up again. Ever.

I'm one of a kind
No one can find
anyone exactly like me

Our experiences of growing up in the same household were as different as salt and sugar in your favorite cup of joe. I'm the salt—that pretty much sums up my life's events. Moments for him are a beautiful memory. Of course, there were the typical teenage arguments between my adoptive parents and my brother about him coming home drunk. But, Noah was the shining star—especially in my adoptive mom's eyes. He could do no wrong. My experiences, on the other hand, were the polar opposite. I was left alone daily growing up. I was left to be in my room, no communication, no play dates, or heart-to-heart conversations. Abuse as soon as I stepped out of my room. Being hit, emotionally battered. My mere presence could send my adoptive mom into a mild rage. I would wait patiently for no one to be around, when I could finally go into the kitchen and make a snack. If she smelled fear, her presence appeared like a hawk. She would obsessively follow me and grunt while cleaning up a crumb or aggressively wiping the sink down. This was a common occurrence. She would get into a state after she used the faucet to scrub, wipe, scrub and wipe. What was that madness? Her quick, loud exhales told me that I was in "her" kitchen. But if Noah came into the kitchen at any moment, for any reason, a feast was to be served.

After years of abuse, I ran away at fifteen, and each of our communications with one another were years apart. We were first in contact after my grandpa had heart surgery and was in the hospital. I got a call from an acquaintance that I needed to be there just in case it was my last opportunity to say goodbye. Fortunately, even after his chest wall was opened and his heart was hand-massaged back to life, he lived twenty-plus more years. He was a fighter. My brother told me then, casually, that his parents and him had spent a lot of time together and even holidays were spent as a family. Their love for my brother had no beginning and it had no end. The mere thought of parents wanting you was so foreign to me. The feeling of being accepted into a family? Unconditionally? I had no point of reference for it.

are you listening? a little feedback would be nice

Having spent time with close to a dozen therapists over the past few years has been mentally exhausting. Each session would start with the same jibber jabber. Then, I would start my story from the beginning. I always get the collective sigh and a *hmmm*. I'm not proud of my complex past. But it's mine. In the past, I had many ways of dealing with my feelings, none that a professional would recommend. They only helped temporarily, only scratched the surface. It took decades to finally open up. I'm still hoping to find a therapist that will be able to show some empathy, listen to my words, have a reaction, and offer some resolution that is helpful.

One word that is biologically linked to my being: abandonment.

Abandonment: a state in which people feel left behind, insecure, or discarded. This state has a biological imprint that activates the physical pain centers of the brain. It can occur as early as birth. This fear and anxiety is called primal abandonment. It happens when a child is separated from its mother, bringing out primal fear which imprints on the brain's amygdala, or emotional memory system. These first-learned feelings, when triggered, can be reawakened by later events contributing to terror and outright panic throughout one's life.

Check. This one is at my core.

Here is an example of a typical counseling session meant to help me deal with this and other issues. Its failure to really hear my cry or understand my deep-rooted triggers will be apparent.

Therapist- *Hi! Good morning—I'm your therapist and you have been referred to me by the VA.*
We have a twelve-week program to discuss some coping mechanisms.
Do you have any questions so far?

Me- *No, not yet.*

Therapist- *It seems from your questionnaire you may have some depression, anger, anxiety, and strong triggers.*
With your cooperation, our program can help alleviate some of this pain.
Let's start by getting to know you.
Can you tell me a little about yourself?

Me- *I'm not sure where to start.*
But I have had something on my mind for a while...
At this point I just need to get it out.

Therapist- *Before you start, we need to get our questionnaire finished and a survey completed.*

Me- *Ok? Well, I need to get this out, it won't take too long.*
I have been referred for a reason. Can I talk this out?

Therapist- *Well, this is your time, but remember our set goals can help these situations.*

Wherever you're comfortable to start and want to share...
Let's take this first session to just talk.

Me- *Maybe from the start, but I really need to discuss an event that happened recently.*
Ok...well I have deep-rooted abandonment issues.
During my life I was constantly reminded I was a bastard...
...and if there was an issue, its 'cuz "she's adopted"—
Anger, she's adopted—
The one thing and constant statement I have heard throughout my life...
"I was never important and never wanted."
Always blamed for being adopted...
They raised me, which could be a great study for a good ol' debate of nature vs nurture.
I did not try to take scissors to my wrist at seven 'cuz it was a healthy environment.
I did not pull my hair out, strand by strand, as a child suffering from anxiety 'cuz it was a healthy environment.
A plethora of dark family secrets.
Constantly called names and beaten from an undiagnosed alcoholic, manic-depressive.

Therapist- *Ok, so we are closing in on time for our session. I appreciate you sharing some of your story.*

Me- *So the situation that happened recently was when I overheard a conversation from an adoptive mom...*
I had taken my daughters to a paint-a-ceramic shop.
Having a great time and figuring out the ceramic pieces to paint,
I noticed a mom walk in with a daughter. She seemed annoyingly loud for a calm environment.
My girls and I went about our business, then a phone call came to that mom.
Loud words were blasted...the conversation made my blood boil.

She insisted on talking about her "adopted" daughter, that she has anger issues, and she doesn't know where it's coming from.

That mom said she got her as a baby, but she doesn't know why she acts the way she does.

She went on and on very loudly, blaming her adopted daughter for all the problems in the house.

I noticed the daughter she brought into the business was just going about her thing. I was twitching in my chair and wanted to leap out and beat the shit out of her...but with witnesses?

I told her to take that conversation outside. She looked at me while I glared with anger, and she stepped outside...

My oldest daughter glanced at me and knew I was upset.

I had to hurry up and get out of that place.

I went off verbally in the car complaining about that woman who was complaining about her adopted daughter...

...but brought the other one, no love for both, honor one and shit on the other. That "mother's" loud complaining went on and on unnecessarily.

I know that feeling all too well: the one who needs love and care is left somewhere else while the golden child gets to be creative and share these moments with that bitch. The issue was her—not the daughter. The girl is troubled and angry due to the hate she receives.

Therapist- *Again, thank you for sharing. That seems like a topic we will discuss, but our time together has come to a close.*

I recommend with an incident like that, you remember you are with your daughters and be happy; the questionnaire will really help push through these moments of your triggers.

Me- *Ok...be happy? Well, thank you so much for YOUR time! I will be happy. I feel so much better!*

Therapist- *See you next week...*

Me- *Can't wait!*

Chapter 5

trust bubble popped

As frustrating as it has been, I have tried to keep going with individual therapy. It has not been an easy process. I would wait months from the VA, then get referred to Community Care, waiting again for an approved facility that could schedule to see me. Then be seen—but really… did they "see" me? Over and over, the process—to be identified, referred, approved and then to wait. Only for short sessions where I never felt understood or even heard. Unfortunately, these appointments are not only in the therapy realm but in other areas of the medical arena. Waiting is an ongoing situation within the VA system. Refer. Wait. Repeat.

The last time, I was ready to be open, to dive into their way of therapy. I was ready to get help. I eventually formed trust with a female therapist. She was a former Marine who got the pain of being in the military—and from a female perspective! I got to express myself, f-bombs and all, laughs and long exhaled, "Yesssssss!" I looked forward to the next week and being able to share and work through the trauma with someone who understood. Struggles, now triggers, developed into anger. I felt comfortable, and it wasn't as painful a process as in the past with the looks of horror from hearing my past. She empathized and did not just shake her head with dull commentary. She was involved. Then, of course....BAM! She told me, "I'm sorry to tell you this, but I have recently decided to leave this practice." Inner monologue: *fuuuuuccccckkk.* Therapists leave. And you have to tell your story over and over and over again. She was going to go into private practice to be closer to home. All very valid reasons. She told me she was nervous to tell me since we started to discuss my abandonment issues last session. I cried. The tears just flowed, and I couldn't help but feel a bit rejected; I was just starting to feel a bit of relief mentally. Too many feels. A sense of mourning and a returned feeling of loss and thinking, "Who is going to help me now?" But I was happy to see her figure out her next career steps. She was going on to do better things. But it hurt. I had found trust and a safe place. Gone. She recommended another therapist. He was new and seemed to have a good reputation.

"Uh huh, ok?" A wolf in sheep's clothing. His pretending to hear me. I will find him to be a narcissistic, rude, argumentative being. As we were introduced, he commented that we only had a few more sessions, even though we had just met. He was all about following the rules, clocking the time spent by the first therapist, even though I would be starting all over again at ground zero. He had no clue about my history, which had taken four sessions with the other therapist to begin to understand, to try and find a place where we could start as a team to unfold my complicated past. Time was running out. I rushed through our first session, going through the basics. I sounded like medicine commercials who rant at the last moment about all the possible side effects, super-fast disclaimers. I tried to catch him up on what was going on. He listened, seemed to show empathy. So, I agreed to continue and showed up the following week.

Strangely, he asked me if I would be willing to volunteer at his former non-profit job (probably because if I get busy and dive into a social setting, the distraction could help, I'd meet some people, get out of my bubble; some other shortcut counselors are taught). He figured this would be a great opportunity to be in a social setting, to meet new people. My isolating introvert self was not too eager about this idea. I felt obligated to go because if I didn't, I felt I would not be embracing his therapeutic help. So, I went. It was around the holidays and the non-profit was having a food drive. I signed up for the event, but my triggers are not scheduled. They show up whenever they want. That day was no different. It didn't take too long since I was in a large, unfamiliar group, rushing around, no introductions and…GO! Hello, anxiety. Back again so soon? It replies with a Clark Gable sharp tone: "Frankly my dear, I don't give a damn." Then, the moment. There was a male with a towering presence. He yelled at his volunteers; it felt loud and sudden. I was sitting at the time—I felt trapped, and I immediately started to cry. I tried my best to get up from a sitting position on a curb. Not so limber anymore. I left the event. Defeated, embarrassed with a side of shame. Did anyone see me just freeze and cry? When I went back to my therapy session, we discussed his plan for the next sessions. He insisted we stay on track, make therapy goals of how to proceed. He had developed an outline for the clinical side of the sessions. I told him I understood, but it had been decades since this trauma, and we hadn't pinpointed where to start. There was too much to go over. I just wanted to have those last couple of sessions for talking and examining and unpacking my thoughts. I kindly argued that after decades of heavy trauma, a goal was cute, but I wasn't ready for goals yet. I was in survival mode still. I have never been able to explain how I feel. Telling myself to be grateful? Repeating to him I have a self-care routine to help reduce my hurting physical being. But I hadn't yet been able to dive into each trauma and understand the why behind it. That particular session was going nowhere, and it felt more argumentative than productive. There were things in my life happening that needed venting before healing *could* happen. I needed to get some things off my chest. He sat a bit straighter in his seat and reminded me that there was a format he had to follow, an outline, that setting a goal plan would help. Seriously, it's not the time, I reasserted, trying to express how the next two quick sessions we had left were not going to take the past decades of pain away.

My mind couldn't settle, and I interjected a discussion I had with my daughter about my end-of-life wishes. This talk had just happened and was at the forefront of my cortex. I told him that it took us a few times to go over since we would start to cry and never finish. I told him about my wishes and the plan to have nothing religious. Just a huge celebration. And what I wanted to happen with my body—the how, who, when. We went into a bit of a back and forth. I sat in shock and started to get offended by his rude interjections, as he started to become snide. "How will you know this will happen? Guess you won't." Really? Awesome, thank you for the happy therapist trust bubble. Not the best atmosphere to have when you're relaying very personal things and getting them thrown back in your face by your therapist. The trust, what little there was to begin with, was diminishing.

Then, I dove into the previous weekend and explained about my volunteer time with the food drive. Unfortunately, it did not go so well. I mentioned to him about my anxiety attack at his old job. He couldn't believe his friend made me that scared, so scared I cried. He breathed hard through his nose in disbelief. "What did he say? What did he do? Why did it make you feel like this?" All questions asked in suspicion. It was a complete mess. I realized then that he was not invested and only wanted to defend his friend. He ended the session by asking, "Do you really think that will happen after you're dead?" referring back to what I had told him, as if my expectations of my own death were unrealistic and he just couldn't let go of that. He really fixated on this fact, like he was saying no matter your personal opinion, it's not welcomed in a therapy session. My mouth dropped and I was raging inside. I wanted to yell and complain to the highest court of law to revoke any license or degree held by this "professional". I stood up while giving him a death stare of my own and yelled, "I'm done!" Not a thing to put in my head. But he knew he needed to have the last word. It just was a horrible experience. He got mad and knew exactly how to make a last dig by bringing up my end-of-life wishes in a sarcastic way. He knew he had the power to say this to me in my depressive state. Fucking asshole. I got up quickly and left that room and rushed out into the hallway. Didn't say a thing to the receptionist. I stopped going to that practice. His unsympathetic presence sitting there all smug made me want to vomit—sitting, twisting in his seat, side-to-side, side-to-side. Not caring a damn about me.

It wasn't until a month later that I could get the words out explaining what had happened to a supervisor. She listened and got a bit irritated—at me! She said she couldn't believe he would treat me like he did. She never apologized. Just constantly, robotically responding, "Ok, ok, yes, ok." Are YOU listening? I screamed in my own head. She reminded me that they had a strict protocol to follow, a curriculum. Back to the fucking goal setting. She insisted on the fault being mine, that if I had upheld the protocol, this would not have been the case. She commented, "It works and is proven. It seems like our goal setting was never in place." Oh my…what the hell? Back to the start.

Still reaching for my purpose.

i tried the traditional house

I have never been a religious person. I have not been baptized for any one God. Oddly, my upbringing was as a devout Catholic on one side; with all the guilt and fake smiles displayed. The other side was strict LDS (Latter-Day Saints)—lineage rooted from the journey into the Salt Lake, eventually homesteading with thirteen wives and fifty-eight kids and friendship with Brigham Young. A great example of Mormonism.

To obey your husband, do what he says…that always made me a little skeptical.

I was not sure how to express or feel grateful in the Word that has metaphorically held its hand on my head, pushing me down. Or to bring praise in spite of the abuse experienced throughout my life. One example of this guilt and blame was when my adoptive mom casually told me in her glorious wordsmith ways that when I was a one-year-old, her father died and it was my fault; she blamed me. In her mind, I was a curse. She felt cursed by God for bringing me to the family. Oh, well thank you for that enlightening mother-daughter bonding moment! Was I to cherish these words? She often reminded me of this type of thing, making me feel flawed from the start—dangerous and cursed, even. Her deep hatred for me seemed to know no bounds. All this, while sharing His love to those outside of the family. So, how exactly was I going to have open arms to a God loved by her? His followers only hated in my mind: full of hypocrisy, loathing, obligation. Behind our home's closed doors were the encircling flames of hell on Earth. What more of a hell did I need to believe in? I had front row seats. This follower of His Word did not know how to love, cuddle, give kisses, have any sort of edifying conversation—just the presence of liquor on her breath.

Years went by and I could not let myself be open to that world of devotion. I was in survival mode. As a teen runaway, self-medicating with marijuana at thirteen and downing bottles of tequila, such was my ritual and devotion. Though temporary, it was satisfying at the time. It made me feel numb and be the life of a party. I could be carefree. I have not been able to be at a point in my life that I can freely extend my hands and thank God. My entire life has brought up so many challenges. I thought it was just my luck. Was I indeed a curse? What did I do in my former life to deserve this?

Throughout my adulthood, I have tried to go to church. I thought a hipster rock band, swaying to the beat would get me to stay. My daughters could meet friends and learn important lessons, I thought, later finding out it was only the doughnuts that gave them that push to go. I couldn't get myself to pick up the Bible or sing along. Stubborn, maybe…we were told to hold up our Bibles and I would fumble around waiting for the coast to be clear. Then, the preaching. I never raised my arms and said, "Hallelujah!" swaying in an almost psychedelic groove. It made me uncomfortable to be next to those who were. Why are they always smiling and being so proper? I felt overwhelmed with the pastor telling stories. Who was this person? The holy what? A father and son, two brothers and a stone? Who's a ghost? Ugh. The time I could no longer sit there anymore was when the pastor got hot-tempered and disgusted about homosexuality, transgender bathrooms, and he began to pressure his audience to sign petitions. I was out. I could not hear this discrimination. Politics should never be demanded in a church, and to provide voting ballots for their prejudice was unconscionable. Making the devout feel pressured to take your view or else. I walked out and never looked back.

I extended my education for a short time in another church. All day groups, one last mass session. The women's group was nice but very judgy—smiling towards me but standing at a distance to not make conversation. I have tattoos, drink coffee, tea, alcohol. Not to mention, being a single mom was a no-no; that was short-lived. Everyone had circles of children. Fathers holding babies, mothers rocking toddlers. Not a place that I felt completely welcomed as a single mom. Or to look for a future date. All were taken. I knew I was never going to stop drinking coffee, tea, alcohol occasionally. I did not want to dive into something where I knew I was not completely following. Having these religious failures in my life, how can I know anything is out there watching over me? How can I be more in tune with faith when there are so many questions left unanswered?

An incident deep in my collection of memories. My memory takes me back to when I was 20, when I had just graduated from the Army's boot camp in Ft. Leonard, MO. This program was called "hometown recruiting." I finally got to go home. I worked in a nearby recruiter's office in Northern California. I was still new in the ranks and was ready to make copies, run errands, talk with future soldiers that were about to take their journey. One day, I had a short break and walked to a CVS store directly across from the office. I was in my BDUs (battle dress uniform). I started walking down each aisle, killing time and window shopping. It's been so long since I was able to shop and not be yelled at by a DS (drill sergeant) on a time limit. I looked up and noticed a woman looking at me. I thought ok, maybe it's curiosity—I'm in a uniform. But as I continued to walk down another aisle she was there, just looking. This was all very weird. So finally, after the eye contact dance, she walked toward me. She told me, "I'm sorry for watching you, but I want to tell you that you have a bright aura and there are a lot of angels surrounding you, protecting you." My mouth may have dropped, and my expression may have been a slow smile. I had never been in this situation. I thought she just wanted to know what branch of service I was in or that she wanted to thank me for my service and say she had a family member who was in the military. I may have just calmly said, "Oh, whoa." She simply smiled and said she needed to tell me. We turned in opposite directions and walked away. It took me awhile to soak in this information.

That conversation may never have been discussed again, but it is occasionally in the back of my mind after incidents of physical trauma. Do I have angels nearby?

I had my first TBI in training at Ft. Lee, VA. There was an incident and my company's drill sergeant came to visit me in the hospital while I was on oxygen. I woke up to him sitting by my side. He spoke few words, got up quickly, and started to cry as he walked out of the hospital room. Diagnosis: mild TBI (traumatic brain injury, since there wasn't a stopwatch timing the time that I was unconscious, less or more than thirty minutes is the scale) a fever, with a side of pneumonia. Was it an angel who slowed down the speed of my body while I fell to the ground? Well, it wasn't my time to give up. My second TBI happened during deployment. Oddly, just recently, the VA reworked some acronyms. They decided to call TBI (traumatic brain injury) ABI (acquired brain injury). If my memory serves me right, being "acquired" in the military is an inside joke used to describe acquiring material goods, maybe undercover or bootleg. That I "acquired" it is a funny thing—like I sought out this lifetime disability? The VA says a brain injury is acquired since our veteran community was not born with the condition. Sigh. I digress. Back to my memory of waking up in a troop medical clinic, not knowing what happened. Angel? Keep fighting, I have a young daughter at home waiting for me, I told myself. During this stay in the sand box, I was the NCOIC and in charge of supply convoys. We had orders and my company needed equipment for almost daily supply drop-offs. Of course, in theatre convoys there were always risks; you had to stay highly alert. One scheduled departure was delayed. I continued to prepare to roll out and got radioed that all convoys would be stopped. "Shit, I need to get this convoy going!" I thought. Later, I found out that a foreign civilian was killed driving out of the gate in an earlier convoy. I couldn't stop thinking that if we had been allowed to go, I would have been the driver of the lead vehicle and would probably have been the one killed. Angel?

Granted, all these experiences are difficult and are often repeated during my sleepless nights. The question is: is someone or something looking over me? Was the decades-old conversation of my aura the reason? I find that I try to slow down my busy mind to feel. Being in the moment. Mindfulness. When I start to drift into a spiral, I come back and remind myself: you are ok. You're home. You're safe. Religion may not be my thing, but I am a firm believer that all things happen for a reason. You may not know why it did, and you may not like it when it does, but I am determined to overcome the darkness. To keep treading the waters. To whomever, or whatever—I appreciate your watchful guidance.

CHAPTER 7

1980

*I*t was 1980. A rough year. Around the U.S., world loneliness echoed. It was not a promising time. The iconic John Lennon was shot and killed in New York. Mount St. Helens erupted on March 27th. Iran and Iraq broke out into war. AIDS emerged as a deadly epidemic; a severe heat wave killed 1,117 people in twenty states. There was a failed operation to free U.S. hostages in Iran. My story began with my first breaths, followed by abandonment. Alone. Later, I was held by two American strangers crossing the border. They had just walked up and over.

"Is this your baby?" the border patrol agent asked.

"Yes."

Nothing else. No security measures. No paperwork needed. The border patrol would just wave them in. A baby in a stranger's arms.

It would be another seven years before I made the journey back to the border town. When the very presence of me was in the way of my adoptive mom's radius, and my very breath ignited her hate. She would constantly scream, racing manically back-and-forth to my adoptive dad while I overheard her, hurting my developing soul deeply. What can a seven-year-old do that is so bad that they are always unwelcome? My adoptive mom had heavy feet; her slippers would scratch and glide across the kitchen linoleum. A robe or muu-muu flowing, her looking like a mad woman who had just escaped an asylum. She would be muttering to herself. It was a long hallway to the kitchen; my room had a clear view. Her presence was strong and fierce. This mentioned "mom" later was diagnosed as a manic-depressive whose actions were erratic and emotions nearly always out of control. I often did not know which of her personalities was on each day's menu. She was a woman of the 1950s robotic chore mode, who would obsessively wipe the kitchen sink, mumbling, just wearing out the coating of that sink. A side of complete anger; dessert closet drinking. She would ramble, "I didn't want her." I tried to ignore the madness, but I knew it was only about me. I hid my view behind the slightly open bedroom door. The footsteps would get heavier. The tone would get louder.

"Take her back, I don't want her, she was your idea."

This strange relationship with my adoptive mom came from her being almost jealous of the attention I received from my adoptive dad. Of the two, he spent the most time with me. She made sure there was distance and coldness. I had no one else. She may have felt ignored. She may have felt my brother, her golden child, didn't get enough attention from my adoptive dad. The dynamic was confusing and, with a blended family and no connection biologically or emotionally on any level, it was distant. Situations which threw her into a manic attack stemmed from me being in her kitchen. I would place an item in the sink and her head gasket would explode. This housewife, whose sole job was to care for her children, failed miserably. She had me clean bathrooms and make sure the house was tidy. There were two formal rooms that we didn't dare go inside; they were for company, whose presence was never known. Those rooms were ghostly, with ruffled flower prints and matching long drapes. I spent most of my time in the family room. She would be upstairs lying down in her bedroom, or in the kitchen, manically wiping down the sink. To this day, if I notice I'm cleaning my sink, I wipe a few times and throw the sponge—I'm not her. Her explosive attitude would become hard and strong. At times I would just be in the house, and she would look at me with disgust. Breathing through her nose, bitterly, at my presence. I would get pushed, hit, mostly in my head, or shoved. I remember getting shoved into a room, trying to get away from her swinging arms, hitting the back door and falling. I held up my hands to block any further attack, and she broke a glass platter over my head. It shattered. The rage. She hated my being so much. I eventually grew very tall and towered over her, but in the '80s, children were not able to talk back or physically respond. Wooden spoons were a thing. Soap was a constant in the mouth. There was an incident where I was kicked out of the house for being present and in her way; I was getting dressed and in my room. Her manic episode needed me out. I was wearing a bra and t-shirt, barely below my belly button. She pulled me out and locked the doors. "You're disgusting, ugly." I was outside, fairly naked, for hours. I waited until my adoptive dad came home. Embarrassingly trying to pull my shirt down, I told him that she kicked me out. Nothing happened. I got to come back inside.

My adoptive mom would yell at my adoptive dad and be in a mental state so extreme, there was no return. She demanded in front of me that I had to go. "Take her back!" "I never wanted that ugly brown bastard." He had no choice but to make the phone calls preparing for my departure. He would never give the same hostile attitude he received back to her. Even after an incident of her rage. She grew angry—yelling, "I hate you"—chasing after me. I'd try to get away, screaming. She threw knives at me, running down the stairs. Totally ok to do all these things in this household. My adoptive dad never questioned the mental state of his wife. He had moments of annoyance, but never a heavy hand nor the capability to stop her. His modus operandi was to work a god-awful number of hours, drink, and bury himself in his den.

Southwest Airline tickets were bought immediately. After the tickets were bought, my adoptive dad and I would be on the very first plane to San Diego and off to a Tijuana Catholic school. Get sized for a uniform, meet nuns, and be silent. I did not speak the foreign language. Adoptive dad brought a translator, so every step would be detailed to me. They would discuss my new home. It was very confusing to simply exist in the states, wobbling on an unbalanced pendulum. Shipped back with no voice, going along with being left. Being young and rushed out of my house to a foreign country, I had no idea what was going on. I guess they are leaving me, I thought, as the day became night. Dad got a call from adoptive mom, and she said to bring me back. What's going on? Loathing me, hating me, and now she wants to bring me back? Another plane ticket back to the Bay Area. This would happen three, maybe four times in my young childhood. Loathed and hated, but always brought back for more of the same.

My psyche at that point was diminished. It got so bad that one day, at around seven years old, I sat with my back to my bedroom door and grabbed my scissors. I was so desperate to not feel anymore and the sadness of growing up in the household got to be too much. I put the scissors to my wrist, exhaled, just wanting to leave this place. I looked at my wrist and mimicked how to do it, long ways or sideways. How could I do this? I wanted the pain to stop. I pressed the scissors down and my adoptive mom walked in. She looked at me, glanced at my arm, and simply walked backwards out the door. So callous and cold. It was a, "My apologies for interrupting, please proceed," kind of gesture. I got startled and put the scissors down.

I'm one of a kind

No one can find

anyone exactly like me

The abuse was not just at the hands of my mom. She was the physically and emotionally damaging character in my story. I had it coming at me from every person in my "home." When I was a young teen, my dad would come into the bathroom where I was showering and linger. The frosted glass was not a total blackout from view. I could see a figure going back and forth at the sink. Moving. I did not think anything of this due to my innocence. As time went on, he was in the bathroom more, and longer. I would get out of the shower, walk up the stairs and hear his den chair squeak. I would look back down the stairs and see him looking at me walking up in my towel. He would not say a word, he just stared. I didn't feel comfortable. It gave me the creeps. I would walk up the stairs sideways, holding the towel closer to my bottom. Glancing down and seeing the quiet stare. Changing direction, or just sprinting up. It continued, and I had to contemplate how the routine of my showers urged his inappropriateness. Would the abuse and wrong behavior stop? Couldn't I just live in a household of complete, unconditional love? It was all too much. My brother during this time was always out with his friends, enjoying a social life. Able to drive and get away for a day. No questions asked, he just became the socialite never having to dwell in the only house I ever knew...and hated. Why in the hell was this happening? The showers. Him not saying a word, just staring. This happened again and again. That heavy wooden carved chair and its squeak as it turned. I hated that sound. I would look for longer towels and look for ways so he couldn't see up my towel. One time, I snapped, "What!?" I was completely disgusted as time went on. I finally told the mom what was happening. She didn't care. She didn't even comment. Brushed it off. The discomfort grew, creeping over into my participation in sports. On the soccer field, we would have multiple uniforms and change on the sidelines if it was necessary to do so, trying not to conflict with the other teams' colors. So, with sports bras on, the girls would throw off their jerseys and make the quick change. I would always glance at my adoptive dad's last location, hoping that he wasn't there, staring. It was so gross. I would quickly learn the way to pull one jersey on and the other one off through the neck to avoid any skin showing. I felt so violated. The feeling of being watched was unnerving.

Finally, I had the courage at around ten years old to tell my family doctor what was happening at the house. She was African American, and I was the only brown girl around. I felt a connection and comfortableness. I wanted her to take me away and have me as a daughter. I remember being scared as she asked how I was. This moment is now a faded memory. I know I immediately started to cry. I told her that my adoptive mom would yell and hit me. She left the room, most likely to put the mom on the spot, who would somehow get out of being in any sort of trouble. We walked out of the hospital with nothing more said. The one time I stood up, reached out, and nothing happened. I was stuck in the family.

CHAPTER 8

monologue, adoptive mom, my written words

*T*his was inspired by a writing prompt to create a monologue in my writing class. It could have been any subject. My brain is pretty quick to deep-dive into the pain I have lived through. I need to get it out anyway I can. I wrote this monologue from my adoptive mom's point of view. In "her voice" as she moved around the house, seeing me as her unholy muse, me as an unwanted commitment she got.

SETTING: *1985-1990. Stage is black, a spotlight for one standing mirror, a spotlight on a closet door to the left of the stage.*

WOMAN *walks out of closet door, twisting the cap of a large vodka bottle, pacing back and forth, glancing and fixing a '50s beehive-style wig. Occasionally taking a swig of vodka.*

WOMAN   This is my life. This is my life? (sigh)

My mother did not talk about how hard this shit would be. She always kept a great house. Ironed and starched her nurse's uniform before every shift, she took care of my hardworking dad... homemade dinners. She took care of eight kids... eight kids.

I wanted kids so bad. Why did God shame me? Why couldn't I give my husband these children he desperately wanted? Can I call myself a mom? I don't have any stretch marks, never felt a growing baby kick. I'm barren. I'm broke. (tearing up)

It has to be me. My fault. God put down his foot and said no to me.

But why? (untwisting cap and taking a swig)

Now I'm stuck with these two kids. They aren't mine. Not by blood or race. *Goddd*. My husband wanted them. Did we really have to adopt two? One was enough. Then, years later, another was found, and we got the call to take the baby. *Jesus*. I had to be the upbeat one. Oh yes, this will be great! Thank you, husband. Thanks a lot!

Sigh. I *do* love one. He is my baby boy. Ohhh, he's so sweet. He makes me laugh. Watching him grow up has been such a joy. I tell him I love him, and we share so many hugs. I can't wait to see his next soccer game.

Now, this bastard. She is such a pain. She came—and my BELOVED dad died within a year? She did that. I know this evil baby did it. (untwisting cap and taking a swig) I leave her alone. I just need some distance. To wrap my head around the very thought of this baby. Ok...maybe I leave her in her crib too long? No. I don't think so. Who cares. I truly hate her. I will not hold this baby who took my dad's life. So glad my husband didn't notice. HAHAHA. I hate her so much. God...why are slamming me into a deep despair. I have been a faithful Catholic all my life. Haven't you noticed? I have prayed. Come on. I exude Catholism. Now I'm stuck with this brown brat baby.

Do I call her an ugly bastard? Yes!! So-the-fuck-what? She is. I am 100% sure her biological mom couldn't keep her damn legs shut. Now I have to take care of her mess. (untwisting cap and taking a swig) I'm so glad my dear husband is not home when I…. may…get a bit angry. It's happened all my life. No biggie. Look, I'm high in life, the joy is great. But once I look at this brown shit of a baby, it gets me so angry. I hate when everyone else around us glances at me and then her. Like I actually birthed it. Jesus, hell no.

She is so odd. She looks at me like I want to talk with her. I'm so sick of her.

So, I have hit her. She deserved every bit of it. I know I should have told her there was broken glass on the ground the other day. She just walked in too quickly. Yes, it was her fault. She should have known there was broken glass.

Hitting her in the head is too easy. What a stupid little child.

I know I can't take her life, but my patience is wearing thin.

Ok, yea, so I tell her…I never wanted her. I tell my husband to take her back. Does this husband do exactly what He's supposed to do? Damn right. He will NEVER leave me. I have told him to take her back…multiple times. But I don't care. I just don't want this. HAHA. (untwisting cap and taking a swig)

I get a few days of peace.

That girl and my husband fly back down to Mexico. Did I say…I never wanted her? LEAVE HER THERE.

I keep thinking this probably won't look too good. What will my family say? When they notice one missing? Damnit. This is the issue.

Now I realize I'm stuck with that little ugly bastard.

Why did she tell me that MY husband is watching her in the shower? Yea right. What a pain. He had to get something in the bathroom. He is such a busy man. I'm tired of these lies. She has no clue what she is talking about.

We are both great parents. We just have one unfortunate, lying bastard.

(untwisting cap and taking a swig)

END OF MONOLOGUE

left in a room

I would have enjoyed stories of my beginning in a better light
Joyful memories of smiles and happiness
My mom would have shared stories of us together
Us laughing at funny jokes
Knowing my mom would always have my back
Instead, pushing me to the ground and stomping on my back
Leaving me alone in my room, wondering if I will ever be enough
What did I do to deserve any of this?
The abuse will never stop, until the day I run away
She would kiss my boo-boos, hold my hand
What I got was her always expressing complete disgust
I was constantly pushed away
"I never wanted you, you are a mistake"
This was the chorus of my childhood
I would have enjoyed our cuddles
But I only got hit
To me, adoption is trauma and abandonment
All rolled into feelings of wanting to know

What is love? How can I change
Into what you want me to be?
I enjoyed the fantasy of having a loving mom
She would share her ice cream, ask me how I was
She would never curse at me
Never call me a bastard
We would enjoy our time together
Never fly me back to my birthplace
A handful of times, being fitted for a school uniform
In a land whose language I did not share
Screaming, taken back to where she came from
So desperate to get away
I put scissors to my wrist at seven
I can't live like this, please take me away
Here I go, no pain, almost there
A warm feeling
Only to stop, with a slight interruption and no words to follow
Never got to finish what I began
A loving mom filled with compassion
What I had, she later apologized for her manic depression
That explanation is not enough
My biological mom left me to grow up in this madness
There wasn't an adoption agency
No proper steps of parenting
This couple was never interviewed
It was 1980 and the rules were not in place
Anyone could find a child, bring it to a new land
Are they the right match? Will they truly love this newborn?
My biological mom did not care what happened to me
I was abandoned, left to be found
Not in a hospital, but on a dirt floor,
Left in a dark corner
This is my story explained to me

I was wrapped in multiple blankets under a heat lamp
My umbilical cord sheared long
Taped around my belly
No dad to proudly show me off
No pink balloons or "It's a Girl" sign
No mom to hold me close
No evidence of my presence in any court paperwork
Just birthed and left there
What did I do to deserve any of this?
Did anyone hear this young babe
So desperate to be held, too young to know anything else?
To this day, it is hard for me to feel
True feelings of love
So many damaged years of distrust
They should have left me in that room

family traits

*M*y adoptive mom was one of eight kids who grew up in Oakland. Her dad was an officer in the police department and her mom was a nurse. Stories of her mom are brief. I was told she worked in a time when nurses starched and ironed their blinding white nurse uniforms before every shift. In later years, I found out the sad fact that she had a miscarriage in the bathroom while sitting on the toilet. She could not take the time to grieve with a full-time job and full-time family duty.

While growing up, I noticed my adoptive mom's annoying habit of talking loudly on the phone; at restaurants, and in casual conversation. We would have to ask her to lower her voice. It was a trained trait. I'm sure it's the fact of growing up with seven siblings, trying to be heard over all of them in a small house. Of course, the decibels would have to increase for any possible attention by her full-time working parents. She was a caretaker for her younger siblings—she dressed them, acted like they were her babies. How exactly did she treat her younger siblings? In my experience, she needed more practice. Complicating things was her demise of a late diagnosis of manic depression—what is now called bipolar disorder. I only found out due to her calling me on a yearly phone call, drunk and slurring her words, saying that she was sorry about how she treated me. This said to me, as an adult—now she's so sorry for what she did to me. It's not enough. It's way too late. I would never have treated my own babies this way. It took fifteen years for the first apology, after I ran away from home at fifteen years old. Thinking about her quirks to this day sends me into a fit of chills. "Pet peeve" is such a lighthearted term for echoes of behavior that will never be extinguished from my mind.

For instance: FEET. I hate feet, and it is because of her. This lady would always take off her shoes on long car trips and let them sit on top of the dashboard like a cavewoman. Gross. Just waving those godawful toes side to side. They were deeply calloused and had thick, long, unmanicured toenails. How could calloused feet be a thing with a housewife? She did nothing active. No hikes, no high heels. Her habit of crinkling water bottles, another focal point of bad memories. She would shake water bottles and crinkle their bodies, untwisting the cap with mad, exaggerated passion, for no reason. The trigger for me is in how she drank it. The tongue curling, her chugging motion. NOOOO! Just sip! Stop making that noise! Stop making everything so damn dramatic! Nobody needs to see you make love to the fucking bottle. Gross! And my least favorite was the sloppy, loud noise of her sucking on hard candy—knocking it from one side to another in her mouth. Why are you so loud with everything that you do?

My beginning is not something to brag about. Silly moments when I sang out loud, or of being held by my adoptive parents. I was only told a couple stories about my childhood. I was told when I was a young toddler that I held a magazine upside down like I was reading it, and they said I would be a reader. Another story was, while we were visiting my aunt, someone left the basement door open, and I scooted myself in a baby walker over to it and rolled down the stairs. Great! Slurring her words from too much vodka, my adoptive mother told me this story about my being a baby. By then, I was in my twenties. Another doozy for my confidence! She told me she would leave me alone, too. She hated me for my first year of life. She rarely had anything to do with me. She didn't hold me and left me in my crib. She blamed my birth for her dad's death. No baby books. No reminiscing about the past. Nothing was ever handed down to me. In my forties, years after I cut off ties from them, I had to come and get a box of items they wanted to throw away; one they had told me to come and get. Inside there were my daughter's toys, clothes that were not mine, and one baby picture. One baby picture that I have framed, and that's it. The only evidence of me growing up.

I didn't have the open relationship of supportive adoptive parents to dig for many details about how I came into this world. Facts were delivered tersely, slowly, and spontaneously throughout my childhood. Maybe a handful of sentences in total. There wasn't the comfort of asking to sit with my adoptive mom and having enlightening conversations. Home life was not a thriving environment with everyone in their spot, scattered about the house. Conversation was limited to only sports games or practice reminders. Everyone was at their TV, just letting the time slip by. "Hey, how's it going sweet girl?" or, "Can I help you with that?" Nope. I had to learn to be not seen and not heard. I was never given praise, hugs, kisses, or a simple..."I love you." My mere presence seemed to bring about a feeling of disgust. I grew used to people being annoyed by my genetic makeup.

This was the childhood given to me. So, I do not have, nor have I ever seen a picture of a cute moment between me and my adoptive mom. No pictures or proof of any love. I already have the deep insecurity of not being loved emotionally and of the trauma that happened. There is no candid proof of any anchoring moment to think back to. It felt like I was a figure floating through the house. My adoptive mom had her spot in the kitchen. It had a tiny, ten-inch TV screen. Entertainment Tonight with John Tesh and Mary Hart was a nightly ritual. As soon as I heard the first few infamous notes, I knew dinner would be ready soon and awaited the dinner call. I could never venture in and disturb the moment of TV reality gossip. It makes me sad that this could have been a great bonding time to maybe share an interest. Talk about our day— laughing, hugging. I never had an intimate conversation with her about anything.

We never shared anything with each other. It was so cold. And at any moment I didn't know which personality I would meet there. Was it a "what do you want" day, or a "you little bastard" one?

When I had to get a bra, my adoptive dad took me to a department store and asked a woman to help. I left with a handful of sports bras. I needed my "mother" to help interpret womanly secrets for me. Getting my period was dramatic, and I didn't know if I was living or dying. There was no relief in the situation, and my adoptive dad was just like, "You're bleeding, uhhhhh? Ok, let's go." Again, not a moment for a guy to handle.

She never came to any of my sports games. At one time, I was playing three sports a day. I had to be relentless. It was hard work. Exhausting. This family incubated a hard-hitting, sports freak atmosphere. If I refused or was tired, it seemed like I would be out of the will by my adoptive dad's tone and threats to hurry up. He had a way about being a sideline coach. I would be running down a soccer field and scan to him as he raised a fist and mouthed, "Get 'em!" I would always just nod my head and go about my business. On the soccer field, there would be running up and down the field, scratching, elbowing, pulling on jerseys. Most times, illegally slide tackling. The aggressiveness was exhilarating. So many cheers and parents yelling at the refs to pay attention. "Come on, Ref! You blind? You need to watch that number 9!" I loved playing soccer and enjoyed it for thirteen years. Unfortunately, I never glanced up to see my adoptive mom cheering me on. No handing my teammates a bag of sliced oranges and a big jug of shared water to pass around for the team. Those white plastic bottles with a long straw, the ones where you would squeeze from a distance and whose water only had a plastic taste. Sometimes, the players would dive into a community bag of ice and chomp on it to hydrate ourselves. Yikes, not very kosher. No oasis moments of my "mom" telling me how proud she was of me, though. No retelling moments during the game that she had been most excited about. Nope. Never. Zilch. I just accepted this fact. My adoptive dad kept me busy doing sports and she did not have to travel, sit in the sun, or cheer for her daughter. I was too young at the time to remember, but some memories from soccer were retold later that when my brother had to travel for soccer, I would stay at my grandparents' house while there were trips to Canada and across the United States. I would be left. Stories were commonly told by the parents of the team, joking about how much fun they had going out and enjoying the town while the boys hung out in their rooms, bonding. I may not have been a superstar like Noah, but it would have been nice to have some family support for my playing soccer in town.

My adoptive dad grew up in San Francisco as an only child. Catholic-baptized with Mormon roots. Irish and Portuguese decent. His father, in the era of the 1920s, received derision and was called a black Irishman due to his tan. Prejudice through the decades. His mother was fair-skinned, had a kind smile, infectious giggle, and reddish hair. Both were beautiful people who I miss every day. They didn't look at me as being brown and not related to them by blood. My grandpa called me, lovingly, "his girl." My adoptive mom hated it because she thought it was unfair to Noah. Just when I finally got some positive attention. But shit, lady, this man was the only one who cared about me!

Not a very glowing experience for Noah was when we were both young and visiting our grandparents. That unfortunate event, I remember, was a time when my brother and I were at their condo complex and visited the community pool. My brother had the great idea to run behind me, knocking an air-filled ball out of my hands. Unfortunately, I ended up tripping onto the cement surrounding the pool. My chin smacked across the cement edge from which my blood flowed into the pool. My grandpa yelled angrily at my brother to get back to the house. He, I found out, hated blood. He ran around the pool, grabbed me, and helped me up. We ran to his cruiser boat of a sedan Cadillac. My grandpa gave me a lot of napkins stacked together to hold under my chin. I felt so small in the passenger seat, barely seeing out the window. I just sat in silence, noticing my grandpa's fast step on the gas pedal, letting the speed slow, and repeat. We would shift forward then back in the seats for the entire car ride. I felt it was a bit fun and watched him mumble angrily. At the hospital, I got a few stitches under my chin. My grandpa was by my side.

I must have annoyed the doctor since I insisted on knowing every move he was making. "What is that for? Will I have a scar?" It may have been nerves, but I just kept asking. I was an inquisitive eight-year-old. On the way back, the ice cream was delicious, and my brother's punishment was the grand prize.

To my adoptive dad's demise, though, his mom coddled him. His sense of nobility started right there. She was pregnant with my adoptive dad while her husband was at Army boot camp getting mission-ready for WWII. Years earlier, a baby girl died from SIDS, only weeks old. This pregnancy, carrying my future adoptive father, was a risk. She took great precautions, scared that, like the daughter before him, she might lose him, too. Being of an older generation, the true pain and struggles were kept 'till death. My grandma never told me about her daughter. The loss was probably unbearable. Maybe she blamed herself or felt guilt. The baby that she hadn't had enough time with, heard her sweet cries, or shared intense love. The excitement of being a first-time mom. That dreadful morning, seeing Rose lifeless in her crib. Unimaginable. I felt like it wasn't my place to push any details. It was when I was younger, around ten years old, that my adoptive dad took me to buy flowers then drove into a nearby town's graveyard. We walked side by side; I held the flowers. He stopped at a wall and looked up to find "Rose" and a short display of numbers—her time on Earth. I only asked who she was back in the car. He said she was his big sister, who died as an infant.

So, when the time came to give birth to my adoptive dad, my grandma took all precautions. The time was too soon; she was rushed to the hospital and had a premature son. At the time, premature births were certain death. He survived. We would joke a lot that of course he was premature—he is never late and always early for everything. His dad was later discharged by the Army due to an accident that occurred while he was in boot camp. He was able to see his son and be with his recovering wife. Things happen for a reason. Spoiled and cherished, my adoptive dad's indulgent upbringing was a huge contributor to his controlling behavior. He was standoffish, flat and emotionless, never present. He was a man who stubbornly demanded attention, selfishly avoided family time due to his work schedule, and remained oblivious to the abuse I was exposed to. A classic '50s household. Wife kept at home, doing the housework, making dinner, and making sure it was ready on time, while he, the man of the house, "brought home the bacon."

My adoptive dad falls into the hard-working boomer generation category. Short stature, but he drank like a giant. Clues leading to this conclusion were not evident until I was older and understood the consequences of alcohol. Our house had a family room with a bar—a high bar with a countertop and a huge built-in cabinet of glasses adjacent to the liquor. It had a small refrigerator under the counter with one sink. At night, I would watch TV in the family room and hear the click of his reclining chair. I knew it would only be a matter of time before he would shuffle in and walk directly to the bar. He filled up his wine glass by pulling the plastic tab and tipping the Franzia box just enough for the liquid to pour out. It always smelled cheap, like it tasted bitter and strong. It was his top choice. So, in my youth I would hear every night the clink, clink, clink of the chair. As time passed on during the night, I would walk down the short hallway into his office and glance in. He would be asleep. I always thought, oh my, he works so hard, he's so tired and needs a nap. Poor dad. As I grew and entered the knowledge of life, well, he passed out. Simply that.

My "parents'" first collision was on a blind date. Friends of theirs thought this match would be a true fairy tale. If I could meet and slap those individuals, I would. My adoptive dad had been caught up in a business engagement and was late. Phoning to arrange their introduction at this business party, they met and quickly became engaged; he introduced his blind date as his wife. Romantic or caveman-like? Always in control. Yea, for me. A match? Maybe at first, when there were no kids. But frustration, no love, and arguments would be the chorus of their next fifty years together and counting.

Is this a learned behavior? Nature vs nurture. This would make great research. My grandpa may have been the bearer of a quick temper, but he was my only ally. My grandparents were married close to seventy years before my grandpa's death. Early in my childhood, I noticed how my grandparents were so funny together. Their love was very evident, and my grandpa often looked for my grandma if she wasn't in clear view. The way they looked at each other was complete surrender. Their love was undeniable, but touch was absent. They would bicker often. My grandpa would get upset momentarily, while my grandma would laugh at him. They knew each other so well—I just giggled at the funny show. It was like clockwork. My grandpa would shake his head and mumble, while my grandma would wink and glance at me, smiling. She knew his quick, harmless temper would be over soon.

The news of his ailing health came to me in his last days. I have only recently had his memory hit me like a shower of memories. It was brought about by my daughter having a college assignment; she had to interview me with a few questions. A particular one gave me sadness and joy, all balled-up into one.

The first question she asked me was, "Think of a time in your life that you had to persevere. How did it get better?" My thoughts rushed to my grandpa. I read my answer as this:

"While I was going through the fire academy, my grandpa was dying, and I only had a few days to see him. But this would involve me traveling out of the county. The academy would not allow me to take the time off. Missing a certain amount of training hours, I could have been dropped from the academy. Within a couple of days, my grandpa died. I was devastated since he used to tell me I was "his girl." He was the only member of my entire adoptive family to express any love and kindness to me. Within a week of his passing, I had a dream of my grandpa sitting in his chair in the corner of my room. He didn't have a smile, but a content, peaceful look on his face. I felt warm and relaxed. No words were spoken, but I immediately knew he was ok. He came to me to allow my grief to be in a more positive space. He wanted to tell me he was fine and at peace. At times I will remember this image and feel happy.

I feel, even within this week, that my grandpa has been trying to reach out. I feel he knows the difficulty I have been going through emotionally lately. I will always love and appreciate his presence. It gives me the overwhelming sense that he knew how much I loved him."

Over the years, trying to continue the relationship with my adoptive parents only came with more and more degrading comments. I needed to do something drastic...and quick. I finally cut the strings in my early thirties with absolute silence. No communication. But before I made this decision, I thought my two daughters needed their grandparents. Unfortunately, there was a huge, disgusting dose of favoritism. With my oldest daughter, who had lived with them during my deployment with Operation Iraqi Freedom, they had developed an almost obsession. It was not so with my other daughter. My adoptive mom continued to loathe in her hatred towards my youngest and would also call her a "bastard" and cursed her existence. It was devastating to see this outright love and neglect, simultaneously. My youngest is a beautiful soul who is delicate and did not need a "grandma" to turn against her. She didn't deserve that. I had to break free after the constant judgment of my parenting. Really? My parenting? They had the nerve. Did my childhood just fade in their minds? One example was when I signed up to use my GI bill to get a bachelor's degree, arranged for help from a sitter from a renowned company and interviewed a fantastic candidate. I was ridiculed by my adoptive dad who said that I was a "horrible mom to just leave my kids with a stranger." Him telling me that I am a bad mom? Ummmmm, because I was getting a college degree, I was a bad person? I was pregnant at the time and told Wendy, who I ended up hiring to help our family, that there would soon be two girls to look after. She had no issue and was herself in college for child development. Wendy was with my family for close to four years. She was an absolute savior and so perfect with my girls. To this day we love to look back at our memories of Wendy. Her shared artwork with the girls still hangs on our walls. I hated to say goodbye after earning my degree. Wendy has since moved on and is now a fabulous mother herself. What a treasure she was!

That day I cut the cord, I had a thousand-pound weight, bad memories and scars, completely lifted. "Keeping your enemies close" did not help in my situation; the toxicity had to be cut. As a child, I had no choice but to accept my fate. I had to forge ahead as a kid with fake smiles and a well-trained Irish Catholic demeanor to not show what was going on behind closed doors. I had to uphold my part of the exterior smiles but keep the dark, secret history inside. I had to protect my girls from that environment. They would grow up, eventually seeing this horrendous amount of dysfunction. The best decision I made in my adulthood was to finally get out. My girls and I have been thriving without their abuse and control. I have forged ahead and tried my best to convey love, communication, and complete adoration. My past made me determined to forge a different path for my own daughters. Everything happens for a reason…

CHAPTER 11

small farm town

I grew up in a small farm town in Northern California that was incorporated in the late 1800s. Not until the '90s did the entire economic layout of this town drastically change. The tech world had creeped in then and laid new foundations of money. The town was beautiful, with large open areas and roaming cows, wooden fencing piled decades before with precision. Cruising downtown with no purpose was a highlight. My town only had stop signs down Main Street. No one seemed to rush to go anywhere. There was a family-owned drive-through dairy at one corner selling easy grab-and-go chips, candy, juice, milk, and eggs from local farms. Teens would come to the driver's side window to ask what we wanted and cheerfully grab orders. Most importantly, on hot days, a tall yogurt swirl cone would make the humidity seem easier to bear. The antique register was a reminder of another time, a simpler time maybe, with a loud cling announcing each sale. The drive-through dairy is still open and running, even with all the current surroundings. My memories of the town are so vivid. Main Street had an old-time feel; saloon-style architecture, cowboy-esque wooden slats in front of a scattered row of storefronts. These few, original blocks would clamp and clop while you walked.

As one would continue scanning this little town, this perfect little town, they'd see a Veteran's Memorial building at one end, a large old glory flying high. As a kid, I never noticed exactly what the building was or the importance, but always knew it looked like a museum. I passed by it thousands of times going through town as a kid, never knowing I would in the future have so much love and appreciation for the building.

Like many small towns, this one loved its sports teams. The children seemed loved and appreciated. Our recreational sports season was the pride of the town. Every team had funny mascots, like fairies or monsters. We would meet at our coaches' homes and make costumes for the yearly parade. Each team had a banner made of felt and PVC pipe as the frame, inscribed with players' and coaches' names. These were proudly carried in the parade. Every game of the season, we staked that banner on the ground to represent us—they were our works of art. Other teammates' moms would always be the motivator that upheld the tradition. One year on the team, I wore a huge paper mâché head with small air holes in the mouth and eyes; I was a Jim Henson Muppet this particular year. I was a quiet and shy girl who didn't mind hiding behind a costume to wave to the crowd, the giant paper mâché head falling back and forth on top of my own head. Me, holding it in position and smelling its scent of newly dried chemicals and glue. On the morning of the parades, the mayor would introduce himself and soccer league representatives would make speeches. The league would gather at one end of the street and wait for our opportunity to walk down Main Street; all of us would get super excited for our moment to be seen. Our coaches would high five us and we would scream our team's name, waving our hands in our uniforms. Parents and town members would wave and cheer us on like we were celebrities. There was music, food, balloons. Little town traditions. Looks can be deceiving, though, and the happy moments were always outweighed by my experiences as a child who needed to be loved and welcomed by those I should have trusted.

Along with being raised in a small farm town came the complete absence of diversity at the time I was going to school. Thankfully, after visiting over the years, the demographic has changed and diversity is now welcomed. My elementary school had only one to two students of different races. It didn't get any more diverse through high school, where there was an incident that led to me moving schools. I ran away at fifteen and would later attend three local high schools, looking for my place in this world. The first high school I attended got the two brown girls there mixed up. I walked into the office and one office lady angrily yelled for me to come over. Another one stood up and said, "Not that one." I immediately left the building.

My classmates were not kind. Some, in fact, were even scared to touch my hand. In 2nd grade, our teacher told us all to come to the floor and sit down in a circle. Easy enough. But to one white boy, a perfect specimen of spoiled and rich who always wore his collared shirts perfectly tucked into knee-length beige shorts, it was the worst thing in the world. White socks pulled to lower calf and those shiny white sneakers. I remember all the details. His parents were often at the school grounds, and it seemed like his mom floated down the corridors. She had perfect, salon-styled hair, and a tight, matching tennis outfit. Her makeup was flawless. What else...well, those shiny, white sneakers, of course. His dad was even worse. He looked like a Ken doll. He was tall, tanned, with the whitest of white teeth, perfectly pressed casual clothing. Ugh. While all the students began to sit down in a circle, I had the misfortune to sit down next to this boy. The teacher wanted us to hold hands. I innocently looked to the side, reached out. He looked disgusted and hesitated. "She's dirty and doesn't bathe," he said, pulling his hand away. I looked down, embarrassed. Wow. My skin color is not dirty. I am brown. I bathe. I glanced at my own hand to see why it was so disgusting. The teacher only responded that he should sit somewhere else. Some time passed before this teacher called up a student who was black, and then me. He put his arms around us, telling the class, "I know these girls are different..." I don't remember the ending, due to age and being shy in front of the class, or maybe I just blocked out the rest. But whatever it was, I didn't feel any better. What was the purpose? Did he think he made the situation any better? He didn't. He just underscored that we were different. That I was different.

I'm one of a kind

No one can find

anyone exactly like me

As the years went on, kids would slowly find out I was adopted and knew exactly how to dig and make forever wounds. I remember a time on the playground swings. The sun was out and ready for us to play on the playground, which was made up of rust filled metal slides whose very touch in the heat made a third-degree butt and arm blister adventure. Yelling, "It's so hot!" The hard plastic covered slides made static sounds down the spiral crackling as we screamed. Why did we keep going on these rickety, old, death-defying contraptions? I guess we were kids and tetanus was not a concern. The rules were laid out if there was a line at the swing set: you could only swing a certain number of times, then you had to get off. Well, that day, I was enjoying my swings when a blonde, blue-eyed, strong-minded girl counted out loud and called me out. I stopped, and we got into an argument. I couldn't just jump off at the exact count but dragged my feet on the ground to a halt. The swing slowly stopped. I am pretty sure we both yelled at each other over the count. This unfortunately ended with her yelling, "At least my mom wanted me!" Woooo!!! I instantly felt embarrassed and in shock. Today, I could have had so many comebacks and personal digs toward her. But back then, I was very shy. I had to think quickly. How can I hurt this girl? A fact about her was that her mom worked in the local grocery store, and I had just seen her unloading a pallet of bread onto the shelves, switching out the loaves of expired bread. Could I use this information? Twist it to the greatest of all comebacks that would make this girl run in agony? Insert: evil laugh. No—no is the unfortunate answer. This is how that went...my first spat of words was, "Your mom sells old bread!" There may have been a moment of confusion on both of our parts. I said it confidently and with anger. I got off the swings and walked away. Sigh.

Why did I say that? Selling old bread did not have the effect I was looking for.

I unfortunately lacked then the quick wit and sarcastic humor I have now. Another example of not being a trained word assassin was when I was in an argument with an African American boy who was the class clown and always obnoxiously loud in class. He made it a daily duty to get very loud while disrupting everyone in class. The teachers always told him to behave and be quiet. He was an active kid who couldn't quite sit still in his chair. Easily distracted. This day was my turn to be harassed. He called me a "bean burrito" out of anger. What about being brown is so bad? So, I called him a "burnt bean burrito." He looked at me with his jaw dropped. Other classmates snickered. End of conversation. Not my proudest moment, but it happened.

A look at this town in the 1980s: there were houses that surrounded the school grounds. These were middle class homes. Manicured bushes, mowed lawns, plain. A little bit further, on the outskirts of downtown, were blocks of the original small cottages that developed as the town's population grew, similarly styled and colored, with a tall cement wall to block the view of the apartments. This area was where we never went. It was filled with foul-mouthed bullies; the kids who would always sit in the back of the bus and throw spit wads while being obnoxiously loud.

On bus rides, I was even quieter. The older kids would rush onto the bus, getting first pick at the back of the bus. I would move timidly to the first two rows, hoping to avoid any confrontation. I wanted to melt into the seat. As the bus rolled out of the elementary school grounds, the noise got noticeably louder, and the laughter got intense. I did not ride the school bus with any of my friends. I lived the farthest away. I was at one of the last bust stops. I would usually look out the window and scan nature, second by second, with the flow of the bus's speed. On one bus ride, a couple of older male kids walked up to me and stood next to me in the aisle. They stood, staring at me with inquisitive looks and smirks on their faces. One gave a glance at his friends, laughing, and blurted out:

"What are you, black or brown?"

I don't remember if I said anything. I most likely just turned red from embarrassment. I walked home from that bus ride and asked my adoptive mom, "I'm brown, right?" She got confused and I told her what happened on the bus. Maybe this would have been a great bonding moment for her, a moment when she could tell me that she loves me and is sorry that happened. Understand how much I wanted to be supported; to tell me, encourage me, to not listen to bullies. But her face just cemented over. "Yes. You are different. You are brown." Ok, I thought so.

During these bus rides, there was a long road that drove throughout the town parallel to where the houses got bigger, with more land—established. I grew up down this road in a country club with golf courses, tennis courts, and a pool. It was a prestigious area. This area was my muse. I was adopted into a household there, which bore a significant amount of pain and abuse. To this day, I cannot go into the area, as lovely as it may be, without feeling hatred. This was where the generational wealth of the town resided. I learned not to say the name of where I lived. I would only get discounted with, "Ohhh, ok. You're rich." Like that explained everything. As I grew up, I just said I lived off the main road, never pinpointing where. I was unfazed by the status of my address. I did not carry that on my sleeve or take out my silver spoon for dinner. I would have rather grown up in a neighborhood surrounded by kids my age. Not the older generation of the club members, who are retiring in the lap of luxury.

Growing up in an affluent area, I did not yearn for food in the pantry or clothes in my closet. I did yearn for love. Hugs, cuddles, kisses, or any form of acceptance from that family. But it never came. I never once saw my adoptive parents tell each other they loved each other. I never saw them hold hands, kiss, or show any form of affection toward one another. Those exact traits were given back to me. I will later learn that showing forms of affection will be decidedly hard in my future. I witnessed and seemed to develop ways to argue and yell. The motto of the era was children were to speak when spoken to. Know your manners, be respectful. A time when parents were charged to put the fear in you.

Finally, in my pre-teen years, I became a friend to another resident in my neighborhood. They moved in and we were inseparable. At times, people would ask us if we were sisters. We spent all our free time together and even went on a vacation together. At this technically advanced time, our households had the capability of faxing. This was a great invention. So very '90s. We would send pages at a time to one another reading: "hi" and "this is so cool." I remember waiting patiently for each page to print. So exciting to slowly read what my friend had written.

We had so much fun together, my friend and I. Laughing was my favorite part of our friendship. Months later, I regrettably and dramatically succumbed to peer pressure and completely shut her out. I ignored her due to another jealous friend asking why I was hanging out with her so much. Soon, after my haunting decision to shut her out, she was a witness to her own mother's death and was almost killed by her father himself. This incident happened after her younger, beautiful mother was allegedly cheating on her older husband. To my recollection, it was only a short period of time after I shut her out. I was dropped off at school walking towards the crosswalk and her mom pulled up next to me in her car. She was a beautiful woman who, before then, I shared a close relationship with. It was a struggle to look her in the eyes. The guilt was overwhelming. She wanted to know why I shut her daughter out and stopped talking to her. I was ashamed and did not say anything. I just looked forward, avoiding any more eye contact. Her mom drove off. I never saw her alive again, and my friendship with her daughter ended. She never talked to me again. After her mother was murdered, I never knew exactly what happened to her. She moved, and I moved schools—our lives simply split apart. I hate that I shut her out. She was my best friend. It's a shameful and undeniably painful regret to have stopped talking to her.

'80s-born and growing up in the '90s, it was a common theme to show up at a friend's house and spend the night, not like today, when parents plan play dates. Sleepovers were the best part of the '80s. Nighttime foolery was the haunted theme of sleepovers. It was the prime time to stay up all night, laughing, and doing the typical sleepover mischief.

My favorite was TP-ing houses and prank-calling boys we had crushes on, hearing their voices answer and then hanging up on them. Funny names and silly voices; we were so cool. Nowadays, it is impossible to do this kind of mischief with all the cameras and recording devices. But then, we could openly run to a house and cover it with toilet paper, throwing it over the tree branches, wrapping the bushes, so much fun. If it rained, the painful cleanup of soggy TP. Don't fall asleep first. Putting a girl's bra in the freezer or writing on their face. Bloody Mary spoken three times in front of a bathroom mirror, or having a friend lay down on the ground and, with the others, lifting her "light as a feather, stiff as a board", completely believing we had lifted our friend up. But if anyone mentioned using a Ouija board, I was out and always found my friends' parents and talked with them, like some kind of confession. I was and still am petrified about that board "game." Rumors swirled that a girl used this board and woke up with scratches on her face and a "V" on her arm for evil. I said, "No thank you to that. I didn't want to be forever cursed."

It was the late '80s and rumors were our social media. Adults could and would put fear in you to make you behave. The stories were cruel and graphic. One example was our bus driver told us to behave on his bus since, just awhile back, a girl with long beautiful hair was sitting on a school bus and her braid was whipping out the window and suddenly her ponytail got ripped out from a tree. So, we were told to keep our hands and feet inside the bus. "Do you like your lovely ponytail, Miss?" Or to hold your breath when you pass a graveyard so no ghost will get your soul. Sadly, and honestly, I still hold my breath. I am not tempting a lost ghost to find my soul. Not today, Satan. Don't sit too close to the TV or you will go blind. Well, I do wear glasses and have astigmatism in both eyes. No, not superstition though, definitely and scientifically genetic. But then again, both of my daughters have 20/20 vision. Huff.

Back to this quaint town, my muse. Hanging out at the local coffee shop on Main Street was a must. It was the '90s by then, and it was a seemingly popular spot to act older and mature. Parenting was nonexistent and they often had no clue or care where their kids were then.

Using a pay phone was a pain. Usually, we waited 'till we put our heads together and thought of a lie about where we were going. Very unlike today's helicopter parents and GPS trackers. This time was so vastly different on so many levels. There was so much freedom. It was a blast gathering and loading up on a super-dosed espresso. My favorite was a triple mocha with thirteen packets of sugar. Yes, thirteen. Eek. This translates to approximately 90 mg of caffeine of purely added sugar. The AHA (American Heart Association) sugar recommendation for women, in a day, is six teaspoons or 25 grams. Luckily, I can say diabetes was not activated. I was amped for hours. Baggy jeans, oversized flannels, thrift store finds with Joe or Butch gas station shirts—a great find. Kids were lined up and sitting on the couches, sipping with mouths full of both foam and deep laughter.

Partying was a must in this small town. Marijuana was everywhere; you knew who to ask to score some. Acid was very popular, but too many stories from friends on a bad trip didn't make me want to try it. I remember one story my friend told me about his bad trip; he was at home all alone. He dropped acid and his chimney started to breathe and the room felt small when the chimney inhaled. Uh, no thank you. Speed was an unfortunate turn for teenage girls who needed to make it down to the advertised 1990's version of skinny. Many girls were sent to different rehabs in my senior year due to low weight and crank or speed addiction. Media showed unrealistic skinny models and it was detrimental to young minds. In today's media, loving your body, being happy with all your curves, are nice messages to see. Body positivity. Not sunken cheeks, hip bones poking through the tops of low-waisted jeans, and clavicle bones sticking out as the picture of perfection when I grew up.

Alcohol drinking started early. This town was where my brother introduced me to weed at thirteen years old, taking me to his friend's birthday party. Everyone except me was an adult. It was in the next town over's cheap tweaker motel. A popular teen drunk fest that night. There was a table with a couple of guys separating the buds and making fat blunts. I had no idea what that was, at that time it smelled like sweet nature—I would soon know. My brother walked me around and introduced me to his friends. They were all very drunk and high. Loud. They laughed at me and said, "She's going to get fucked up, can she hang?" Pfft, the drinking commenced. Time started to pass, and my brother told me drunkenly, "I know you are going to get drunk and high at some point, so I will take care of you." We got this. I would walk around drinking and look at the hook-ups, laughing. Kinda gross and sloppy. I was thirteen. My brother got way wasted and was stumbling and slurring his words. We had a hand signal and would put our two fingers in front of our eyes and wave them towards each other. I was drinking happily, and his wave got sloppy. Yea, I could hang, and much better than most of these seasoned teen drunks. I took my first puff of THC. I thought I would die, I coughed so much. Then it was like riding a bike. Not a problem. My brother spent the night throwing up, his girlfriend helping him near the toilet. Baby, I thought. I'm unexpectedly good. I walked around and noticed the partygoers had slowly passed out. I was hyped for hours and hung with the last of the awake teens. Finally, my turn to slow down; there was no room for me anywhere. I slept on the stairs. What a grand time.

I spent the following seven years partying. When I could get alcohol, I would. I spent many party nights getting carried to my car. Bottles of tequila would be my choice, just straight; it would hit me like a truck, and I would be super amped, according to the atmosphere and mood. I could be the life of the party, dancing with everyone, laughing, not giving a shit at all. One party we were all gathered outside, I was high and drunk and kept hearing this noise. I laughed hysterically and pointed behind me. I asked, "Who let the goat out?" annoyingly, a few times. My friends started to laugh and told me it was a dog. "You're fucked up, Kitchi." Memories. My best friend would end up lying next to me making sure I didn't throw up and choke on my own vomit. I was completely a lush. Numbing my pain. Stealing my best friends' parents' liquor. One parent had spent time at Betty Ford. I found out this fact in later decades, thinking maybe I contributed to his thinking he may have drunk all the missing liquor and not knowing it was his daughter and I. Teens. No empathy. I knew how to numb my pain. The hurt from over the years could be hidden by drugs and alcohol.

Farm town, boring time. Nothing to do at times. Teenage mischief became my priority. Either shooting frozen paintball pellets with friends at an empty parking lot, chasing each other at high speeds, quick turns, screeching stops, so much fun! The lucky shooter hanging out on the side when the opportunity arose to hit the other car. Marking our cars with a graffiti array of colored paint. Whoever had the most paint on their car would lose. Of course, the local police did not like our fun and games and consistently lit up their police lights and turned on the sirens. We would always laugh and have a talk with them.

"So, what you are guys doing?"

(duh)

"Oh, we are just hanging out and talking."

(covered in paint ball mess)

"Yea? Ok, you guys can't be here."

(laughing) "We are leaving."

Never did stop us.

(we will be back)

Growing up in this town may have also saved me from a possible stint at a rehab. The small-town police officers seemed to not want to bust the local teenagers. Maybe they could scare the crap out of us; with a mention of our names brought familiarity of knowing our families. As a high schooler and a runaway, I would drive back, knowing the areas, the spots. Finding an empty parking lot at a local round table pizza on one occasion, I brought a boyfriend. We had pot and wanted to put it to good use. So, we lit up using my trusty, well-used, small hand-held blown glass pipe, swirled multicolored design. A lovely purchase from Telegraph in

Berkeley, a staple to find drugs, tie-dye shirts, cheap slices of pizza, kids running loose having a great time, among others. We had the windows up. Puff...puff...pass, just taking in the swirl of the THC cloud. We were in heaven and would glance at each other with heavy eyelids covering blood shot eyes above heavy smirks. Relaxed in the car seat and melting into our bodies. It felt so good. As soon as the pot hit my mind and felt like I was floating: TAP, TAP, TAP. Holy shit! We are both fucked! It was the local police. Two officers were standing at each door. I was the driver and reluctantly rolled down my window as a huge cyclone of a weed-filled cloud flowed out of the window. This is not good. They told us to get out of the vehicle. We both stood outside. Individually, we were asked to move with each officer. My boyfriend was a few steps from the passenger door, and I was told to move towards the front of the hood. The officer asked my name and what we were doing. Duh, right? Getting high! You know this! The effects of weed hit me hard. I could not answer easily. I licked my lips profusely and tried to get saliva to produce in my mouth. Cottonmouth was so bad I couldn't talk. I finally got it out—we were going to get pizza. Then, I got mad looking over at my boyfriend who completely gave in and started to cry. He had his arms folded and head down, just blubbering. He broke my lovely high. What the hell! Not even any pressure and he broke. Now we are both screwed, I thought. I do remember hearing the officer chuckle a bit after I tried to speak, but to this day, I cannot see their faces—only the shiny badge and gun belt. Luckily, they both knew we were so high and just out for some teenage fun, not intending to sell. They decided to take the baggie of leftover weed and dump it onto the ground beside the parking lot. I looked at them in horror and was so mad. My weed was being littered into nature. Nooooo! I wouldn't be able to distinguish between the garden particles and my stash. It was night—I was too high. Then, glancing at my boyfriend, crying and scared. I couldn't believe that baby shit.

The officers told us to leave. We both got into my car and drove off. Matters could have been so much worse. We could have both been taken to teen jail and gotten into big trouble. Of course, at the time, I only concentrated on how I could get more weed. I can laugh now. Teenage years. Developing brains and invincibility. That was not the beginning nor the end of my delinquency.

After a non-conventional teen cycle of life, I worked full time after graduation at a deli, hostess at two restaurants, and finally one year before I joined the military, I was a cashier at a DIY warehouse company. Continuing the partying, marijuana, and alcohol. This incident should be out of the scope of prosecution due to the statute of limitations. So, here I go. While taking breaks at this company I would sit in my car and make a ciga-weed, smoke it, and often enough feel the effects as I walked back into the building. I'm not too sure how I actually helped any customers, with blood shot eyes I repeated their questions, telling them, "This one is the best." Kinda feeling bad for my whistleblower moment with the bakery lady in my past, but I didn't get caught. So, this one time I stopped to help a driver on a forklift. I was a spotter, and unfortunately, this employee was not an experienced driver. He made the wrong lever change and dropped the pallet on my foot. Shit! If anyone got hurt on duty those individuals would immediately be told to get a drug test, company policy. NO exceptions. Well, crap, considering I was high as shit. No good deed goes unpunished, and it bit me in the ass. So, I gathered up the paperwork we were given and was sent out to get a drug test. I was freaking out and decided to try my luck with some pills—niacin. I took a handful and drove around for over an hour. I was hoping to draw out this test and hopefully the pills would do something in my body to not make me pop for the drugs. I arrived at the building, walked in, and by that time, my skin was burning, it was red, and I started to itch uncontrollably. Side effects were a full-blown situation. I had to have looked awful, like I was jonesing for drugs. The drug test employee smiled at me with a bit of a "uh huh" vibe. I was in such pain. I'm pretty sure she knew I did something, since she told me the other employee showed up hours ago. She asked, "Where have you been, did you get lost?" I told her, shrugging my shoulders, "I got lunch since I was hungry." I peed in a cup and ran to my car feeling like I was on fire! Some time passed and I was told the other employee was fired. He didn't take any illegal drugs, but a prescription pain medication that was not prescribed to him! I was shitting my pants, thinking, "I am a legit pothead." I never got called into the office and I was in the clear. How the hell did that happen? I don't know. I would eventually leave this job and enlist in the Army.

CHAPTER 12

will she want me back?

I was five-years-old; I remember my adoptive parents sitting me down. They called for me from the kitchen. I was in my room. At the time, I was too young to know those tiny steps would be life changing. I remember it was nighttime, after dinner. Thinking back, this talk may have been invoked by me starting kindergarten, in case the subject came up—family tree projects, friends asking questions, eventually making cruel jokes. I was the brown girl in the Irish family of fair skin and small stature, who would eventually be the tallest in the family. Stories from my adoptive mom would involve telling me that when she strolled me around as a baby, people would look down and look back up at her not knowing what to say. My dark skin did not fit my new family's mold. Tonight was it: I would learn why I was different, and it would become a source of confusion, setting me along the constant journey to know more. Who am I?

I remember the walk down the hallway—light brown textured wallpaper, framed pictures of deer (a passion of my adoptive dad). A long, narrow pathway. My room door was at the end of the hallway. A T-shape. My bathroom and the master bedroom were at the end of the hallway.

As I walked down the hall, I noticed them looking at each other, waiting for the other to talk. I stopped where the carpet and linoleum met. The dad pointed to our dinner table, the table being our one family spot. Our household was old school; mother kept as a housewife, father worked hard as a consultant to uphold a nice lifestyle. Smiles outside of the house. But inside, she would sneak liquor throughout the day, numbing her deep pain and always taking it out on me. Later, after I understood the effects of being drunk, she had a way of slurring her speech that I came to recognize as a cue to be on my best behavior. Bored, lonely. Isolated and unheard. I took note…never, ever wanting to be controlled and kept. Never wanting to be anything like them.

I remember sitting at the dark, wooden, hexagon-shaped table. A glass and gold hanging chandelier. The room had a view of the high bar, and a kitchen cut out from the hanging cabinets. Behind me was a living room that was decorated to match; lots of maroon, cabbage rose print, and ruffles on pillows and skirts on the sofa fabric. We never went in. It was cold and uncomfortable. This particular room would be a scene from another story told to me, when a raccoon came into the house and was in the room when I was an infant, lying down. My adoptive mom explained she saw it come close to me as it wandered around the room. She left me in there and got a neighbor to help. Following protocol, I was taken to the hospital to see if I was bitten and had rabies. Luckily, just a few months prior, the injections for the rabies vaccination had changed from multiple shots in the stomach to only one. I was vaccinated as a precaution.

He finally said, "We have something to tell you." She just nodded and said, "Yes, we do." She kept the awkward moment going and began, in a sad voice, "We must tell you…that you are adopted." I had no clue what that meant, but they were both sad and looked uncomfortable. Sidenote: this is reminding me of all the new viral clips of pet owners telling their dogs that they are adopted…getting "a reaction." It's so stupid. It's irritating to see it's so hilarious, with laughing in the background. There are those who do find out and, to them, it is life-changing. Being adopted can be a beautiful thing, yet now there are people equating the situation to their rescued dogs. In my case, I remember immediately crying and not having a clue why. Classic family-style, they just stared at me. No hugs, or kisses, or we love you. Just awkward silence. I was grasping the sides of the cloth placemats to soothe my feelings with touch. Waving my legs in the brown, wooden, padded seat to comfort myself with movement. I finally asked, "What does this mean?" They responded in a how-to book style. We got you from Mexico. We are raising you. You had another mommy. Brain overload for a five-year-old. Who am I? Another Mommy? Will she want me back?

I remember this follow-up did not help; I felt even more confused and had way too many questions. Questions to this day that still have not been answered. I never brought up questions about my birth again due to uncomfortable feelings and somehow feeling guilty.

From time to time my imagination has often pictured why I was given up and left at birth. I would like to imagine I came from a forbidden romance. My parents were ordered to marry different people. So, after their love child was born, they made the very difficult decision to leave behind the image of their love. Only after a parent's death will I be discovered and become a princess. So, I would like to thank being an '80s child, prone to the vastly unreal Disney romances, expecting to be claimed for royalty and for my kingdom to come.

Technological advances have turned my fantasy into new enlightenment. The discovery of DNA sites would soon uncover my secret family tree answers. This was my chance of finally knowing who I was and where I came from. It took me awhile to have the courage to get a kit. Spit in a container? Is that all? In that tube, the answers to my forty years of questions? Ok, let's do this, I thought. A small fee, and within weeks I received a kit. I opened the magical box and read repeatedly the steps to send back my sample. Signed, sealed, and delivered. Then, the agonizing wait. It took the advertised six weeks for my DNA to get processed. My email had a message from the DNA site. My heart pounded and there it was, my pie chart. My DNA. 38% Spain, 51% Indigenous Americas/

Native American, and scattered European areas. This was amazing! All my life, I had been told I was of a certain ethnicity, but it turned out that I was not.

Flash forward and I am having breakfast with my daughters after we visit a popular trampoline amusement park. I wear a simple workout outfit and a Billabong hat, trucker-style, with one white feather printed on it. I bought it in a surf shop. Innocent enough, I thought. I ordered our drinks and noticed an elderly couple sitting in the booth in front of us. The wife had her back to me, and her husband faced me. He kept glancing at my hat and shaking his head, apparently in disgust and disapproval. He waved the waiter over and demanded, pointing his finger at me.

"Why is she wearing that hat? What does it mean?!" The waiter could only glance at me and give an unexpected look.

My immediate thought was that I was just wearing a simple feather; it did not have anything to do with anything, like distinguishing a specific tribe. There were no writings that could offend anyone. This particular area is known for its Native American-owned casinos and reservations, and he couldn't imagine himself eating in a place with other, possibly Native individuals? This was extremely racist and ignorant to me. He seemed so upset and kept looking at me in an aggressive manner. The meal suddenly turned uncomfortable.

The waiter looked at me in embarrassment and shook his head while placing our drinks at our table. Minutes later, they left, and I watched in anger as this decrepit couple passed me. He huffed at me on his way out. I know for a fact if my daughters weren't there, I would have raised all hell! I just sat in shock and the wife glanced over as she left, a look of sympathy on her face. I sat for a moment and started to tear up. What is it about me? I called our waiter over and he apologized at a rampart pace. I explained to him that it was just a Billabong hat. He said it didn't even matter—the gentleman was cruel and shouldn't have been so vile. Apologies, apologies. He left for a moment, and I could see he was chatting with another female. He came back and said our meal was "on the house." Since they were gone, I hoped we could enjoy our meal. But eating a free omelet just didn't help the fact that this racist individual felt the need to point me out since he felt uncomfortable, having no cultural appreciation or even knowledge of a people who had been victims of genocide among so many more atrocities. His uneducated outburst was volatile, unnecessary, and left me feeling confused and angry. It was just a feather! It ruined my whole day. The comped plate of pancakes was just not enough to forgive the feeling of prejudice. I even donated the hat to Goodwill so I wouldn't feel the way I did that day. That old man won. Years later, I can still feel the pain of just wanting to fit in. My tall stature and brown skin make it hard.

With the results of my DNA chart, right in front of me, my ancestors' journey. Totally and completely unknown to me. This information was life-changing. With this site, you could see your DNA matches. This may have been where I hesitated for a moment. I could possibly see a blood relative. I clicked on the area to see my matches and there was one close match. It read: first cousin. After years of not knowing who I was, here, right on my screen, was a photo of a cousin? I stared at his picture. Do I have any same features? I ended up messaging Mateo, my cousin, and he was as surprised as me. "Hi, it's a girl." I knew I had to take things slow, not to rush him, since I knew no one in his family knew I existed. I didn't want to scare him off. After some time passed, Mateo welcomed me to the family. There was a phone call and we talked for a few minutes. I was so nervous. He was happy to find out about me. We were only a few years apart in age. If my life had been different, I could have possibly been raised alongside him. Sharing family stories, having pictures to identify with. He told me my possible last name. Very cool. I was excited to see where this was going.

There was a lot of investigation on Mateo's part, and I am so very thankful. More time passed and no one on the paternal side wanted to accept that there was this stranger looking for her father after forty years. The time was flying away, and I was anxious to hear if anyone wanted to meet me. I emailed every few months that I still existed and was interested in meeting. Mateo would kindly respond he was trying to talk with his family members, but there was not great feedback. I heard the word "scam" and that hurt. This paternal side told Mateo that it was all ridiculous and not real. But I am real, I am here, through science. I thought about how the situation could seem a bit unreal and how the discovery of me, after all those years, with spit in a tube, could be unbelievable to them. They could not get themselves to trust the technology, which broke my heart. This back-and-forth went on for two years. I am not a patient person, and this scraped at my soul. After some time of painful silence, there was finally a lunch with a possible dad or uncle match. My cousin has a large family, and on one side of the family, all four of his uncles—unfortunately—completely shut out the idea of being my dad. The shock of it all may have been too overwhelming. No other information was given, and no further interest in me. I wasn't there to demand any money or disrupt their lives, but meeting with my biological dad was a dream. So, on the mother's side of the family, there was one possibility who was open to meeting me. Sebastian had asked questions about me since his sister mentioned to Mateo that my picture looked like her. My saving grace; she gave me this chance to meet Sebastian.

That day came, two years in the works—the day I would meet a blood relative. The outfits were strewn across my bed. Ok, casual, not business, not too revealing, sensible, cute, but not too cute. My mind was in overdrive. Makeup, just some eyeliner, not too heavy, not a time to experiment, but long enough to cover my eyelid. Oh my god. Bracelets. Just a couple, not too clangy, not too showy, bright-colored? Beads? The drive was worse. What time should I leave? Early? Recon the restaurant? Wait in the parking lot? Yikes. What if they look at me and say never mind, this is a mistake...

I drove to the restaurant. Parked in the back. It was in an area that I had not been to before. The city had a busy, rushed feeling and one-way streets. I rarely drove down to the city. The restaurant was known for their pies that were colorfully advertised on their windows. It was old and had green-and-brown decor. A huge glass case full of pastries in front of the register, with lines of booths and tables. The kitchen was placed in the back left corner, with open-style architecture. Clearly seeing the chefs, waiters rushing around, and the sound of the chefs' bells for placed orders. The two of them were sitting at a booth, smiling, looking at the menus and talking. I backed away from view. I did not at that time have the confidence to just walk right up. I was screaming inside my own head. I noticed them both but was too scared to approach. I texted Mateo, *I'm here.* He stepped towards me, kindly smiled, and shook my hand. It was so strange. I put my tough skin on and didn't want to break down and cry. The meeting was long due to the translation. The show, *Long Lost Family*, indeed messed up the idea of that moment; all of us locked eyes onto one another. There wasn't a long run down a hallway, and there weren't hugs and sobs. I timidly walked up to the table and sat down. The possible dad or uncle spoke only Spanish. I looked at Sebastian a lot, trying to find any physical similarities. It felt strange to be there. He was nice, calm. Had a safe smile. He showed me a picture of his kids, but I quickly glanced and gave them no chance. I was there; they had had enough time. We figured out Sebastian would have been only nineteen years old at the time I came about. He mentioned that if he had known about me, it wouldn't have been like this. Just another thing to be mad about toward my biological mom. I only had basic questions and was not sure how to go about the meeting. Sebastian made sure to tell me he was a hard-working man and had a letter attesting to his character in a reference-style note. I didn't want to get nosy, but as a hard-working individual myself, I knew this was an important fact that he wanted to emphasize. Maybe we both didn't know how to go about a meeting under these circumstances. My cousin expressed how much he loved his uncle and that he was like a second dad. He actually paid for his college and was a great mentor. Life would have been significantly better to have this man as a dad, I thought. I could have grown up in an environment filled with love and support. Culturally, I could have had an identity. Up to that point, being told I was one ethnicity and then having 0% of that ethnicity felt a bit unidentified, and in that "other" category.

I was completely confused by the Ancestry site as to who I really was. This DNA match could supply answers I needed all my life. I tried to describe some of my childhood but didn't want to bring down the tone of the meal. We enjoyed breakfast, laughed, smiled, and I dreaded the time as it expired. As we walked out of the restaurant with selfies taken, I didn't want it to end. Sebastian walked with me behind my cousin and in broken English told me he "would be there for me." I immediately started to tear up. Not once in my childhood by my adoptive parents was I ever given such kind words. NEVER. This man who could be my dad was wanting to be a part of my life? Unbelievable. I drove home in a cloud of happiness. I looked at those pictures almost every day, hoping Sebastian was my dad. He and I were the same shade of brown, same height, similar smile... could he be? Or was it just me wanting this so much?

As agreed upon at our meeting, I went to a local paternity site and gave my cheek swab. The results would only take 3-4 business days. Unfortunately, by the time they made plans to go to the paternity test, the global pandemic started. It's been over two years now and the borders have closed and opened on and off to only essential things. Now, thinking back...I hate that I didn't grab a spoon or DNA-infused item from our breakfast. Tell them to test that. The DNA lab told me they can find one's paternity from an item of clothing, even. Rrrrr, dang it. Unfortunately, the distance of time and quarantine stalled, and future communication came to a standstill. I emailed every few months in the first year after our meeting. Heard nothing back. So, I decided to take a break from communicating. Again, unwanted. Again, ignored. What is it about me? I may never know if who I met was, in fact, my dad. I have tried not to think of more abandonment. It's hard not to.

It's been closer to three years since I gave it another chance by email. I had to update him on the paternity test. The company that had my DNA closed without any notice or chance to change offices. Nothing. The $350 I spent—gone. I called plenty of times, demanding an answer. But the owners didn't care. Lost. I wanted to see if they were still interested in taking the test. I could somehow go to another company. My cousin mentioned that his uncle's passport had expired, and he would not be able to cross the border. So, it may not be me, but the obstacle of his passport. I will take that information and ruminate on it.

The thing is, HOPE was still there; HOPE that my story wouldn't end there. I'm waiting for the day I get a call that they want to continue the process, see if our bloodlines match genetically, not as scam, to get a result that Sebastian is my DAD. I'm excited to begin this journey, meet other family members. Get a sense of my genetic makeup. The who I am and the why I am. What a different life I would have had if not abandoned at birth! Those pictures will have to do for now. Yearning for the moment I am accepted by them.

mirror challenge

An interesting writing prompt was given to me while attending a veterans' writing group. At the time, I was still struggling for my purpose and sense of belonging. I started with the women's group before the main group. Testing the waters and different personalities. I knew I had a love of writing and wanted this opportunity to jolt my creative side even further with knowledge. The women were open to expressing their feelings. It was nice to be with similar experiences. My first few groups I wanted to share, but I did not have the courage. Finally, with some encouragement, I started to read a poem. I glanced up and saw a room full of puckered mouths and sad eyes. So then, I couldn't finish, and I started to feel anxious, and tears poured down. Another member picked up where I left off and finished for me. They told me it was powerful and that I shouldn't stop writing. That was the confidence I needed.

As time went on, I went to the main group, too. This group had a variety of military war-era veterans. One distinguished man was a three-war veteran: WWII, Korea, and Vietnam. The sheer life experience present in these individuals is incredible. I have encountered many Vietnam veterans, retirees, OEF/OIF, pilots, Purple Heart recipients, former first responders, and retired government agency workers within this group. The stories pour out of the members. It is very cathartic to witness the events of these individuals, knowing that I am not alone. The tears, even forty-plus years later after their participation in a war, are still cried as if it happened that very day. Regret, survivor's guilt, death, friendships, families, brotherhood and sisterhood. We can relate to PTSD, the hardships, the effects, and shared camaraderie of serving.

During the women's group, this interesting quick write was introduced:

"Write as you would look at yourself from the future, past, or present."

Here is my starting point:

My biological mom, she is pregnant with me; I'm witnessing her being torn and thinking of her own future, of everything she'll miss out on. Selfish. I'm releasing some anger and telling her what she ultimately did. Thanks, muchas gracias. Bravo, lady!

Obviously, a mistake. It may have been just a night on the town. A girl's night out. But now you have *me* growing in your belly. Did you cry when you knew you were pregnant with me? Did you hate what was growing inside? It's a shame that research was not shown to you about how well a baby is connected to its mother in utero and that the whole thing should have been magical. Research has shown that during a mother's pregnancy, the baby feels what the mother's body goes through with the same intensity. These messages of emotions prepare the baby for the world. In my opinion, Mom, you prepared me to be a pessimist and warned me only of the strong, heavy, unbearable emotions of this world. Your signals of love and happiness could have been better. Did you always know you would leave me in a basket? What a cruel, barbaric way to treat your baby. Since being pregnant, having held my own babies, there is absolutely no way I could walk away! Maybe my circumstances were different, but I didn't have the opportunity to ask, so must assume, you did not care. Just discarded. Nine months and the plan was to leave? I have no record of birth; I was not born in a hospital. Not a note or a given name. No identity. Was I hidden, were you embarrassed by me, scared of who knew? Did you have any good feelings of caring for me for all those months? When I moved in your tummy…was it emotional or traumatic? Too many questions to ask…I'm sickened to know the truth. Are you happy in your life? Do you ever wonder about me? How many other babies did you toss away like me? Or was I the only one, and you kept all the rest? Remember…as the years go by…I will always hate you; I will never ask to meet you…this growing baby in your tummy will be way better off not knowing you. You set me up for a lifetime of hate, abandonment issues, and not knowing how to love. Take care.

Me as a baby: *Now, having been in this American family. Thanks again to you, biological mother, cheers, salud. Adopted by this family. By people who will loathe me, not love me.*

In turn, Dear Self, you will never be what they wanted. Just an ugly, brown bastard of a baby. Don't listen to them, though—you are beautiful! Blamed for the new adoptive mom's dad's death after only a short year in their presence. A sudden heart attack was the culprit for her dad being dead, not you. She will resent you, though. She will tell you that you were left in a crib, untouched. How could a baby take a life by just being? Babies ARE life. What is it about me? Unfortunately, Dear Self, you will always be someone to blame. This hate will continue. Constantly left alone. Who will love us? That question will not be answered, just more confusion. Don't try and reminisce about the past, there are fewer than a handful of pictures of us, no baby photo albums to look back on. No stories of our first roll, crawl, or step— those things, like you, will just simply not be cared about. It will be a pattern that continues throughout your life. But, Dear Baby, as I look at you, I think how bad this shit will be. You will develop abandonment issues and not know how to love. The story is always short due to lack of memory. These adoptive parents don't have any stories to tell. They didn't care about us. Elementary school is full of ups and downs and kids are cruel. They will slowly find out that you're adopted. They will ask what it is, but feel it is their obligation to say, "At least I was wanted, and you were given away." Fifth grade will give you a reality check and a foreshadowing. There will be a boy, and you don't mark the "Yes" box to be his girlfriend. He runs up to us at the bell for recess and pins you against the wall. Yelling at you, asking why you didn't say yes to him. Demanding. He's a popular boy and can't stand the word no. So, you do what you need to do and knee him in his balls. It is GLORIOUS! But he drops to the floor and circles in a fetal position, "Ohhhhh, it hurts." You look at the teacher and both of us get thrown into the principal's office. A male, who completely sympathizes with the other boy, doesn't care he pinned you and wouldn't let you leave. It's suspension for a day. But it will be ok. You've got a Gameboy and lay in your room, winning. No school.

Taking up writing, a beating. Not so wonderful memories. The writing prompt is sure diving into my soul. Looking back and looking at myself at these ages is emotionally draining. I'm remembering the triggers of incidents. It makes me sad to look back at myself, so young. The past is never forgotten. The teen years. Yikes!

To Teen Me: *Standing in gratitude to my biological mother, who didn't realize her actions, hat tipped to you.*

This may be the beginning of a spiraling time. When you smoke weed at thirteen, it will be life-changing. Introduced by your older brother, thinking it would be best to get high with him, so you know what it feels like. Someone to trust while being high. Then, after, you'll learn to smoke like a champion, alcohol will be the next step. You'll then drink like a champion at thirteen, too. Can't wait to drink. Tequila will be your favorite. You will be the girl who has to be carried to the car and dropped off since you will always be passed out. You'll have a great set of friends who do not judge and are always looking out for you, though. Some nights, you'll meet late at night under a star-loaded sky and get loaded yourself. They will drop acid, and you will smoke pot and drink. The nightlife, drug-induced trippy chats of tie-dyed skies and flipped universes are not in your acid trip. It all goes way over your head. But, in unison, your drugged-up comments are: "Ohhh, mannn, yeaaaaaa, sweeetttttt." Not very enlightened or world-changing but in agreement with how trippy life can be. We will always have fun! Acid is a clear choice for many of your friends, but you will stay away from it, from rumors of tripping out years later. It makes you nervous. The thought of being at a grocery store in the future and having an old acid trip and tweaking out will not seem fun. Stopping is never an option, though. You will run away at fifteen. I know we are survivors. So, I can't warn you not to do anything, because you will do everything. Thank the gods we are out of that house! The night we do leave home is in the middle of the night, but don't be scared. You will literally run with no shoes on. Your best friend's family will be your first stop, and it is a ten-mile sprint, walk, jog on a two-way road, winding through country roads. It is in the middle of the night; the road will be lit up by the spaces in between the tree lines and the glow of the moon. It is hard to see and your jumpy movement down the road leaves your heart in a panic. Any noise, and you turn around. Leaping onto the side of the road thinking your adoptive parents are the oncoming traffic. Completely horrified and in shock by the cool of the night, your best friend's family will open the door to find you hypothermic and afraid. Your best friend will be scared, and her mom will try to grab your arm but you're so scared, you'll pull back and cry. She will embrace you and say you are safe. They will be nervous but understanding. You will be free, but it comes with a lot of transition and hard work. A few months there while we get a small grip on the new reality. Our best friend will be our lifesaver. Most days, she will witness you laughing and enjoying the drunk-induced ride. Smoking weed every day, not giving a shit. Not a care. Our teachers are coaches and will give us passing grades so we'll continue playing. Playing hard, getting high, and working through multiple sport teams: volleyball, soccer, swimming, track, cross country—and the championships always on the line. The coaches let some grades slide. Our coach will tell us in class to study. As you walk out, he will mention everything will be ok and, "Let's go get our rivalry team this week!" Emotionally, you will struggle and often get angry and run from any conflict. You will still feel out place, and this will lead, eventually, to trying three high schools. Trying to fit in and find an accepted niche. No luck. These years will be a blur and most of the time will be completely erased. At fourteen, you will start to model and get an agent. There will be a great opportunity and you will be an extra in a movie starring multiple A-List actors. So much fun, and the movie scene can be paused again and again so we can notice how young we are. Around seventeen years old, a couple of sexual harassment cases will happen. The company Foot Locker will pay you $1,000 just to shut up. Being groped, rubbed from behind by the manager's erection with unwelcomed touching, which was caught on tape. His career is on the line, and he does not want to have any charges or get fired. You will meet a corporate lawyer and won't understand what he is saying. You will be paid off to conceal what happened. At nineteen, you will work as a hostess and be sexually harassed by the kitchen staff. One time, you will walk back to the timecard area and an employee will grab your arm, pulling you towards him. This disgusting, dirty man will try to shove our hand down his erect pants. You will break loose and run out. We quit. The manager will call back a few days later and apologize. Too late. I know this is a lot. I am always at a loss. New habits of running away will be our muse. There will be a set of people from work that will attach themselves with you, leave. Do not succumb to their wanting to be your friend. You will be heavily supplied with drugs but will be unknowingly helping to transport their supply to buyers. The "cool" nights at tweaker motels and that very distinct chemical smell is not good. It will be meth cooking in the bathroom. Stay away from these guys. The developing anger that will be expressed with be blended with weed and anything that can get us drunk. During early high school years, sleeping in your car, cleaning apartments to stay in an extra room or on their couches. Senior year and steadier times. All these ups and downs in our teen years; feeling alone, abandoned, and struggling to work full time as a student while our friends had no idea of our struggle. Successfully pushing away anyone who asked, "Why are you so mad?" You don't know us or our past. When, exactly, will shit get easy? Not yet. So many other tales, too much to write. It's all jumbled in my thoughts. The teen years were extremely hard, let that be that. You will come out of all of this. Life settles later on, Little Me. Trust me.

CHAPTER 14

mental dodgeball

*G*enerational pain, trauma from the past. It was easier to push deep inside than to reach out. I unfortunately took way too long to seek help and re-work my brain that is hardwired from pain. This is a struggle. When I grew up, the constant was, "You're a bastard, your mom's a whore, and take her (Kitchi) back." Love was nonexistent for me. Not in my favor. A hug. So simple. In my youth, hugs could have set my entire thought process on a different path. Two arms outreached, and with a step towards your loved one, you grasp them. Basic. A stupid hug. I cannot take the responsibility to give a hug. I was not raised with such nonsense. I had never in the fifteen years I lived at their house witnessed the parents kissing, holding hands, offering any sort of touch. Instead: avoidance, loathing, alcohol, negative comments, arguments. I avoid these steps due to the discomfort. I wish I was embraced tightly by my "mom", feet dangling in the air while we laugh, and I can't breathe from the death grip of love. My household was cold and silent. No forms of affection. I tried not to get in the way.

Meeting new people is tiring. I notice groups of people going right in. I can easily be in a new environment and be completely exhausted physically and emotionally. I will take the next day or so alone, doing absolutely nothing. Enjoying the decompress time. Witnessing others enjoying these hugs. I stand off to the side and smile and nod my head, shifting past. Avoiding contact. Phew. In adulthood, I became a natural at avoiding the greetings of new people or seeming to be busy just at the moment of contact. If I walked into a crowd, sooner or later one in the group would talk and the flow would move past the potential for my connection. My greatest victory is to stand too far away and greet. It would be a weird, long reach. It's just a hug to most people. It's mental dodgeball to me, with my past and unhealthy relationships. Building the trust to let go enough to embrace is difficult. My daughters know, unfortunately, to not go behind me or grab me from behind. I have an emotional reaction if caught off guard. My sense of being trapped by their tight arms around me makes me feel like I can't move or breathe. I feel bad after, but I have to tell them to let go or not that way. "Just calmly slide in if you want to cuddle, be gentle." I ask them to give me a moment so I can prepare. Many times, the very movement of their arms coming closer triggers a strong response to flinch. My older daughter has seen this too many times and says, "It's ok, Mom. I am just going to hug you. I love you."

My love language is acts of service. Words do nothing for me. I have been so beaten in the past that words themselves are not validating. But, putting action to those words shows me an incredible amount of love. Simply, with...love. Being close, having trust, extroverted and spontaneous? It just isn't my thing. That has made it hard to develop friendships and, worse, relationships. Receiving any sort of compliment? So uncomfortable and I immediately feel small and lower my head naturally. "You are so strong Kitchi." I cower, then I feel like a fraud. Any sort of emotional boost was non-existent growing up, so I am not sure how to react. I realize opening myself up can be tricky. First, there is an invisible thousand-foot wall to be crossed; a moat filled with crocodiles, walking into a booby-trapped trail. But, after that, I am all yours. It may seem like an Indiana Jones scene; it feels like an emotional ride to me. I have been actively trying to jump into social situations, wading in the waters. Letting go of the overwhelming chest tightening of "getting out there" and looking for my person, a friend that could, in fact, be a life changer. Support, someone to lean on.

My adult relationships are very sparse but have carried the same complaint of me being too distant. Arm's distance apart. Upset at the fact I do not carry on with devoted displays of affection. Not holding hands for a strange amount of time (to me), maybe the occasional squeeze of affection, walking a few steps in front. I do carry myself proudly and not daintily. I show an air of confidence, but it's just a mechanism to put outward. My insides are mush with low self-esteem. When I do have that overpowering affection towards another, I start to stutter-step, extend an awkward arm, and ask, "Can I give you a hug?" It has been a joke on so many levels with friends I have known over the years, "Ok, Kitchi, I'm going to hug you. Don't make it awkward." It's just a hug.

I show my love and appreciation with acts. But, simply speaking the phrase "I love you" is so mentally exhausting to me. I have been kicked and knocked down in some situations after others said they "love" me. I feel a shield self-preservation go up. Since I do not know what is going to happen next, it is another shuffle step and moment of silence to work up the courage. I feel I have hurt relationships in the past by not being able to say the words or even be able to give a pet name. It sounds so ridiculous to me to call someone "boo boo", "sugar muffin", or "baby cakes"; affectionate-sounding pet names are so cringy to me. But it seems hurtful to some to not be able to share an inside name with each other. I cannot promise I will become an overly excited pet name caller but will try and be creative with the names. For example: wait for it… Working on it…Geesh, even in this moment, I cannot give myself any slack and type any. Ok, here I go…love muffin….NOPE, not ready. It's all just too much.

Another little kink in my reality is that I have some food complications. It developed in early childhood when I would eat snacks and my adoptive dad would make eye contact with me; he would blow out his cheeks, making an exasperated sound. His interaction would be demeaning. It was not funny to me, nor welcomed. Not a great gesture to a growing girl whose self-esteem was already low. I know I have "food hiccups" from these moments. My way to cope with my depression and a sense of control in the chaos of my past is to try to attain a goal—my intrusive thoughts are about daily meals and snacks. I plan ahead to space out the portions that I can have. Weighing myself daily is a must. I have a strict goal weight. These numbers will plan the rest of my day. Either I will be very mad at myself and get angry for eating that extra slice of bread, or constantly picking at the extra pull of skin and wobble of my upper arm. My mommy pouch is there to remind me of more skin folds. It is difficult to be held, arms grazing my sides or tummy can be extremely uncomfortable. Bad thoughts of, "Do they feel the fat?" It sends me into defense mode. If this magic number is not achieved, I will hold back or lessen the meal intake to get back on track. It all sends me into a slight range of depression, then I eat more, and then I get frustrated. If I have obtained the goal, great, I eat extra and then spiral the next day if my weight is up. An exhausting ordeal. It could be the combination of making me feel bad for eating from childhood trauma and adulthood abuse. Either way, these habits and behaviors can take quite a toll on my mind, body, and relationships.

Which brings me to an unfortunate incident that made me a victim of my own mind games. A former boyfriend, whose stature was "big-boned", showed love through cooking. He made great food, and his family was the same. They would come together to have dinner, share secrets and laughter with each other, help each other. What was this atrocity? Families who were close? I couldn't get used to it, this strange environment. It got to be uncomfortable. So, this situation with food got me to my boiling point. I thought he wanted me to gain weight. I couldn't handle the thoughts and our relationship came to an end. I felt overwhelmed. I needed to achieve below my goal weight, then binge for reward. Back over the goal weight and back at depriving myself.

The only two events that I fully indulged in were both of my pregnancies. I gained seventy-five pounds both times. The mental note was, "I'm eating for two. It's for my baby." So, the indulgence gene may be there, too, but I don't want to tempt it. Both of my girls became my priority. Love was pouring out of my pores. My mother nature genes kicked in high gear and made sure they were and are both loved. My oldest daughter was the first baby I ever held. I was scared, before them, to hold a small, fragile newborn. I was young and inexperienced. I didn't want to break her. It turns out gaining over seventy-five pounds for each baby helps in a small way. Army nurses were concerned about the weight; I reassured them the baby wanted all those breakfast sandwiches. Breaking both of them was not likely. Both girls were solid, chubby littles. Both twenty-one inches long and both eight pounds, with a few ounces between them. My obstacle was trying to fill them up. I wanted to hold them and make them feel safe. Generations often unknowingly repeat mistakes by accident or genetic code. I couldn't imagine leaving my girls, abandoning them. Not being able to watch them grow into beautiful young ladies. Having them feel discarded. The curse will stop with me.

Surviving what I have gone through is my struggle. I do not want my setbacks to deny my daughters their happy existence. At times, we will joke, sharing my dark sense of humor. They will say something along the lines of leaving something behind or throwing it out. I will say, "Sure, leave it, just like me, easy enough to just leave it behind." They cringe or look at me and say, "Aww, mom!" I laugh. It is all fun and I remind them that I love them. The girls are old enough to understand the story of my origins. I do struggle in some areas of physically being there for them, but if they need something, my love language of acts of service soars. I make a point to tell them they are amazing, and I am so proud of them both. They are both equally beautiful souls—so caring, so empathetic, and so bright in their respective talents. Each has amazing strengths and I want them to build that confidence of a "yes I can" attitude. We have long talks, getting to the bottom of any problems. Communication is key with them both. Their age difference makes the issues very different, but I make it a point to help or just listen and be an active supporter. They are not the monsters of my past. I know how important it is when they rush into my arms. Their warmth is contagious, and I love them so dearly. I have learned about compassion and being a momma bear to protect my girls, even if I didn't have it for myself. I am determined to not have my childhood repeated.

CHAPTER 15

signed on the dotted line

I grew up in a small town in Northern California.
In the '80s it was dairy farms
Anything military-based was foreign
I don't remember in elementary school honoring the brave
No recognition for hometown heroes
I did not know anything of that world

I grew up in a family that never wanted me.
Adopted from a foreign land
The parents showed no love
To me or to each other
One would scream, "Take her back!
I never wanted you!"
A '50s household determined to fake smile
Nothing is wrong here
Behind the closed doors
Is a different story

As my childhood turned into teenhood
A runaway, always the partier
Having fun, social scenes
A bit rough around the edges
Alcohol and marijuana to numb the memories and pain

As a young adult I worked full time
Making rent for a room
As a deli clerk in the local grocery store
I was 20 at this time
I looked down our workplace behind the counter
And stood in a moment frozen in time
Do I want to be here with all the other older ladies
Packing deli meat, fixing sandwiches, frying the food
Until my retirement?

One phone call changed it all
A recruiter called
He introduced himself as a staff sergeant in the U.S. Army
He asked if I wanted to see the world
Wow, well this seems legit
Oh my, I would see the lies in between the lines very soon
I signed up and left two weeks later

Shaved head
Ready for the Army
A short conversation with my beloved grandpa
He cried when I told him I enlisted in the Army
He and his brothers were all soldiers in WWII
He wanted me safe
I was "his girl"
The only one in the family to show me any attention
I assured him it's a different Army

Six years the Army had me, a sergeant
One deployment
A combat veteran
Honorably discharged, with some forever unwanted gifts

Chapter 16

hey private!

After I ran away at 15, my life was full of things I had to do just to make it—working full-time as a high school student to pay rent for a room, homeless for a moment and sneaking into a fast-food restaurant to sleep in the ball pit of a playground, living in my car for a short time, struggling to feel happy. Finding a place to sleep was a bit challenging. On and off traveling around and parking. I was once caught. Unfortunately, my history teacher, from the second high school I went to, was walking around in Berkeley and tapped on the window while looking into my car. "Kitchi?" saying my name, in a confused manner. He decided to walk to a shop and grab me a burrito and asked if I had "somewhere to go." I replied that I was just "waiting for a friend." What a lie, he and I knew it. That next Monday came, and I had his class. He looked at me with sadness. I did get a passing grade in the class, not from my above average performance, but as a kid whose life took a hard road. I was typically getting high and drinking 'till I went into a complete spin. I worked at a local grocery store as a courtesy clerk and helped in the floral department. I learned to adapt, work hard, and grow up fast. I have learned that things, good or bad, come in pairs and to be prepared. Events over time have been just that. I was the captain of my high school track and cross-country team. I loved to be social. Friends were important to maintain. Parties were a must. I didn't know, but the hardest years were yet to come. I will learn about life, power, influence and figure out...I don't have it figured out.

I was 20 when I enlisted in the Army. It had been five years since I last saw my adoptive family and I contacted them to let them know I would be enlisting into the Army and was leaving in two weeks. That was the extent of my conversations with them. My grandparents had also been a part of the separation; I decided to also let them know. My grandpa was the only one in the family who cared about me going into the Army. After I ran away from home, I only saw him a few times, on short visits. He once saw a tattoo I had gotten on my ankle and said, "You got a stain on your leg." I guess I didn't do a good job on covering it up. I felt bad and I hoped he knew I loved him, but it was better for me to separate from the family. He cried and worried that I would get beat in training due to his and his brothers' experience at their boot camp before their deployment in WW2. No one talked about their service. It was as if it never happened. I reassured him that it is a new Army. I would find out his concerns were, in fact, valid.

I had never seen anyone in a military uniform. The very thought of the military was foreign to me. I grew up in a small, rural farm town. Ironically, when Noah received an Uncle Sam postcard, wanting him to be all he could be, I cried that it was a considered possibility for him, not wanting him to leave. Ironically, not knowing my own future, being only ten-years-old at the time. A full decade later, and I would be making an oath to my country. To be all I could be.

I had no idea what to expect in the military. There wasn't a class before I enlisted on what the differences of each branch were. No military history lesson. Not unless you had family who could tell you about it based on successive generations of enlistment. I had no clue. I needed a purpose; I was stuck working multiple jobs with no chance at any college. The military, I thought, would be my chance. This came with many outside struggles, emotional obstacles. I would learn some truths quickly just in the first month of my training to become a soldier.

There are many circumstances that are heartbreaking. The unfortunate reality for some soldiers is the rate of suicide. Within the timeframe that I was at boot camp there were two soldiers who took their lives. There were only whispers of the situations, but we could never ask any questions or make any inquiries. I remember as time progressed, one soldier in my platoon was ultimately discharged from the Army. He decided not to participate, argue, and consequently left with a wide smile and wave to us all. Some soldiers who demonstrated a mental health decline were put on suicide watch. Their battle buddy would have to be with this soldier everywhere: bathroom, shower, chow hall, barracks. They could not leave their side. No shoelaces, belts—they would always look so defeated. That soldier would even have to sleep in the hallway, on a cot, near the DS office and night watch. Eyes always on this soldier. The very same months I was there, 317 soldiers had been evaluated for depression and or suicidal tendencies. 211 were in fact identified as suicidal, with 146 soldiers held on "suicide watch." Even mail call was an event to be delayed or kept from the soldiers due to upcoming tests and the possibility of hearing bad news from back home. This could also have been the cause of the deep dive into the mental health of some soldiers. I remember after the range, we got to have some letters from home. They would strategically know when to release letters. The concern was they didn't want any "Jody letters", or news that your girl dumped you or has been cheating on you.

It was Fort Leonard Wood, Missouri. It was a time of year when particularly high heat and humidity would hit you in the face when you went outside. The air was thick, and a second layer of sweat would envelop our bodies. There was a huge number of incoming soldiers at the time I enlisted. All of us were on hold, waiting for an opening to be assigned to a platoon. This was called "Reception Battalion." We were all wide-eyed, looking at one another like, "What the hell did we get ourselves into?" Drill sergeants (DS) would walk statuesquely, turning their heads and bodies almost robotically to catch anyone looking out of place or doing the wrong thing. You could never tell where they were targeting on, since the brim of the DS hat blocked their line of sight from everyone else. Like a hawk, they would dive towards a recruit and yell at whatever it may seem was wrong. Even if it was as small as slouching in a chair: "Put both feet on the ground, hands on your knees, straighten your back, you ain't back home, you are MINE!" Of course, we all did something wrong; this environment was so brand new. We were all issued an Army regulations book; it was small enough to fit in your side pant cargo pocket and we spent hours reading, or trying to. Drill sergeants would remind us to always keep our "Bibles" with us and make sure we all memorize every word. "You will be tested." It had all the specifics on everything Army: uniforms, conduct, marching, weapons, etc. I seemed to read it, but nerves didn't help, and it was a distraction to look at. "Hurry up and wait" was a learned behavior. Rushed over here and there to "hurry up and wait" for hours. We were put into small co-ed groups to start our paperwork, get our uniform fitted and issued, plus receive shots and haircuts. The medical lineup was a room packed with females who would walk in a line circling the outside of the room, pull down our shorts just enough to expose our top of cheek, and lift a shirt sleeve while getting multiple stabs by rough personnel out of uniform. Most males on haircut day, I noticed, weren't too excited. Walked in one door seeing many locks, fros, long shoulder- length hair. Then they came out the other door—one style—buzzed. They would walk out rubbing their nicely buzzed cuts and white untanned heads as in shock.

We would get marched to every appointment, chow, and temporary barracks. Those temporary barracks...they were so aged—tall wooden structures, paint peeling off. Inside was a long, narrow room with dozens of bunk beds lined up next to each other. I was closer to the exit on a bottom bunk. The wool blankets were scratchy, and I didn't want to waste time in the morning making up the bed, so I slept on top of the sheets and blanket. There would be drill sergeants posted at the end of the room near the exit. I would hear some light chatter at night. One night, I saw this female start to walk down the row of bunk beds. I thought maybe she needed to use the latrine. The drill sergeants noticed her and yelled at her: "Hey PRIVATE, what are you doing?" This female did not answer and kept walking. I heard a shuffle and one responded, "Oh shit! She's sleepwalking! Don't wake her!" The female seemed to moan, and the drill sergeants guided her to a chair. I kept my head down and pretended to sleep as this happened right in front of my bunk. I never saw that female again. She must have been sent home and got a military discharge. If a service member has a physical or mental condition that impacts their ability to perform their assigned tasks or could put others at risk, like with sleepwalking, they can be discharged.

This new environment was overall stimulating, and though I was around all these new soldiers every moment, there wasn't any time to chat, laugh, or get to know anyone. It was hectic and sometimes scary. Using the latrine was a quick, rushed experience. Everything had to be precise and rushed. A female drill sergeant would surely come in as you were sitting down, yelling, "Push and squeeze females, hurry it up." Soon, I would learn that this post had a nickname. It was called Fort Lost in the Woods, Misery.

As time passed, our group had orders to start boot camp. For our initiation, and to add a sense of confusion, we were all rushed around with our rucksack, our duffle bag filled with gear. Drill sergeants came right up to our face, not even inches away, yelling at us to all hurry it up. We formed one line, and running one by one, we were all crammed into a cattle truck. The metal was hot, and there were only slits of window space. All of us had to stand, our gear at our feet. For hours we were driven around, the curves in the road bouncing and shifting our bodies into one another. I could hear some sniffles behind me and a question of, "Where are we going?" Some tried to get a little shut eye, others stood within an array of wide-eyed glances.

We finally arrived at our destination. Bravo Company, 2nd Battalion, the Undertakers. We had two drill sergeants, both male. Boot camp was about ten weeks in duration with three phases. Each phase had a purpose. As written in our graduation pamphlet: "The objective is to begin the soldierization process by teaching the new soldier discipline, spirit, and basic combat skills while toughening them mentally and physically."

From the very beginning at boot camp, we were all soldiers. Our cadence echoed loudly... "The Army colors...the colors are green...to show the world...that we are mean." As I marched, I would get a sense of pride. I knew I found my purpose. This exact fact of finding our purpose will be a challenge after getting out of the military. We would soak in all the information and knowledge; we would be immersed. It did not matter what biological traits we had. All soldiers were punished equally.

So, it began. The soldierization process started quickly when our platoon got faced with a lesson requiring cooperation and teamwork. Strategically, the head DS, Garza, yelled, "ATTENTION, HALF RIGHT... FACE." We got several lessons a day and soldiers would do the wrong thing then be made as examples, especially of what not to do. A smoke session ensued. To be "smoked" meant physical punishment, platoon or singled-out individual, to teach us not to do something wrong. Every day, any time, throughout the night. No one wanted to be an example. Our DS would call out who made the mistake and in cadence we had to "thank that soldier." I remember this experience being an equal opportunity whooping. Male or female, if you made a mistake, everyone paid for it. Many, many early mornings on the intercom throughout the barracks, "Everybody out, you have 3 minutes to form up outside in your BDUs, GOOOOO!" Anytime we could be called out, in any government-issued uniform, and at times be told to change multiple times. Running back and forth changing in the barracks, running back outside. Then the dreaded moments of waiting for the DSs to look back into the barracks building to see if any of our quick changes led any soldier to drop an item of clothing or have it out of order. If that happened—it always did—the sounds of wall lockers and bunks being flipped were stereo loud. The yelling and howling of how we are, "Unsat, disgusting soldiers, who smell like feet and ass!" We all knew we were in trouble. Of course, our punishment meant some intense "smoke" sessions. It could be anytime of the day or night, and we only had minutes to make the barracks perfect and in order. If we were unsuccessful to change in the allotted time, the smoke sessions ensued. I didn't talk to anyone to get to know them except my battle buddy. She was by my side the entire time. Together, we endured the heat of the pavement on our hands that was literally blistering. Tough as nails, she got one the size of her palm, but hid it to prevent any attention. Finally, when the DS noticed her hand after she kept lifting it up as she was doing push-ups, he wanted to see her hand. She shifted and stood up. Then she held out her hand. The DS could not believe it. He then proceeded to ask why she didn't tell him about this. He made a speech to our platoon that this private was tough and pushed through the pain. She responded that the pavement was hot. He knelt touching the ground and said, "Shit! It looks like it is! Platoon! Attention! Fall out and form back on the grass off the pavement. MOVE!" She was sent to medical while we were still punished. Blister popped and wrapped, she came back and wasn't in so much pain.

On another noted occasion at 1 a.m., after hearing the intercom yelling, "You have two minutes to be outside, summer PT uniform, MOVE!" We stood outside the barracks waiting for the drill sergeants. A soldier suddenly passed out in formation. A DS ran over and started to yell at her, but then hauled her off. The soldier had been bitten by a brown recluse spider.

Time passed and we were going through our phases to complete bootcamp. The one and only time I got into any trouble was in the chow hall line. Our platoon had lined up inside the chow hall. There were two entrances, and we would be lined up on the wall side of each entrance in a wooden wall barricade. It was neck high, and you could see what was going on. We would line up back to front, breathing on each other's necks. It would always be packed. Another platoon would be finishing up eating; we were allowed to come in once that other platoon left, but only when the DS allowed. That day I was so hungry after a long day of punishment. We were lined up and I glanced with my eyes only to a table where a soldier was eating. I just wanted to see what was for chow. As soon as I glanced, I felt frozen and slowly looked up to the other side of the room. There he was, a DS locked in on my eyes. I quickly moved my eyes forward and held my breath. "Shiittt!" was my inner monologue. He ran over and with his DS hat, he hit me on my head and yelled, "HEY PRIVATE, get outside and start running around the building!" I exhaled and left the building and started to run, still hungry and now with no food. Something must have happened to him since I never saw that DS again.

As our rotation through boot camp, we all had the privilege to work in KP (Kitchen Patrol). It was a bummer to assist the kitchen staff, take orders, peel potatoes, throw away trash, all while being harassed by other DSs. The only kicker was we got to take an extra allotted time on chow. At this point we all inhaled our food, did not breathe, and tried to fit all in our mouth in one scoop— if we even had time to use a utensil. I remember my KP duty, a DS yelled at us to go get a plate and sit down. The group of four of us ran and sat down, we looked like a zoo exhibit, we shoved the food in our mouths, slightly glancing up to see if we were going to get yelled at to leave. At this point, one DS turned his back to us, and his shoulders went up and down. I did not process it until years later since I was so desperate to eat, but he was laughing at us. We were animals!

Along with the phases of bootcamp, we would be trained intensely on our new career paths. Soldiering standards met. One qualifying factor was the rifle range, which was an interesting time. This was the first time I ever held a weapon, at bayonet training. The DS told us, "If bayonets are ordered, hell will touch the ground. Your new love is your M-16, love it, name it, take care of it." We were all extensively introduced to our new "love" and made sure how to break it apart, clean it. During our instruction we would line up outside of the armor room and one by one get our assigned "love." We would run out of the room while yelling, "One shot, One kill!" Then off to the back of vehicles that would drive us all to the range. The sun wouldn't be out yet and we would be clanking in the back of the vehicles in full, battle rattle gear. As we neared the range the sun would start to gleam, and the mist of the cold morning was in everyone's breath. One particular day at the range will never leave my mind. It was just a couple of days in, and there was a tower on the range where a DS had an intercom system set up to talk with everyone. It was loud and you could still hear instructions even when all the weapons were firing. "Move slowly, do not run, walk to the end and stop, DO NOT MOVE!" Once all the soldiers in this group had stopped at a number on the range, we stood there waiting for instruction. "OK, now slowly left face while keeping YOUR WEAPON DOWN RANGE!" The instructions were so basic and easy to understand but in an environment like this, my grip on my weapon was tight. We all slowly did as we were instructed. Only a couple soldiers were yelled at to keep their weapons downrange. The count of soldiers worked out to be two per lane. One soldier would sit on a bench a few feet from the soldier who was firing down range. There were a handful of DS pacing on the firing line helping soldiers clear a jam in their weapon, help tightening up group shots and we were getting instruction to move in one straight line down the range. This time I was sitting on the bench, waiting to fire. A female who was firing was listening to instruction at the end of her session. The DS yelled: "Now everyone get up slowly and KEEP YOUR WEAPON DOWN RANGE!" I was getting ready to go up to the line when that other soldier in front of me completely ignored all instruction. She walked towards me while pointing her weapon at me. I shifted back a bit and just then, two DS sprinted and tackled her. They were in her face, "What the fuck are you doing PRIVATE? You could have killed someone! Get the FUCK off MY range!" They stripped her of her weapon and with her head down, she moved away from our group. The DSs looked at me and shook their heads. That someone could have been me. Well, that was the last time I saw her. Not sure what happened.

Time would pass and new habits would be formed. Drinking full canteens and holding them upside down until nothing more trickled out would become routine. A regulation-measured wall locker, always kept with precision. If there was one shoe not perfectly lined up, beds not properly pulled tight, a string hanging off your uniform, a pocket not buttoned, a "dust bunny" (lint for example) on the barracks floor, socks, underwear not folded in a regulation roll? The DS would find any and all errors. Then the shouting, the wall lockers being knocked over, beds flipped, items kicked. Soldiers cringing at the violent scene. Finding any time at night to shine boots; cans of polish, lighter, water, rubbing circles for hours, whatever it took. "I better see my face in those toes!" would echo from our DSs' mouths.

Marching was the only mode of transportation. We marched everywhere. Classroom instruction, rucks, PT, chow. It ended up being one my favorite things. The DSs would have such loud, often funny cadences and thunderous voices. Cadences for example: that poor "yellow bird, with a yellow bill, perched upon my windowsill" that seemed to always get his little head smashed, it seemed nice and sweet in the beginning. Or singing, "When your granny was 91, she did PT for fun..." and up 'till she died, "Saint Peter is there at the pearly gates." There were loads of meaningful cadences along with "Captain Jack", "Army Colors", "I left my home for the Army." It was our new way of life. Becoming soldiers. Our platoon could run and or march with great on-step beat. Making louder footsteps, hand claps and in cadence felt so motivating. As time passed and our weeks were getting closer to graduation, a particular cadence became very popular to all of us. We would sing the cadence with some lines being: "Sound off, two, three, five more weeks and we'll be through, we won't have to look at ugly, ugly you!" Nearing graduation time it became very motivating to each closer day. Then, it became, "One more week and we'll be through, we won't have to look at ugly, ugly you!" Then, even better, "One more day!"

CHAPTER 17

it's the small things

When we are young, we are taught about our five senses. Senses are crisscrossed with emotional processing. Most people have turned a learned sense into something good or bad from an emotion. In my case, memories, flashes of the past during the day. Thoughts of anger, my career taken from me, shame, being discarded, loud sudden noises, crowds, traffic, feeling of being trapped, strangers walking around me, strangers looking at me, people standing too close in line to me, bouts of sadness, hopelessness, fireworks are dreadful reminders of the mortar explosions, the list is very long. My senses have imprinted new emotional responses.

As a child, playing with sparklers and waving them through the air spelling my name, I enjoyed the fireworks show. Now, the loud pop and sizzle display can send me back to my deployment overseas in a negative way. A handful of years ago I thought I was ready for a firework show. I was with a group of friends that invited me. We got there, parked, set up a nice spread of food and games. The atmosphere was cheerful, and the parking lot was spaced out and everyone was having a good time. I thought, yea, I can do this. Time was passing and the sun set, and it was getting darker. The announcement of the firework show was to begin in five minutes and the group decided to go closer to the top of the hill. I walked with them and stood there as one pop and sizzle went up after another. I shuffled back a bit and felt scared and nervous. No one reacted, so I stood there and noticed smiles and cheers. Ok, maybe I can do this. Then the blast of freaking hundreds of pops and sizzles. Oh, hell. I scrammed backwards. I ran with my arms imaginary holding my weapon and I sprinted looking for my battle buddies. Of course, they weren't there but at that moment my reality was back in deployment. I was out. A friend sprinted behind me trying to catch me. He finally caught up and he pushed me into his truck and blasted music. I sat in the front seat, covering my ears from the fireworks, just crying. This was the most embarrassing thing. I stayed in the truck for almost an hour. I finally got out and found the group, who was trying not to make eye contact with me. Even more embarrassing. I couldn't drive and had to be dropped off at home. I wasn't ready.

Another unavoidable sensory overload was at a local restaurant. Natasha, my eldest daughter, and I decided to go to a local breakfast shop. We stood in line and ordered our pastries; I told her to get a table since the crowd seemed to come all at once. I sat down, distracted by getting my coffee and settling in at the table. Within moments of sitting, feeling trapped, I noticed that the crowd was getting uncomfortably big. The tables were crowding in all around me. The customers came from all directions, circling me, walking in front of me, at my side, in every direction. I couldn't watch it all. My head was overworked. I felt so dizzy and began to become nauseated, my heart started to pound, and I had pain in my chest. "Tasha, I am going outside for a bit, I'm not feeling too good." Natasha is very aware of my reactions to crowds. It was too much that day. I ran outside, tried to breathe while not trying to hyperventilate. My heart seemed to speed up. I waved to my daughter to come outside. As she walked outside, I told her, "Let's go. I need to go to the hospital." I thought the whole car ride that I was having a heart attack. Natasha kept a calm voice, "It's ok, Mom, I'm here. We are on the way." We went to the nearest hospital. I was put in a wheelchair, they took some tests, asked about my past. The male doctor came into the room and reached out to my hand and my instinct was to immediately pull back. I was a bit jumpy, and he had reached out fast. He looked at me with sadness and empathy. "Hi, Ms. Feenix, I am going to be your doctor for today. It seems your tests have come back all in the normal range. Can you tell me what caused the pain and dizziness?" I told him, "My daughter and I were in a café and I felt overwhelmed and couldn't breathe." The doctor responded with, "Ms. Feenix with your medical history and what you are telling me, it seems you had a panic attack, which can in fact feel like a heart attack. You did the right thing to check. How do you feel now?" "I feel better now, thanks." He looked at me kindly and sympathetically. Whoops. I felt embarrassed.

So many of these senses have left my body in distress. Even a simple can of tuna fish can bring back bad memories. A simple glance at the tuna fish aisle will bring me back to deployment. During my stint overseas there was a suicide bomber who dressed up as an allied soldier who walked into the chow hall and blew himself up, killing a handful of soldiers. The chow hall was destroyed. I spent the next four months or so walking into a small truck trailer that was a mini mart or PX to buy tuna fish packets and snacks for chow. I did not want to go back into the chow hall. I felt unsafe. Head on a swivel. If I see the tuna fish packets, I will remember that time.

There are too many incidences of me driving and triggers making it nearly impossible to do so without feeling the overwhelming rush of sweat, freezing. Motorcyclists who push the throttle to make a loud, sudden noise. Through sitting in traffic, at a light. It makes my entire body shudder and tense up. I get so caught off guard I will start to cry. I tend to flashback to my convoys in the road. Noticing everything around me. Trash piles on the side of the road still makes me weary, loose debris that moves across the lanes makes me hold my breath. I get tense, try to avoid the debris. If I have no choice, I will drive through it and feel overwhelmed and angry that in a sense I put my daughters in harm's way. At times a stupid leaf will be picked up by other drivers tire and fly at my windshield. A stupid leaf and I feel I cannot breathe. The fact it is coming straight towards me is all I need to get scared and my anxiety to rise.

These senses have all been a part of my life. It's overwhelming at times. When people witness some of my unique behaviors it can be embarrassing. I try to make a joke or quickly recover but it's a part of me. Senses have been intertwined with humans for survival. It is crucial. There is a sense I have for a particular smell. It was during boot camp. Memories can be a good way to remember positive and happy situations. There are different ways to recover these moments and for me, in this case, the significant memory is smell. Senses can be heightened with memory recall of a past experience.

Luckily, not all the senses are alerted in a negative way. I like to think of these times. Happier times. With my mind constantly heading toward the pessimistic, a few positives can help. At times, smells can leave a mark, transporting me back to a time, an era, my youth.

One smell that will always remind me of hard work, dedication, and achievement fits inside a palm-sized Kiwi shoe polish can. During our first steps of processing into boot camp, we were rushed around a shopette with a small list of items to get. Holding a hand basket and a generic ATM card given to us with an allotment from the Armed Forces Bank, we rushed around scared and bright-eyed. We couldn't make eye contact with anyone; we were there to get our supplies, quickly. Drill sergeants were screaming at us, "Hurry up Privates!" Our freedom was the property of the military. Shower shoes, brown towel, soap, soap container, shoe polish, running shoes, etc.

"Soldiers you better hurry up, buy it, and get out in formation!" a drill sergeant screamed. There was no way that I wanted to be last, get smoked, and be called out in front of the entire formation.

From the very beginning it was branded into our minds that our boots were to be shined. We had a quick smoke session to learn how our boots should look. Drill sergeants would pace in front of the formation and give instructions. Showing us from the front leaning position (push up position) how their boots looked. Trying to remember how to shine them with sweat dripping down my face in the peak of summer in Missouri. I got the drift. Shine, shine, shine.

"I better see my face in those toes. There better not be any scuff marks!"

Late nights after lights-out seemed to be the one and only time to shine our boots. Every night, taking thirty minutes or so to spit on the heels and toes of the boots. Use a dab of water, borrow a found lighter to heat up the polish. putting one hand in a sock circling. Any trick to get a deep shine. Making the heels and toes of the boots shine like glass. My battle buddy and I would switch our flashlight cover to red and pray to the boot shine spirits to make those toes shine. Always looking out for any heavy boot steps from incoming drill sergeants. When that happened, we would have to jump on our bunks and fake being asleep, trying to not get everyone in trouble since we were up past lights out. Issued boots were a dull black, and it was hard work to break them in. I would twist that Kiwi polish handlebar snap open lightly and hear a low popping sound. Lifting the side of the can open. Then the strong, industrial smell of the black shoe polish. This will forever be a smell that takes me back to boot camp.

Chapter 18

my niche

At boot camp my platoon had two drill sergeants. One: the head DS, Garza, had a deep voice, shaved head, and eyes that peeked through the rim of his head gear. He could do inspections and stare into your soul. "Private, why are staring at me? Do you think I'm pretty?" My ultimate favorite was..."Have you lost your military mind?" If any soldier seemed to be lost or did something so stupid, they would be called out loudly and corrected on the spot.

One continuous call out was to ask if anyone had a complaint. DS Garza would yell, "Do NOT SPELL MY NAME wrong, it's DS G-A-R-Z-A! Do not have a piece of lint or thread loose on your uniform! God help the platoon!" His cadence was crystal clear, loud, and he would robotically move in his highly starched uniform. Creases that were perfection. Another DS—I don't remember his name, but the nickname was "The Hawk." He could be in your face one moment and circle around yelling at another private in the next moment. He earned his nickname. He was the silent, a stealthy DS. Funny thing is, the very last day of our boot camp rotation, he inspected me, looked at me, and asked if I had been in the platoon the entire time. Stared at for an uncomfortable amount of time while he tried to remember who I was. I was so quiet, he hadn't even known I was there. Success never got called out. I also looked completely different by that time. Sadly, I was issued the standard government-issued oversized, one size fits all, brown rimmed "birth control glasses" (BCGs) and had a shaved head. I looked like the brother I never had.

As time passed, our platoon completed each phase. The training was more in-depth in combat life-skills. Using the gear correctly was key. Military knowledge was key. After a few weeks, we were told we had only minutes to file into formation outside the barracks. We were marched to a multi-purpose room. All the current platoons of this battalion were sitting high backs, hands on knees, head straight forward. Different officers came to talk. One standing like a giant walked side to side. His pace was intimidating. He confirmed news that had been in the newspaper. He knew we couldn't see a newspaper or call home, but there was a world event. He yelled, "We are at war!" Shifts in seats, some gasps, others seemed excited. I sat in confusion. He told us that we were ready to be deployed. He mentioned that we were "the first to graduate and the U.S. is calling for us to be deployed overseas, our duty is to be the soldiers that we have trained to be..." I thought, have you seen us? We are all just working on marching commands and are failing at that. Whaaaat? He told us we had five minutes to get back to the barracks and pack up. Buses leave in fifteen minutes. Dismissed. We ran into the parking lot, obediently. Formed up. Marched back to the barracks. As I walked into the barracks, some were crying. Some seemed happy. I knew immediately it was just a joke. We could not possibly represent the U.S. Army without having graduated boot camp. The U.S. should not depend on our platoon for any war infiltration. We will lose if we get deployed. You wouldn't want my platoon to represent the U.S. Army...eek. We hadn't been trained in our jobs yet! But, I packed as told. So many tears by other females, preparing to get prematurely deployed. Within the allotted time we marched back to the multi-purpose room. The same higher ranks came up to the stage.

They told us that it was all a ruse. They wanted to know why some of us, the soldiers, came into the Army. If it was for college, then we would have enlisted for all the wrong reasons, they said. Some were ashamed, blasted, and I sat there. Unfeeling and thinking I passed this test. But many tests were given throughout boot camp. You had to adapt. Challenges arose, mental exhaustion set in.

The time came when we were trained to put on a gas mask properly, making sure it was ready to put on while placed in your bag. If the day came and the hand signal for gas was motioned, we were ready: pull up on the Velcro top of case, pull out mask, cover your face with it, pull straps overhead, tighten it to your face, seal it. All the steps we practiced. Over and over again. Then one day, all our training would come together. The entire Delta Company marched into the woods; the gas mask strapped to our legs. Immediately I got a weird feeling of…we do everything for a reason. It seemed like we marched for hours. It may have been my adrenaline. This time, there was a group of eight DSs I had never seen before, all from the other platoons. They arranged us in a tight sitting circle in a spot in the middle of the woods where trees had been cleared. The atmosphere was calm. One by one, the DSs demonstrated the use of smoke colors and why we use certain colors for signaling medical, wartime, helicopters, etc. The colors of the smoke were bright, and I remember the slow "sssss" sound of them being released.

All of us were so packed, our knees were touching each other. All that time, I had my hand on the mask bag; trust nothing. Then, the time came. I saw a head nod from one DS. Oh shit, it's going down! Immediately some drill sergeants walked backwards, grabbing their masks, others seemed to walk towards it. A canister of CS (tear gas) was popped off. I remember grabbing my mask and pulling it out, placing it on my face and making sure that I sucked and blew to seal my mask. It was sealed. At the very moment, being so packed close, many soldiers did not get the hint and seemed to be in so much distress. I cannot forget the horror on their faces. Some struggled to seal their masks, as coughing sounds echoed. Others pushed, grabbing their battle buddies, and yanking on uniforms to pull themselves up. Such desperation and cries. I saw soldiers run off into the woods. I was packed in the middle of this chaos, noticing a select few like me, watching the horror. Looking around and being grateful for remembering the training. Calmly sitting, hoping to any god that our masks were sealed, and that they would keep the falling white pepper burning particles in the air from being inhaled.

One male soldier, directly across from me, did not get his mask on. He was not in my platoon. He was trying to hold his breath, only took a deep breath in, his eyes becoming so watery. I looked at him, through my mask, safe. I could hear my own breathing and smell plastic from the face shield, plus the feel of the weight of the filter system. He looked like he was melting. He couldn't get up, so he desperately reached out to me, grabbed my uniform, and tried to grab my mask. I thought, "Oh noooo!" I pushed him away and yelled at him to put his mask on. I will never forget the look on his face. The CS canister particles flooded this male. Knowing that even though he felt like he might, he would not die. The look on his face is what I can look back on and laugh. So, Ft. Lost in the Woods came true. Aside from the soldiers who ran into the woods, the rest of us were formed up and marched back to the barracks. It took a few hours to find those missing privates. Funny moments were scattered throughout bootcamp. The military taught me to pay attention to my surroundings. I was ready to become the best soldier I could be.

Graduation finally came and it was an exciting day. We all got to dress in our Class A uniforms with our earned graduation ribbon, grenade, and rifle medals. We all looked super sharp. Took loads of pictures, promised to always keep in touch. Unfortunately, soldiers would be sent all over the states for their schools and quickly lose all contact. It is just the nature of the military for friendships/partners/families to be torn apart, by the needs of the military. I had only recently seen one soldier from boot camp closing in over twenty years after, at the local VA. She looked like she hit some hardships; she was homeless, I heard from the uncomfortably loud discussions she had with office representatives. She had been screaming in the lobby for an unknown issue with her bags. "Don't touch my fucking bags, you're going to steal my stuff." She did not recognize me, but I remembered her clearly and hope she has gotten assistance since.

Families flew in from all over the country and overseas. I went to dinner with my battle buddy's family, and I really appreciated her for the great meal and freedom for the few hours we got to enjoy. It was a whirlwind immediately after walking through our graduation. I, along with a group of soldiers, was bussed over to Fort Lee, Virginia from Fort Leonard Wood. We were all shuffled to bus lines and gave hugs. We were then able to get our civilian bags from months before and able to take a look at our clothes with colors, which was a shock due to seeing only grey issued PT gear and our BDU's camouflage. I grabbed my contacts, needing to be rid of the government issued glasses. On this journey, I excitedly threw away my BCG glasses and wore my only pair of contacts. At least I started to look halfway presentable. I still had a shaved head, which I decided to keep during training due to quick showers, never getting in trouble for one follicle coming down below my collar. It was very convenient. The bus ride was full of sloppy, sick, sneezing soldiers. The one bathroom was not any better. Unfortunately, and embarrassingly, I got pink eye in both eyes. I woke from a nap and both eyes were shut with goop. I had no choice but to take out my contacts. I am very nearsighted, and for the next few days, I had to follow groups around hoping it was my platoon. Everything was so blurry, and I could only focus on big movements of multiple people. If I heard a loud voice and saw fellow soldiers, I would follow the sound and hope I had the right platoon. I stayed back noticing anyone looking familiar and listened for, "Fall in!" Only then did I know the message was for me and took my place in formation. After a few days, the cadre noticed my embarrassing predicament. Both eyes disgusting, me with my arms out trying to find my way. Yikes. I was rushed into medical; I got drops to relieve the pain and discomfort. They ordered more BCG glasses! Crap, once again—those things.

Eventually, no pink eyes, I was ready. After the in-processing for all the new soldiers, we were assigned a unit. A brand-new assigned platoon, and I was officially in AIT (advanced infantry training). This was our school where we would learn how to do the job we enlisted for. I saw my battle buddy from boot camp, but she was in another platoon. Only in passing or a quick pass to go to the PX (mall or Post Exchange) is where I got to say hello. AIT had more freedom which you would earn by doing what is expected, staying out of trouble. The cadre did not humiliate soldiers, but guided and emphasized the importance of accountability. We all got to see them as humans and to observe them and learn from them.

Every day we marched multiple times into this huge, prison-like courtyard. Four cinder block multiple floor buildings, barred windows, maroon trim, facing each other. The buildings had a sand pit in the middle for soldiers who needed to be taught a physical lesson. A paved walkway surrounding this pit. On one occasion, a large group of rocks on the side of a building was moved to the other side for maybe a DS power move or boredom. This area was where we marched each day before class, after class, and for mail call. A funny mail call time was when this Colombian soldier kept getting these brick-like packages, sealed tightly. The DS would call this soldier out every time and examine the almost drug paraphernalia-inspired package, asking where he was from. There would be a low level of laughter from us. The DS would shake it and make him open it on the spot. It was always cookies, and the DS always got a snack to "make sure it was safe."

We would be proficiently marched into a circle around the pavement, still marching in place, then sharply turned to face each other in designated platoons calling out echoing cadence. All in step, turned with precision. Four platoons calling out cadence. This was the best time. A loud, thunderous beat; the cadence was thrown by a musical DS. DS Williams was our cadre in charge. His voice was so melodic. I loved singing the cadence from his beat. Motivating. My happy time. My favorite memories were the cadence called for...

"I left my home"

(DS called out) I left my home; (Soldiers repeated) I left my home

I left my home; I left my home

To join the Army; to join the Army

The day I left; the day I left

My momma cried; my momma cried

She thought that I would surely die; she thought that I would surely die

(Repeat initial top verse, and add family members to cadence)

It is somewhat solemn, but I had goosebumps when a hundred plus soldiers were all in step, sounding off in one heartstring-pulling cadence. Most missed home and longed for family. Some lines were more operatic, emphasized. It was beautiful. Usually, it was sung at the end of the day, after chow before we were dismissed for the night.

My responsibility in AIT would soon take shape quickly after all the soldiers got used to our new cinder block home. As we were assigned to our platoons, we got to meet the soldiers that we would know for the next rotation. There were soldiers from Haiti, Colombia, the East Coast, West Coast, everywhere. My roommates: one was from Texas and had such a happy, hyper disposition, and the other...well, I could not understand one word. She was no doubt from a deep southern part of the States. I had to apologize all the time for not understanding her. One day she just left; I got back to the barracks and all her gear and wall locker were empty. It turned out she had to go home quickly after she was called to testify in a court case. We had no other details, but it must have been something serious; we never saw her again. So, in this particular room, there were three beds, and only two were assigned. Both of us had a wall locker to store everything. Each item had a place and, in that place, it was either rolled tightly and or lined up according to regulation. We could put up a couple of pictures on the inside of the wall locker door. Shoes that were laid under our bed had to be in a specific order. Boots, running shoes, shower shoes, all lined up, no toe broke the perfect line of the bed frame. New habits were formed, for sure, due to the punishment that came when anyone had anything out of place. To this day, clutter, piles of clothes, unorganized situations make my skin crawl. I avoid certain shopping stores due to the chaos of how they do not keep up with the clothes, items being thrown on the ground, sizes all wrong and in the wrong places.

My training school would be for automated logistics specialists. I was supply— specifically trained for the warehouse environment. It was fast-paced, always busy, and in the future, our training would allow for a smooth support order to be distributed correctly and efficiently. The next thirteen weeks (about three months), we were trained. Days were filled with classroom lectures and hands-on demonstrations. It was a bit of a relief from the level of punishment at boot camp. We were finally, fully baptized into the Army, and soon, I found myself entering the depths of leadership.

As the military is laid out, we had to have a platoon guide, or PG, in charge. This position was demanding because the PG led the whole platoon. The responsibilities included accounting for everyone in daily attendance, making sure all soldiers were keeping up in class, making sure all were in formation after a weekend pass (which, most times, there were two or three stragglers always sprinting towards formation), and handing out any important information given to directly by the cadre. The day came to decide who in the platoon would take the PG role. We had to take a PT test, a written exam. There were twenty-two soldiers. The results were in. The males seemed to get ready for their victory lap, all smiling, sitting up proudly. Then my name got called for beating everyone in the tests. I did it. It was a bit shocking from just a few months earlier, before boot camp, not being able to hold a few push-ups and then beating everyone in the platoon. We had so much PT, so many "smoke sessions", that push-ups came naturally to me by then. I was the PG for our platoon! The males were then a bit quiet, but all gave me a hit on my back, "Oh shit, PG!" Again, with this small taste of success, it was a happy time. During AIT, there were so many mistakes made by other platoons' PGs. The DS would call on them with questions, making fun of them if they didn't know, and embarrassing them. One constant was roll call. Before we would leave anywhere, we would first do a head count and make sure we knew where our soldiers were. At times, there could be one in sick call, two running an errand, three on clean up duty. If the PG did not know exactly where to account for their platoon, it was quickly and swiftly corrected. Then, the dreaded, "YOU'RE FIRED!" would come next. I was never fired. As PG, I continued standing in front of our company formations and in class settings, calling out the cadre attendance and issues. I was the face of the platoon. I wore the pinned rank that designated my position. Other soldiers got a bit jealous of my performance.

I took my responsibility as PG especially seriously. I wanted to be a true leader, to make sure my soldiers were each doing well. I thrived and I loved the routine and discipline of the military, considering my wandering spirit before. I needed to do my best and to push myself to new levels. I ended up also overseeing the floor of our barracks building. I was responsible for making sure the hallway was always clean, waxed, and polished. No trash. Our rooms were held to a strict standard of cleanliness. It was all stressful, but I loved the pressure and shouldered my responsibilities for myself and others like a pro. Before Christmas break, the female drill sergeants screamed at us to get our building ready for inspection. They told us if we did not paint our rooms and hallway, we would not be granted a pass to go home for a few days. The other females grabbed paint cans, brushes, and scrammed down the hallways. There were not enough supplies, and I had to make the decision for the other females to grab a shirt and dip it into the paint can to get the paint on the walls. Desperation. We had no help. No way to ask for more supplies. Get it done by any means. So, we dipped the shirts in the paint and started. Painting the hallway and our rooms.

Unfortunately, as happy as I was with my newfound freedom and competence, the military environment was not ideal for my future health. The barracks building had a secure layout. The windows could not open, the bars on the windowsills made it Fort Knox just in case of a suicide incident. So, with our floor being painted, the fumes were so massive, headaches followed. We had to live through the weekend with the fumes. Unfortunately, I did not make it. Within twenty-four hours of these fumes, I started to not be able to breathe fully. I coughed consistently. Then, it was lights out. I remember lying down on my bunk and coughing so loudly my throat felt like it was closing. I ran out to the hallway and collapsed on the third or fourth floor. It's been over twenty-two years since my 1st diagnosed mild TBI. I remember slightly waking up and fading out, then being on the first floor, not knowing how, and lying on a gurney. Flashes of ambulance lights, an oxygen mask, and one female drill sergeant screaming at me, "Why you trying to hurt yourself, private?!" Just following me, pointing her finger and yelling.

I was a bit confused; it was hard to breathe. I woke up the next day in the hospital. I had pneumonia and a fever. I was on oxygen. It was not a good look, not a place where I wanted to stay. I needed to get back to my platoon. I couldn't risk the chance of being recycled to another platoon, graduating later or not at all. I wanted to be back. The next few days, my platoon would be in the field as a graduation requirement. I was stressed at the time, but I was so weak and couldn't breathe without the oxygen mask. Within a day or two our drill ser- geant, who I will never forget, stepped timidly into the hospital room and looked amazed at how bad I looked. He sat next to me. I breath- lessly and painfully asked him to keep me in our platoon. He started to cry. He just sat next to me and asked if I was comfortable. The shock of his soldier being on oxygen and having pneumonia could have been a bit too much for this DS. I could barely speak at that time. I felt weak and would inhale slowly and shakily for the oxygen to flow through the oxygen concentrated mask. I must have looked a bit sickly, maybe pale. I wasn't saying, "Aww. Thanks. He really cares," but I was scared about what the doctors might have told him before he walked in. Did he know something I didn't? Was I not doing good? He told me he would do his best to keep me in the class and on track to graduate. I was happy, and he left. After the field problem, I got to come back. I lasted the entire training as the platoon's PG. Despite the one setback, I completed the PG leadership role, and it taught me to be accountable for all the drama and ups and downs of a working platoon. As I was promoted through the ranks as an enlisted soldier, I was very motivated to keep standards high. In turn, during my enlistment, I would honor the Army core values. I was still so thankful that I graduated with my class. Here, I thrived. I found my niche. The confidence I earned when given leadership roles during my military service was among the first successes I had in life. They would serve me well in the future.

CHAPTER 19

the sandbox

I took a drive to my hometown some time ago. As I drove through this once-small town, I recalled what was torn down and noticed what newly built shopping centers had appeared in their place. The winding roads now have rows of scattered, dilapidated barns. In my 1980s–1990s youth, it had scattered dairies and farmlands with lush green fields. Some things have not changed, like the wooden plank sidewalks along the Main Street stores.

One building I did pay attention to was the Veteran's Memorial Building at one end of Main. By then, I was a combat veteran myself; I'd left the town twenty-four years prior. I took my first visit to the building extra slowly, appreciating the tall, gothic-style structure, white interior, large deep brown beams, long wooden benches and tables, and a large stage. On display were pictures of current VFW activities, member appreciation certificates and plaques, and the history of the building. As a youth, anything military-based was foreign. In elementary school, there was never a moment to honor the brave. No recognition for hometown heroes. I did not know anything about that world. Now, knowing the sacrifices, there resides a deep feeling of love for my fellow brothers and sisters-in-arms. Within that connection of shared service, there is a comradery forever that can never be taken from me.

Though my military chapters are written and forever imprinted upon me, I can look back and acknowledge my accomplishments. My past military service as a female is rolled up into a swirl of emotions. I feel honored that I served. I worked hard to become a sergeant within three years of enlistment, and it was a priority to keep all the Army standards. Handpicked for schools and leadership courses, I kept the values in the forefront. Mission-minded, not losing my "military mind." I have one deployment under my belt for Operation Iraqi Freedom and an honorable discharge.

Before my deployment for Operation Iraqi Freedom (OIF), there were months of training for a combat environment with a year of "boots on ground" in the sandbox. We were shuffled around during the processing of our paperwork, filling out our last wills and testaments, any last-minute medical issues, which can be a decision to stop your deployment status. In fact, one sergeant was not deployable due to an unknown diagnosis of sleep apnea. He was sent home. Another soldier's wife told the command she would kill herself if her husband left. She would not be able to handle her husband leaving. So, he got orders to go home, undeployable. During deployment there was a female who tried and was successful in getting pregnant. She was then sent back home to care for the child, but her plan was for an abortion. She was successful. Long days of training, sleeping in huge tents, using porta-potties, chow hall menus, huge bins of free Red Bull to keep all of us wired. Every soldier got their initiation into what the combat zone could be. We had classes in the basics of first aid, the terms of war, firing range, security protocols, our mission. An eye-opening class was some videos of propaganda showing Iraqi elementary school-aged classes singing, in sync, "Kill the westerners." Pictures of the then-president with devil horns and blood dripping from him indicated that we were the enemy and had to be killed. Something to breathe into, something to prepare for. This environment was going to be nothing like anyone at that time had explored. I knew one thing for sure: I wanted to come back home and be with my daughter, who was only a year and half at that time. She was my motivation.

My maternal grandma, I found out, had supported me in this journey as she thought would be best; being such a religious believer and so devout, she would have a prayer card printed for me, wishing me safety on my military deployment. An action that would make me smile, knowing she took the time to think of me. Growing up, my visits with her were sporadic. It was an adventure for little me, sliding in the back of a leather-seated sedan. Seat belts, not important, and I had free range climbing all over the back seat. A metal beast that seemed to slightly glide and bounce. I could go back and forth in the back, looking at all the cars and glancing at the Bay Bridge. A toll worker would grab the money, and off we went. The Bay Bridge, enormous, miles of wires, and a repeated sound of a small "dah-ding" over the separations of put together freeway. Treasure Island, then the yellow lights of the tunnel. Against the backdrop of the city, it was scary and beautiful driving into the clouds of fog. Unfortunately, I would never see my maternal grandma again after my deployment, as she died and within a few months of me being overseas. I will always appreciate her last loving gift of my safety.

While in combat training, there was the opportunity to become a certified combat lifesaver. There was an option given to us for extra classes away from the training for a selected amount of time. Not in the desert with flushing toilets and buildings? Sign me up! "Combat lifesaver certification, bus leaves in ten minutes." Ok, I'm going. It turned out to be an interesting classroom instruction. First Aid, CPR, tourniquets. Then the moment came when we all had to partner up and stick an IV into our arms. My partner was a 6'5", 255lb male—I thought, this will be easy. He's so big he won't even feel the gauge of the needle. So very wrong I was! I started to prep. The instructor was with me, I was talking through the steps, "Ok, so now I need to…" As I glanced up, my partner was starting to get ghost-white and a bit sweaty. An onlooker pushed him upright and I pushed that needle in. Almost in sync, two other soldiers went down. Both soldiers hit the ground. One looked like he died in his chair and the other swayed off his chair and fell. Not a great course for them, but a great laugh for everyone else. We joked if we felt sick or needed medical attention, to move away from those two. But we all ended up certified and were required to carry a medic bag.

Training was ending. We were prepared as much as we could be in a short amount of time, bonding with our new brothers and sisters. A few days before we got the date of our departure, we got the OK to get bussed to a restaurant as a bon voyage. The percentage of males over females was high, so of course, the prime choice was Hooters. Nevertheless, I wanted to get off the dusty installation and have a meal. The chicken wings were touted to convince the few females who were pressured to have Hooters as our possible last meal that this was the right decision. The restaurant was full of waitresses gliding past the young soldiers. Hair curled, makeup, lashes, and those "uniforms" of persuasion. The males seemed to be drooling; and to think, it had only been a month away from home and their testosterone was already in full force. Our deployment orders were for up to eighteen months. It was going to be painful for them. A waitress flirted with a soldier sitting next to me and she shifted her head and pushed her body on the side of my arm. Then, her hair whipped past me and she asked, "What are they doing here?" I looked back at her in disgust. Hellooooo! I am in the Army, too. Females are soldiers! Sigh.

With boots on ground, this new environment and platoon were going to be my new family. At the time of deployment, I was 23 and a supply sergeant with a secret clearance. Only one other supply staff sergeant had this type of clearance. In the beginning of the deployment, we went on convoys to get the lay of the land; the routes from camp to camp and intel meetings on road conditions/closures and possible threats. As time went by, I oversaw the convoys, and I knew what a great responsibility that was. They were exhausting, mentally and physically. The heat of the sandbox was so high. Waking up would be an easy 120 degrees, and the temperatures would only rise during the day. The sandstorms were blinding. You could see in the distance a sheet of dust/sand, and it came in quick. I drove at full speed, with no rules, not braking for incoming traffic. My M-16 was locked into its holder by the door frame, always at the ready as I drove the vehicle. An eye in the mirror counted the vehicles behind me. Listening to any radio callouts. Metal rock playing in the background. It kept up our spirits in an environment that nobody else would understand.

Our convoys were four to five days a week. Three to four vehicles were packed with supplies; equipment that had to be protected due to its high security. On occasion, there was a long list of personal supplies that I bought for soldiers who never left the camp. Some soldiers would find or hunt me down and give me money and a list of things they would want. Most times it was candy, noodles, DVDs, batteries, Gatorade powder, things that would sell out fast at our own camp. I could easily spend hundreds of dollars of their money on beef jerky—essential items in the sandbox. I knew they were stuck and didn't have any other chance to get these supplies, so I did what I could and carried back loads of bags.

A certain route to a camp would always lead to a shack right outside of the gate. I made sure to stop at this small, outhouse-sized shop filled from floor to ceiling with bootleg DVDs. It was close enough that the military could stop, park, and walk close and check out the "store." $5. It was so popular. Most of the selections were produced from a person holding a camera during a theatre experience. It was rare to find a new DVD that wasn't copied, or even worked. It was a gamble. I bought *The Notebook*, and watching on my computer with headphones, cried my eyes out. Emotional ride. New movies that were still in theatres were obviously shot with a handheld camera, shaking, at points drifting up or down. The quality was horrible. At times you could see a person casually walking into the view of the camcorder. So awful. Again, bad quality. But provided temporary relief in being able to transport us to a funny or romantic place instead of a combat zone. Most of the movies that the camps sold to us were so expensive.

I was the only female in my convoy group, and the one in charge. With this great responsibility, I knew I had to take a step back. Take a breath, knowing that with one rotation of my vehicle tire outside the camp gates, we could come upon an incident that could change all our lives. I walked along the convoy line, one by one, checking that our vehicle order was set. I would call a short formation for any updated news on what camp we would go to first, where we would drop off supplies, how long we would be there. I'd provide any important information that my soldiers might need to know. In our vehicles, a call would go out on the radio for each vehicle to check in, and steps were taken for the safety and communication of all. Meticulous maybe? Yes, being prepared was key. At that time, it was commanded to have sandbag floors, a cheap way of protecting us from explosions, no doors, with no armor on our vehicles. We were told it was just in case RPGs were fired at us. The whistle through the air would give us time to roll out of the vehicles. Well, that lasted for at least six months, and our soldiers were being killed. Then, the new command order was to keep the sandbag floors, but to add doors and find any armor we could add to our vehicles. Luckily, the motor pool had talented skills and found scraps of metal to add.

The order came too late for many soldiers. Finding a safe vehicle driver was another failed mission. In this journey, I fired a SPC due to his horrific driving skills. "Hey SPC, stop riding the side of the road!" He just squinted and looked scared while letting me know, "Yes, Sgt." Not even moments later, "Hey, SPC, do you want to kill all of us? Get off the side of the road." That infamous portion of the road that was known to have been planted with small mounds of IEDs. As soon as we stopped, "You're done!" I kicked that SPC out of my vehicle and I drove the rest of the deployment. It only took one anxiety-filled convoy to know that SPC would never drive again.

One convoy, while driving through a highway, the cars were starting to stack up in light traffic. I had a quick interaction which taught me how women are not appreciated in this part of the world. The traffic was steady. Vehicles were driving alongside us. I had three male soldiers with me in the Humvee. I glanced to my right, noticing a woman in a hijab, sitting in the back seat of a civilian car driven by two males. She looked at me; I gazed back. Our lives were so drastically different. I had the freedom to drive in the military and a rank to be in charge. She had no rights. We both were both covered from head to toe—me with armor, and her with religious garb. Two different sides of the world. Though it happened so fast, I think back to it from time to time, proud of my service and the freedom this country gives us.

As a soldier on deployment, there were the details of 12-hour tower duty, radioing any activity other than normal, hearing mortar rounds that were soon to be just another noise near camp. The unfortunate detail in 120-plus degree weather guarding gates. High alert always. I was not trained for security details, but since our battalion was more of a permanent party, we were in the rotation of these duties. My deployment included so many ups and downs. High alert was transferred into my DNA. Leadership was mandatory as a sergeant in charge. The lives of my soldiers were my responsibility. I did not ever want to have to explain to my command and or a soldiers' parents why their son or daughter died or got injured. I did not want that on my conscience. One time we were delayed by a shooting outside one of the gates, and a civilian national got shot and killed; there were intel of IEDs. Our convoys were lucky to have no losses. Convoys were only one facet of my deployment, but I'm proud of my soldiers who worked together and had each other's six with successful missions.

My schedule was packed, and I needed to find an outlet when I did find some extra time. To clear my head and distract myself from the constant doomsday challenges of deployment. I would volunteer at the USO tent. The USO's tent was so amazing! It was the only tent that was carpeted. It had different areas set up with computers, a huge screen TV with movies playing and comfortable seating, along with an area to play games on multiple TVs or check out movies. My job was to stand at the front desk checking in boots and other gear, handing soldiers over their cubby numbers. I worked with a couple civilian contractors. One was a stateside contractor and the other a Filipino woman who had married a Kuwaiti man. She told me stories of his abuse while we worked. She was a beautiful young lady who had a dark, abusive past. She felt comfortable enough to confide in me about her husband who would lock her in the bedroom if male company came to the house. She held her arms over her face, showing only her eyes, and said she didn't like wearing her "ninja" clothing or niqab, a veil for the face that leaves only the area around the eye clear. He would beat her if he was mad or just wanted to beat her. She would eventually find out her husband was cheating due to a clever way of seeing if the soap was used, since he always washed himself more carefully, obsessively, after an affair. She would push a finger to imprint the soap. When she checked and the impression was gone, she knew he cheated. She did eventually divorce this man. I felt sorry for her; she said she was temporarily stuck there until she could save enough money to go back to the Philippines. The stateside contractor had the freedom to visit town and buy food. He brought some "Mexican" food, and I hogged it down. He wanted to thank me for continuing to volunteer. Chow hall food was doable, but a cheesy, smothered burrito…I was back at home. I savored each bite, enjoying the taste of a tortilla, shredded chicken, rice. It was heaven! The three of us had a great time sharing stories and laughing. I really appreciated his kind gesture.

Reflecting on my time as a woman in the military, it was a constant struggle trying to be accepted. My six years were packed with many bad situations and some good. Despite the experiences of being discarded early in life, and of these playing out again later in life, I'm proud of my service. No one can ever take that away from me. I didn't expect my journey in the military to be this way, but the violations started the moment I signed on the dotted line. Property of the Government. These biological traits would jeopardize my career in the military. I would, in the future, have to fight for acceptance from my fellow male counterparts.

The benefits of serving in the military include a college program called the GI Bill, formerly known as the Serviceman's Readjustment Act of 1944; this was a law that provided a range of benefits for military personnel returning from war. I signed up to use this benefit, searching for a new outlook on life and a career for the betterment of my family. A purpose. These courses not only help education-wise, but I only heard this for the first time from veterans discussing their VA claims. It was seven years after my enlistment at that time. I had no idea what they were talking about. So, I asked questions—a lot of questions. Answers were given and I had a road map. I could file a claim with all my service-connected medical issues. They did not tell me this process of my initial application would take four years. One-and-half years after I mailed my full packet of medical claims and records, the package was lost in the mail. I called and asked what was taking so long and they told me they had never received my packet. Of course. I argued that it had been a year and half, and no one reached out to let me know to send a copy again. It was what it was, and I sent the packet again.

Years after my VA disability was established as a combat veteran, I still needed that confirmation. I called the local DAV office to ask if I could say it. "Am I a combat veteran?" I mentioned that to other males who I talked with, some laughed, some shook their heads, told me I wasn't a combat veteran. The representative asked if I served in a combat zone and for my information while he tapped on his keyboard and told me without any doubt that, "Yes, Ms. Feenix. You are, and whoever told you otherwise can kick rocks." He mentioned that it was disheartening to hear me even ask this question. Me being me, low self-esteem, I asked again, just so I could have final confirmation in saying that I am. "So, I can?" "Yes, you can." I told him, "Thank you."

I feel I need to bring my DD-214 wherever I go. See? See it! Yes, that is me. I'm a female veteran. For those who complain there are few "thank you for your service" statements handed out these days, there are even fewer received as a female veteran. Appreciation is across the board biased toward older veterans or male veterans. The embedded patriarchy is the world's strongest material, as impenetrable as a metal wall. Females have been taking turns generation by generation, on duty, chiseling this wall. It's unfortunate and not fair how females still get treated in this country. It seems I need to wear a military inspired shirt and show my ID for a discount for a simple meal on holiday occasions. Then even, some presume I'm a military supporter or a wife or have no actual military experience. But a male will never get questioned. The little things are important to me. These incidences add up. I feel more and more frustrated at not being accepted.

Another example is a hat I would like to wear more. It is my OIF hat. When I wear this, I get side eyes and looks of confusion. Like, "Is this lady wearing her husband's hat? It's not for her to wear." I have gotten too many rude looks from males. Phones being set up to take my picture. I wonder what their captions will be to their posts? "Stolen Valor" or "Why is this lady wearing a war hat?" It's not fair. I should be proud and loud. I'm a female veteran. I was deployed, I served, I was honorably discharged. Though it was cut short due to trauma, I am proud of my accomplishments. I only wish the public, as a whole, would accept me and my fellow sisters-in-arms.

zero tolerance?

The next confession took me close to fifteen years to finally say. I sat across from different VA psychologists during the claims process; I had to recount my past. Situations that I had to dig deep from the back of my mind, memories cemented and never to be recounted, were unearthed. The time had come, and I had to account for each abuse. It was all extremely painful to discuss in great detail. The smells, times of day, pain, and sounds. My account of the world of being a female in the military. Abuse, power, patriarchy, no one to talk to.

I'm who I am because of my trauma. I had to get to a point in my life to be honest and vocal about being a victim of multiple rapes. My stressors are at the surface if provoked. I want to emphasize that I am not trying to say anyone's trauma is not important. This is not a competition; I will gladly give you a win if you take my trauma away. It is unfortunately my story. I can't sit here and fake being ok. Not anymore.

My recruiter was the first of the three abusers who took my youth and trust. The first uniformed male to rape me had established a persona as an outstanding soldier, a highly intelligent, charming, squared-away soldier. His pressed uniform had creases that could cut you. His boots had glass-polished edges that could have been taken from a page in an Army manual. He was my introduction to the procedures of the U.S. Army. I was excited to leave my hometown for a new adventure. I was promised that I'd see foreign places. I was blinded by hope. After I signed my enlistment papers, I left two weeks later. It was quick. I took the ASVAB, hating the fact that I am not a great test taker. My list of potential jobs was decided, and it fell between some un-interesting positions with Supply and the Military Police. SSG Carter asked if "I wanted to be hated or loved." "Loved?" I responded, not knowing why. He said I should pick Supply. Everyone "loves Supply." So, there that was, Automated Logistics Specialist, Supply. Just before boot camp, SSG Carter invited me to join him and a few other recruits for dinner. It was scheduled the night before I left for the Military Entranced Processing Station (MEPS). However, SSG Carter had an ulterior agenda.

He picked me up at my home and told me we would meet everyone at the restaurant. During the car ride, we made small talk; in response to his questions, I offered polite, respectful answers. After we had driven for a while, we stopped outside of a hotel. There had been a change of plans. I thought nothing of this. I completely trusted him, me sitting there in the passenger side of the government vehicle, glancing around, waiting to leave.

He got out of the car, walked to the trunk, and grabbed a brown paper bag, which I would soon learn contained a six-pack of beer. He got out, opened the hotel door, and waved from the door, motioning me to come. I didn't think anything of this. Meeting the other people after this stop? I went as told. He took me, not to a restaurant inside, but to a room. After we entered, he placed the brown bag on the table and took off his jacket. I stood there wondering what was happening. I glanced around and then he shoved me onto the bed, ripped off my pants, unfastened his pants, pushed my back on the mattress, kneed my legs apart, and raped me. He ended up holding me down and just thrusting himself on top of me. I felt frozen and wanted it to stop. I couldn't move and didn't think this was real. My body was tense. This man was a monster and could care less that I was shaking, confused and scared. No words were spoken. He pushed himself off of me. I pushed myself to sit up, leaning back on the headboard, covering myself with a sheet. A blank look, waiting for a command or to be allowed to get dressed. He sat at the table on a chair across from me, opened the paper bag, grabbed a beer, and drank it with a blank look on his face. I was so scared that I could neither move nor speak. He returned to the bed and repeated the steps, after which he again sat at the table, cracked open another beer, and drank silently. Nothing was said. After he had drunk all the beer, he ordered me to get dressed, and dropped me off at my home. I left for MEPS the next morning.

Just recently, I did some spring cleaning, and I went through a couple of bins in the garage that held paperwork and clothing items from the military. I came upon my enlistment papers, including my MEPS paperwork. I had pushed and squeezed that trauma into a place where I rarely saw or felt it, but now it was right in front of me. My recruiter's name, SSG Carter, which after twenty years I had forgotten, was right in front of me. Even his signature. My heart rate pounded. Is that actually his name? Yes, it is, right there. I was immediately overwhelmed with anger and sadness. I cleaned out the old and felt the need to purge, but I put this paper in the pile with other documents to keep. I'm not sure why. It enrages me that he may have had a full military career and possibly raped other new recruits. He changed my life forever, before my military career even began.

But begin it did. Perhaps not surprisingly, the Army proved to be patriarchal. It turned out this military branch was not ready for females in leadership roles. Women were mocked and subjected to sexual innuendo, harassment, and assault. I heard again and again, "Ha ha ha! Lowering the standards, I see." "You got that promotion by what...your mouth?" "You need help with that little lady." Another male trying to push his way into my duties. "Getting cold in here, I see." Working with our jackets off, looking at our breasts beneath our t-shirts. The harassment went on daily. Rarely accepted as a soldier, I had to constantly prove my worth.

It turned out serving in a combat zone was just one obstacle that a female soldier had to overcome. We had enemies on both sides of the war. Not only insurgents, but also our own soldier brothers, were targeting us. It seemed like hunting season. It did not matter what the female looked like. Short, tall, fat, or skinny. Wearing desert camouflage uniforms (DCUs), combat boots, and boonie covers, the latter being the floppy hats that resemble those worn by fishermen. We were walking filet mignons, surrounded by males with mouths foaming, ready to pounce. Females were being dragged into empty tents and then raped. This resulted in a command order that women walk in groups. Ours biological traits impeded our futures.

I had so much anger and had no sense of care for myself. It was literally beaten into me throughout my life that I was not important. Unwanted consistently as a baby, as a child, and into adulthood. That recruiter suffered no consequences for taking advantage of me and depleting my worth that will forever cause me to have personal setbacks in trust. Self-care was not preached, not the cultural phenomenon it is now at that time. Instead, I ran into multiple bad relationships thinking from my past that this is what I deserved. No one loves you and you will get used to it, like your past. This is what is yours. You do not deserve any better. I was at the absolute lowest of low self-esteem.

Fast-forward many years and being single for close to seven years— no dates, nothing. I have reflected on my past. I'm working through it. Making me a priority. Concentrating on my girls. Keeping life uncomplicated. I have grown to love my ability to prioritize my happiness. I have the power to do what I want, when I want, no one there to abuse, to exert their control over me. Knowing that I deserve someone who is gentle, proud to be around me, and patient; that I, like so many others, have complications, and an understanding of this is crucial. I am not in any rush. I'm enjoying putting me first for once. I deserve peace.

In the past few years, thanks to the "Me Too" movement, sexual assault and sexual harassment have become a focus of attention in social media and the news. Both men and women have shared their trauma truthfully. Finally, sometimes years after the fact, they have found the strength to recall the pain. So, too, it has been only in these past few years that I could say, "It's my time. I need to speak the truth. Me too."

MST, or military sexual trauma, is referred to sexual assault or sexual harassment experienced during military service. "Being pressured or coerced into sexual activities, such as with threats of negative treatment if you refuse to cooperate or with promises of better treatment in exchange for sex. Someone having sexual contact with you without your permission, consent, such as when you were asleep or intoxicated. Being physically forced to have sex. Being touched in a sexual way that made you uncomfortable. Comments about your body or sexual activities that you found threatening. Unwanted sexual advances that you found threatening" (U.S. Department of Veterans Affairs, "Disability Compensation for Conditions Related to Military Sexual Trauma (MST)", PDF updated March 2022).

I served in the United States Army for six years. I was very motivated and worked hard to take steps on an exciting journey towards my retirement. Unfortunately, my time was cut short. My career was taken from me. I've been diagnosed with a plethora of conditions that will last a lifetime. Multiple occurrences in the military brings me to my own "Me Too."

There have been studies to understand the recourse of MST. One is an article written on the military.com website on November 5, 2019, titled "Military sexual assault more likely than combat to result in PTSD." It reads, "According to the IG's (inspector general's) report released Monday...45% of women and 65% of men who reported being raped met criteria for PTSD compared to 38.8% of men who had PTSD from experiencing combat...A 2016 report from DOD (Department of Defense) office of People Analytics found that 28% of women and 23% of men who say they experienced sexual assault took steps to leave or separate from the military." One who stepped up and recognized this as an increasing problem was Senator Kristen Gillibrand, who in May "got to the heart of the issue" while then-nominee for the Army Chief of

Staff, General James McConville, sat before Congress for his confirmation hearing.

"I am tired of excuses. I am tired of statements from commanders that say, 'say zero tolerance.' I am tired of the statement I get over and over from the chain of command:

We got this ma'am.

We got this.

You don't have this.

You're failing us."

YES, *they are. I know.*

Chapter 21

who can be trusted?

Most of my recurring nightmares involve the second abuser, my Non-Commissioned Officer in Charge (NCOIC), a staff sergeant, at my first duty station, Fort Carson, Colorado. My company received orders for a field problem at the National Training Center in Fort Irwin, California. My NCOIC purposefully picked a set of five new female soldiers to serve as a logistics/supply squad. This meant we would remain behind, working out of a warehouse in support of our company's logistics and supply needs, while the rest of the company was out in the field.

We all traveled by bus from Fort Carson to Fort Irwin. Once we arrived, the majority of the company went out in the field, while the rest of us remained behind. Our quarters were two trailers, one for the five females, including me, and the other for the NCOIC. One by one, he commanded each female to help him run an errand. The night came when it was my turn. He entered our trailer after we had retired, tapped me on the shoulder as I lay in my sleeping bag on a cot, and told me to get dressed for a supply run. I immediately got up, put on the winter physical training (PT) uniform, and met him outside as instructed. We climbed in the military vehicle, with him at the wheel and me riding shotgun, and drove into the darkness, dust surrounding the headlights. The drive took us past all the other supply units' fenced in area. A gate separated each different company. It seemed like an endless drive and our unit's gate was near the end of the line. We arrived at a gate that was chained and locked shut. The staff sergeant got out to open the gate. He kept fumbling with his fingers through all these keys. He looked down and then at me. Trying a few keys at a time, each without turning the lock open. I just sat patiently, thinking I could have been asleep by now in my cot. It was late. He kept fumbling with those keys as he walked back to the vehicle. He told me to look for other keys in the back. The back of this government vehicle, which was a caravan, had been converted to hold supplies. The van only had one bench in the back. As I began crawling back, my NCOIC pushed me from behind, headfirst into the bench. He forced my head down with his hands and pulled down my PT pants and my shorts. He made grunting sounds as he flipped me over and held me down while he orally violated me. He started to pull down his pants with his free arm. I laid in pain from the initial head blow to the back of the van. I could not scream. He quickly lifted me and pushed my head into the window, the seat, the floor, he flung my hips and legs every which way he wanted. I was a rag doll from his abusive hand. He forcefully penetrated me while pushing his upper body onto me, my head squeezed down into the bench and side arm rests by his hands. I could not move and felt frozen. Afterward, I was bleeding and injured, but I had no one to tell. He was my superior. In the days that followed, I suffered more rapes at the hands of the staff sergeant, and they became increasingly violent. I suspect my fellow female sisters-in-arms did, as well. As time passed, each of them looked more and more like a shell of a person. Yet we did not say anything to each other. I developed migraines that are debilitating; the nausea will make me vomit. Loud noises and light are deafening from being thrown around in the van, but since I did not lose consciousness, a diagnosis of TBI would not be recognized. Every day I have a dull, constant headache. Other days it gets to a point where I need to lay down in a dark room. It's just a reminder of the abuse and power that I will continue to live in.

I was the lucky one. I escaped the clutches of my NCOIC. I woke up one morning with a swollen neck. It only got worse. After a few days, I could barely swallow, couldn't eat and went to the medic for an examination. Since I was at a training post, they did not want to take any chances. I was consequently sent back early on a bus back to Fort Carson for surgery. I was told one salivary gland was taken out due to multiple calcium deposits blocking the gland. Thanks to the pending surgery, I experienced no more violations committed by the staff sergeant. After a week, my company returned to Fort Carson. While shopping, I ran into my NCOIC at the Post Exchange. He was with his wife, and he waved me over cheerfully and introduced me to her, as if nothing had ever happened. I looked at her and could only say, "Nice to meet you." I wanted to cry. This woman did not know the pain and trauma that her husband had put me through. I had to stand there and smile like her husband was such an outstanding human being. I had to see this NCOIC everyday back in my platoon. Nowhere to go but to dwell in his presence. I would have to respect this NCOIC and obey his commands. It was gut wrenching.

I could not tell anyone in my chain of command. I could not quit my job. The military has you locked in until they say you have orders for another post or relocation. I had to live with the emotional state of repeatedly being raped. The challenge was to gain friends and maintain relationships. Not feeling worthy of anything but abuse—it was my reality. Walking through a crowded room with mostly males gave me anxiety, rushing past quickly to avoid any eye contact. I still cannot handle idle eyes. It puts me in a rage. The harassment was still present, and that lowered any self-confidence I may have had. The constant word battle of being a female in a male military. It was hard. We were never good enough. Our bodies were subjected. It never stopped. No one would stop anything, even being an eyewitness. Heads turned and the abuse continued.

For a long time, I did not know how much I was suffering. I felt alone. I pushed the trauma deep inside me. My military training had told me to suck it up, to not feel anything, that it is not that bad. But that was a lie. After years of trying to block these traumas, I was furious at what happened to me. For years my symptoms hovered within me, putting me in a dark place.

The third, and last, abuser was one of my superior officers, a lieutenant, during Operation Iraqi Freedom. That day, we were scheduled to leave for our up-to-eighteen-months boots on ground; we filed in a long line. Walked onto the plane. Our battalion had a long flight from the states with everyone in our DCUs (desert camouflaged uniforms), Kevlar vest, Kevlar helmet, M-16, and all our extra duffle bags, gear stowed below. The flight was uncomfortable; half of the seats were broken with ripped seat cloths with flight attendants being very attentive to the males, flirting and making sure they had everything they needed. Men in uniforms, going to war, the cliché. I would ask another male to get snacks since I seemed to be overlooked. One stop into Ireland. We were reminded we could not leave the terminal. Landing in Ireland was beautiful; it was overcast and so green. Huge cliffs. Ocean waves crashed into the steep cliffs of the ocean's edge with sea mist spraying up. We all stared in awe from the terminal windows.

Then, we were off again to our final stop and new home in Baghdad, Iraq. For some reason, someone played the song "Bombs over Baghdad" over the flight speakers. An excited amount of adrenaline and warrior mentality put us in a rush of whooping and yelling. My journey to the great drop off at Baghdad airport was in the middle of the night. We all had our full battle rattle. Landed. Filed in a long line while noticing other long lines of soldiers coming off planes. The landing area was dark with scattered city lights run by generators, a scene that would become very familiar. Generators everywhere and the loud song they carried with them—hmmm. All day and night. Briefings followed, then, the hurry up and wait. The command had our lives in their palms. The first convoy was going to our in-processing camp. On this convoy, there we were, driving through downtowns, a fairly large city, multi-storied buildings, and us. The roads were empty and didn't give me a whole lot of reassurance. My eyes were wide open, hoping the route was safe, and then we started to circle around and around. We got lost, a handful of our vehicles got separated, and we tried to keep with the lead vehicle. I remember circling a vehicle with another soldier I knew; we both shook our heads and lifted our arms out of the doorless Humvee. Oh shit! These officers who had the maps and directions got us lost! I'm only hours into my first deployment and our command could have gotten us all killed. So, after circling and getting our convoy back online, we made it to the camp.

The next week, we got time to accumulate to our new surroundings. We all tried to sleep in our new time zone. Staying hydrated was key, too. With the weather at a constant 115 degrees or higher, there were pallets of water bottles just dropped and left. Sandstorm-weathered, dusty, crushed, warm—it was our water source. Delish.

In that week we discovered our new camp life. I remember another soldier had brought the series of *Sopranos* and we took on those personalities for a good moment. One soldier would stand sarcastically, waving his arms in and out, "So, you telling me, we gonna be here for eighteen months in this bullshit?" Another replied, "Forget about it. We gots our chow and deese here movies—couldn't be betta."

The time came when we were going to have a unit changeover. We were able to get our sleeping area and make our new tents our home. We lived in 100-men tents, whose maker was contracted by the U.S. Government. These tents were soaked in kerosene for waterproofing. Allegedly, the contract had no requirement for the tents to be waterproof. But it adds fuel to fire, literally. Our tents could burn in less than thirty seconds if they caught fire, and the 100 men and women along with it. We were conditioned to live with huge generators that would power the air conditioners and there was a consistent *hummm* in the background. Loud and constant.

On convoys, I would get to go to different camps and explore their facilities. Some had flushable toilets, and that was living in luxury. Most camps I stayed at had porta-potties. These were so disgusting at times that if the hajis (someone who had made the pilgrimage to Mecca, but in military slang, we used it to describe anyone of Arab descent) didn't pump them out, the shit would be piled high above the toilet seat. The graphic pictures that were drawn inside as crude decoration, *ohhh my*. So many lady parts, so many positions and angles. My thighs were so strong after deployment from holding myself midair above the seat during all those bathroom stops, my own body weight plus full battle rattle. Hovering over the stink hole, not wanting to touch anything.

During our in-processing time at the camp, the outgoing soldiers sold or gave away their shelves, cell phones, trunks, wall lockers, etc. I immediately saw an opportunity to buy a cell phone for myself—a Nokia. Blue, clear case. It needed a calling card called KD. I couldn't exactly go off camp casually and buy these phone cards at will. I needed to find my source. Quickly, I was acquainted with Mohammad, a man who worked as a contractor in the chow hall. We would meet, nod our heads in a "come meet me outside", greet each other with a handshake that covered the fact I handed over a $20 bill for a calling card. Success. We both did not want to get in trouble. On this phone, I could also call the states.

We were made mission-ready. Companies were convoyed to different camps and set up. Everything was new. I would wake up to 120-degree weather. In the beginning, alarms sounded to get cover as a warning, then as time passed, the tension seemed to subside. Just some more mortar attacks. It was just another day.

My platoon sergeant was a towering male whose presence was intimidating. He had a nice deposition but tried his hand at abusing his rank and power. There would be times of only us in the motor pool tent, where I oversaw supply matters. All the company vehicles were positioned in the motor pool with us. The mechanics, supply, and technicians used this tent. One incident, I was busy printing off paper. The printer was behind the platoon sergeant. Usually, it wasn't a problem to grab the papers, but this time he was sitting at his desk. I stood up, asked if I could have the printed papers. He turned his computer chair around, facing me and placed the papers on his lap. He creepily smiled and told me to "come and get them." I sternly said, "Can I just have the papers?" He would rarely come into the tent after that interaction. I was not going to be a victim of his inappropriate statements. I had grown to have a "don't fuck with me" look; I was so tired of being harassed, assaulted—my shell was broken. My happy outlook on humanity was depleted. It was hard enough to be a young sergeant in charge of males. I was tested. I was shit upon. But, I was in charge.

As time went on, there was one particular officer who wanted to know everything about me. I had to oblige due to rank. Answered his questions respectfully. For me, I was annoyed to have this shadow. He knew my whereabouts and had his eyes on whom I spoke with and my route and even the time I ate chow. A few times, I would walk around a corner and there he was there. "Oh, hello Sgt. Feenix! How are you?" I responded respectfully, "Good morning/afternoon/evening Sir, I'm good." It started to become uncomfortable to keep "accidentally" running into him. He would just smile and linger. For him, it was a search for things to control. He had no need to be anywhere I was. He took advantage of me, using his rank and power. I was groomed for his weird presence and narcissism. He would slowly give me compliments. "I like your smile." "You're doing great!" "If I was your man... I would..." statements. "I would buy you whatever you need. I would be that strong man you need." I never responded in a laughing, flirting, welcoming manner. I had to be respectful based only on his rank. He had other intentions. Then, the dreaded night of my last abuse and rape, which sent me over the edge mentally. My emotions were drowned in sorrow and abuse. That night, I was packing up my side of the tent or office area, since we were moving our motor pool, and I wanted my stuff all together. I was rummaging through files and filling boxes. Then, for no reason at all, I noticed he came into the tent and just glided towards me. He casually walked by the boxes with his fingers grazing the tops. It looked like he wanted to say something, but just lingered there. I said, "Good evening, Sir, can I help you with anything?" Lingered some more, nothing said. I didn't know what to do at that point, he didn't respond and just stood there. I started to move away and then he came from behind, overpowered me in the tent, smacked his lips a few times, grabbed my arm and violently forced himself on me. He held me down with his arms, kicked open my legs. I couldn't speak at the time, but soft words in pain to "stop." My speech and body froze, and I couldn't move. As he raped me, he was rough and he repeated over and over, "I know you want it. You're lucky to have it. I'm your man, yes, this is what you want, No one will ever find out." At his level of rank, it was absolutely true. No repercussions. He situated his pants on and didn't even give me a glance. I waited 'till he left. He checked the side flaps of the tent and moved out. Into the moonlight. Just aggressively taken and left. What is it about me?

A few days after, I was conveniently moved to another camp and a different company. However, before I left, I observed the lieutenant as he walked about the camp, his head held high, unscathed, untouchable. As for me, during the rest of the deployment I was deeply depressed, jumpy, anxious, contemplating self-harm. I have been violated so many times. I cannot take the abuse. What is it about me that those monsters have no choice but to decide they will take a piece of my soul? I am a fraction of myself due to these violations. Joy is harder to obtain. I quickly feel the emptiness and a feeling of life being ripped away. I passed out twice during deployment and ended up in the medical tent. I don't remember anything besides the slight flashes of spots, then time unknown, on a medic cot, no one telling me what happened or how I got there. Just, "Can you get up, make it back to your tent?" I responded, confused, "Yes?" This would be later diagnosed as another mild TBI. Having lost consciousness for an unknown time. As a sergeant, I had enough to think about in the middle of a war, including the responsibility I shouldered for my soldiers on convoys. This trauma made completing my already challenging duties all the more difficult.

It took eleven years for me to reach out for the help I needed. The VA claims process itself was mentally exhausting. During that process, I hesitated to talk about the multiple rapes that I endured. Once the VA recognized that I had experienced military sexual trauma, I began therapy sessions, slowly working on myself. I underwent cognitive behavioral therapy, which required that I repeatedly recount every detail of each rape. My therapist and I pinpointed one incident at a time to go over. She asked me to get as comfortable as I could. I sat in a chair, bent over with my hands on the sides of my head, eyes closed, getting as small as I possibly could to vocalize these events. It was hard to maintain eye contact with the therapist. I had to give a full description of each incident: what the perpetrator looked like and what he did, what my body went through, the pain. My homework was to listen to these recorded sessions. I never did. I spent an additional six to twelve months after this therapy in a deep aggressive spiral. I was so angry I wanted to fight, brawl, rip anyone to pieces, anyone. It was not a good time for my mental health.

A piece of me was taken each time I was raped. I had already had a childhood of not being wanted, now my adulthood brought in being discarded once again. I have not been the same since. I live with this every day. Reliving those moments is ongoing. When I see a stranger with characteristics of an abuser, I still break down. Decades later, I'm finally open to working on myself, to making myself a priority. It's extremely hard to trust anyone. I have a lot of anger, depression, and suicidal thoughts. "Relationships" that I was in, not knowing being abused should not have happened. It has been a very difficult road for me.

I am a veteran. I am strong. I have survived. I will tell my story. Yes, me, too: I will not be hushed anymore. I will no longer apologize for being female.

CHAPTER 22

four paws helped save my life

With all the trauma that my body and soul has been put through, I was tested to the brink of letting the pain overcome me. I felt desperate to find a way to bring happiness back into my life. Trying to not always fake the quick smirk of, "Yea, I'm good, thanks," but to reach out, be honest, "Help me, please. I'm barely treading water." I had been participating in random hobbies, trying to be social only to find myself completely torn by the groups of strangers, which gave me anxiety with no resolution. It was not working. Then, I researched a local veteran's service dog program. Let me check this out, I thought. Maybe this could be life-changing. So, I applied.

This journey would involve two beings and our road towards each other. The two of us were born in two different countries. Forty years apart. Yet, these two will find each other. Their journey will happily collide at a perfect time. Both at a young age were given up on and abandoned. One abandoned and the other constantly on the move, trying to forget their past traumas. Struggling to find someone to love and be accepted; not knowing why our very presence gave so much room for hatred towards us. One, age unknown and caught by the humane society, was put into a shelter, eventually not claimed as anyone's companion. Possibly overlooked by potential adopters from days to weeks. Good thing for me, they kept walking. I hate to picture his cage of the past; I have grown to know so much loyalty from him. Alone in a cage. This shelter had limited time, sadly. A kill shelter, it could have led to him walking the green mile. The other was me, abandoned at birth and adopted by a family whose manic rage was always my fault. Both of us had a huge understanding of not being wanted. Being discarded, for us, was common ground.

What changed his path was a call from a local service dog program to "take a look at this once-wandering dog." I would love to reach out to this individual, whoever saw something in him, saw a purpose, and thank them. They saw the potential and good nature of Milo, and with the partnership of the service dog program, it was a match. Thankfully, his stay at the shelter was quick, thanks to his calm demeanor. A show of his bottom lip and teeth, seemingly like he is smiling. At times his lip quivers and it seems like he is talking. This always makes me laugh. Sitting in this cage, legs stretched, and front paws delicately crossed waiting to see what's next. Records show he was found dirty and had lots of weeds intertwined with his fur. He is a German Shepherd mix, with black and dark golden patches covering his soft fur. He has small ears with fur like "ear wings" on the sides of his face and caramel golden eyes. My angel. The trainers arrived and met Milo. They checked their criteria to see if he would be a good candidate to be a service dog. Walked him on leash, gave a few commands, checked for any aggression, approved his temperament and drive to start training. Milo is touch motivated, and after a command he makes a hard lean on my side and looks up at me. I always grab his fur and pat his head. A "good boy" makes his body wiggle, and he struts around—so proud of himself. He was born to have a job. Other than that, there is no background of where he could have been, how long, or what kind of situation he may have lived in. Just like me, both of our beginnings have little to no information. Both have no record of birth; we were both later given a name. This nonprofit service dog facility is specifically for post 9/11 combat veterans. Having a VA (Veterans Affairs) rating of a service-connected disability was one of the qualifying factors to be considered. They "rescue shelter dogs and train them to be psychiatric service companions for wounded combat veterans...every 63 minutes a veteran commits suicide...every 11 seconds, an animal is euthanized..." This organization "saves lives, two at a time." After my acceptance into the program, I was one step closer to having the courage to make my mental health a priority. A chance for a purpose. Milo, even the possibility of him, was the missing key to push me into social settings, having his support to guide me through an anxiety attack. His constant nose bumps or jumping up to tap with his paws at my chest to ground me. Reminding me I'm safe and to focus on him instead.

An important part of my attempting to recover from trauma has been Milo. In a service dog program, the introduction sets the tone for the rest of the training program. This period is referred to as the "dating process." I met a lot of different breeds, whose reactions to me at times were a bit cold. A back towards me, not listening, sounds in the background were more interesting. Some of my personal bad dates with guys could be described as the same. Not the one for me. This part was a bit discouraging, seeing how different dogs reacted to me. It seemed more my sensitivity tolerance was being depleted. I was hoping for that special moment; running to each other, playfully running around and looking at the sunset together. Nice little dream. That would not be the case—not just yet. At the time, the biggest dog I had ever owned was ten pounds. A purse dog. One that barked nonstop, loved to snuggle on the couch with you and had a funny habit of drinking too much water, tummy bloated and needing to be burped like a baby. Large dogs were intimidating to me. Milo definitely changed my mind about size.

At first, I needed to understand the initiation, the program steps, and to give my full commitment. Once matched, it would be another six to eight months preparing for the journey outside of the fenced-in yard. At the program, there was a huge variety of trained medium-to-large dogs. This was during COVID-19 and eventually, during the lightened up terms of quarantine, meeting outside at a park was a safe mandated precaution. The start was very rocky; I remember holding onto the leash with a death grip with each dog. I could not relax my grip, and I didn't want to lose a dog while on a walk. I was hyper-focused, unable to look around. The mental strain was overwhelming. I remember thinking to myself, does this get easier? My jaw hurt from clenching, the pain of holding the leash tightly for over an hour. I tried to give off any sort of pseudo confidence I could to my trainer, who saw right through my inexperience. After each session, I was emotionally drained and wasn't sure if it was part of my journey to have a service dog. In turn, my trainer gave me that confidence and was only understanding, brilliant and extremely knowledgeable.

It was finally my turn to meet my future buddy. One by one, we greeted each other. One large dog playfully jumped at me, and I gave out a girly scream. This was embarrassing, as I squirmed, putting my leg up in a blocking position, not being used to large breeds. Sorry, not this one. Another dog was a gentle breed but ignored me from the start. Sorry, not a great fit. A couple dogs were highly alert, and it drove my anxiety extremely high. Not what I needed. My trainer took all my needs and concerns into account. She brought up a dog they had recently adopted. He was not quite ready to be matched, but she was confident his personality would fit me. I was the first veteran he met.

The gate opened and there he was, tail wagging, excited; he came straight to me. This was a great start, I thought. He calmly glided by my legs, leaning on me gently. Falling onto his back, tongue hanging to the side. I giggled and petted his belly. His name given by the sponsor was Milo. He eventually sat directly in front of me, and I stroked his face. His gaze locked into my soul; I collapsed in my seat, tears flowing. I had found my dog. The dating process ended.

Time passed, and slowly Milo and I were working through our goals as a team. We first passed our Canine Good Citizen test. We received a ribbon and took advantage of the photo op. My trainer was there every session, just a few steps away, encouraging us and giving us both praise. She would be there to discuss any of my concerns, any questions I had. We had become friends, and I am thankful I had a trainer who I could completely trust. She would always remind me, "Remember to not pet Milo after he doesn't listen. Correct it right away!" It was so hard in the beginning to not pet Milo. But, I had to remember why the training rules were put into place. Sessions were timed perfectly to end right at the point of being taught a new command, stopping on a "good note." At the end of each session, I would get the opportunity to pet Milo and I would just cry. Or throw a ball to him and let him scoot and zoom around the yard. That was always a funny sight! Overwhelming feelings would always come over me. I felt like a mess most of the time. My trainer was the best, and she knew being out in public and in new environments could cause triggers to come to the forefront. She had so much patience with me. For two-and-a-half years, my trainer and I spent hours walking around a park, learning new commands, trying to work up my courage to feel comfortable back at the training facility. In the beginning, it gave me a lot of anxiety being locked up in a yard with a lot of sounds and movements. My trainer worked on my confidence and gave me support each time we had a session. We spent so much time together. It turns out Natasha, my oldest daughter, and her had the same birthday, just ten years apart. Both were strong, outgoing, independent, intelligent young ladies. It was no wonder we developed a kinship.

Months later, after training with Milo, the program's veteran representative called me. He was proud of my commitment and the progress he heard about our training sessions. He knew I was having a hard time emotionally. He would kindly answer phone calls time after time from me, at some of my low points, and would listen; give me some referrals and tell me he was there for me. He happily told me that Milo would be my match. I immediately broke down and embarrassingly couldn't stop crying for a few minutes after the phone call. During the call, I asked him if he "was joking or made a mistake." He kindly responded, "I would never joke about this." The facility accepted the match, making it official!

I got a letter telling me Milo would indeed be mine. There wouldn't be any other veterans meeting him.

My buddy. My companion who pushes me to go outside and enjoy social settings, which I otherwise knowingly and absolutely avoid, without apologies. The distraction of Milo sets my jumpiness and high alert, modus operandi down a few levels. If needed, he would be there to regulate me and compress me back into a calm state. Those unexpected noises and the dreaded nighttime fears, being afraid to close my eyes, preparing for a quick and violent awakening, gasping for air— my Milo's mere presence will relieve these symptoms, easing my panic attacks while waiting in lines surrounded by people. Movements in crowds from the front, side, at the back, and across the room can all be very overwhelming sensory experiences and can create a dizzying feeling. Sweatiness, a feeling of being in a sauna and wanting everyone to move back. Anger and feeling so overwhelmed that I have to leave quickly. Milo will allow me to focus on him and the background of all these kinds of chaos fades. I now always have him by my side, helping guide me through the unexpected. His puppy enthusiasm gets me excited for the day!

> Stranger: "Aw cute dog…Can I pet him? Does he bite?"
>
> Me: "His name is Milo…I'm sorry, he's on duty right now."

We both glance down at his calm demeanor, sitting in a trained heeled position. He will be slightly leaning on my left side occasionally looking up. The stranger will notice a variety of military service themed patches. On a large bold print patch: "SERVICE DOG— DO NOT PET."

This has become a daily conversation in my life with Milo by my side. The journey to meeting Milo was long and emotional. More than a handful of therapists all trying to help with no winning strategy. Different remedies in trying to approach my healing process, but each only offering temporary relief. Each therapist having to rewind and share each of my traumas again and again in detail. This did not put me in the best frame of mind.

The years prior to this were tough and I needed to make changes. The deep sensation of suicidal thoughts were beginning to become more realistic. I call these moments "fuck it" moments. To me, it's as strong as a gust of wind pushing you—those times that I am struggling to stay afloat, thinking if I could just let these "fuck it" moments take over, I could feel relief. Since I am not able to schedule a panic attack or call a therapist for treatment at a moment's notice, Milo will be there. Brushing him, falling into his glance, or giving him a meditative pet session with his body as compression, I can now rely on his company and feel safe. I struggle with these emotional and physical impairment lists that I received from the Army; I know, unfortunately, that they will last a lifetime. Milo gives my day-to-day purpose. He has made my deep, hidden considerations of ending it all take a backseat.

Time has passed now, and I am sitting here, writing, a week from my year anniversary with Milo. He is sound asleep right now, an occasional dream prompts his paws to move in a running motion, loud snores, blowing air from his lips he takes a loud, deep breath. I am reflecting on our journey, and it's been nothing but a 5-star Yelp review. Though my diagnoses will be with me for a lifetime, I am grateful for Milo and his constant presence. He has helped me in a lot of aspects of my life.

Being a female combat veteran, now with a service animal, there are still prejudices. There isn't a whole lot of understanding, but loads of ignorance, which I've have been confronted with on many fronts. Now, with a valid trained service dog, many people have questions and doubts, wondering: what exactly is wrong with you?

Some examples of what I get while walking around with Milo include:

- "Is that your service dog?"
- "Why do YOU need a service dog?"
- "Oh, you're training him?"

- "Did you get him in the Army?"
- "Oh, the Army gave you a dog? That's cool!"
- "Is he REALLY a service dog?"
- "I know someone who bought their dogs a vest on Amazon, soooo…"
- "Is he your protection dog?"
- "I guess you can put a vest on any dog."
- *Whistling…* (To which I want to reply: Stop whistling and making sounds to get Milo's attention. He doesn't give a shit about you. He is not here for you. You are distracting him from his duties.)
- "Oh, he's an emotional support dog."
- "Look son, watch out! That's an Army dog."

It's so freaking frustrating. Most of the comments from those who really have no business weighing in on anything related to me or to Milo are dead serious; the lack of education they evince, the judgmental nature—all are hurtful and extremely ignorant. On Milo's vest I have my accolades, including my ribbon bars, military affiliation, and veteran groups I belong to. People glance at them and comment on how proud they are of Milo's accomplishments. Or young military personnel who whisper, "I wouldn't put those ribbons on that vest. My accolades I earned are proudly placed." Or the consistent pointing and laughing from the same age range. During one incident, I ripped into a group of nineteen-year-olds, reminding them of their age. These young personnel were not even born when I was in Iraq. I told them to respect all veterans. "You weren't even a thought in your parents' minds when I was overseas."

I even had a military-based hotel argue with me about my service dog. Of all the groups, on an *actual base*. I told them when reserving a stay, I had a service dog. The man responded, "Oh, okay. So it's an emotional support animal." I told him, no, "He is my service dog." The conversation went back and forth. I was so upset and frustrated. Legally, there are only two questions an establishment can ask in this type of circumstance (under Federal Law and in accordance with the American with Disabilities Act of 1990):

1. Is this your service dog?

   Me: Yes. PERIOD.

2. What task does your service dog perform?

   Me: He's a psychiatric task performing service dog. PERIOD.

Businesses may NOT:

1. Require specific identification for the animal
2. Require a doctor's note or any private medical record documentation
3. Ask about the person's disability
4. Charge additional fees because of the animal
5. Refuse admittance, isolate, segregate, or treat this person less favorably than other patrons

Refusal to provide equal access to people with disabilities with service animals is a federal civil rights violation provided by the Americans with Disabilities Act of 1990. Violating ADA laws is considered a federal offense and civil penalties may be up to $75,000 for a first violation or $150,000 for each subsequent violation. Intentional discrimination or lack of good faith efforts to comply may warrant compensatory and punitive damages.

Luckily, I have the support and care of the service dog program and emailed the head trainer regarding the hotel incident. She quickly responded to this business with a professional windstorm of brilliantly coercive emails and voicemails. Short in stature, but mighty in knowledge and tactfulness, the head trainer emailed me with updates and I am thankful for her professionalism, since I was too angry to be anything but volatile. I immediately received a response from the base hotel apologizing and saying that "in my file" there is a note on how I have a service dog. They apologized for the treatment and said the "man" I spoke to was new. Pffft! That may have been a PR move, but I did see him at check-in for my stay and gladly walked in with Milo and put down my government ID with my rank and disability rating of INDEF (indefinitely). He avoided all eye contact and reluctantly put down the check-in paperwork.

It's so draining to get these continuous comments in my life. The trauma is real, the struggle is real; it makes it worse when my validity in society gets hit with real prejudice. I will have to continue to receive these comments and struggle to fit into the mold of why I have a service dog. The education of service dogs needs to be more of a public thing. Knowledge will help alleviate those veterans from having to answer stupid questions.

Fast forward to now, and time has flown by—Milo and I have been on our adventure for over a year-and-a-half at this point. But there has been a recent unfortunate incident. I am at an emotionally tough point in my life now and am writing this with an extremely heavy heart, a week after a great personal loss. This loss will forever be one that I cannot fully cope with and if I had known of her struggles and demons, I would have done anything for her. My trainer, whom I have just written about, took her own life. She was my savior at the program— my rock. I leaned on her and she gave and gave. She had never once given me a sense of her own self treading water. She was "the legend", and she will be so terribly missed. She had such a great laugh, and her sarcasm was super witty and undeniably *her*. I can only tear up right now typing these letters; she will forever be remembered.

I told her during my stint at the program that this had been my longest relationship— she and I training. She always gave me the time to just cry, and her presence was just enough, with an empathetic smile and her encouragement of, "It's fine." My world has been turned upside down, and I am in a dark place, not being able to see her again. I want to scream to the world how much she was loved! The world has gotten dimmer not having her "joy" in it. My one regret is that I did not reach out and let her know how much of a positive impact she made on me. I read this at her memorial:

If I just pushed send

It hurts to my soul, so devastatingly, so
Knowingly...this phrase will haunt me 'till my end
If I just pushed send
I thought back and forth, days after days to send an email
I could have started it as
My Dear Friend...

I want to let you know how much you meant to me
you were such a light in my life
Your laugh, sweet smile and gentle presence
I miss you so much and our sessions of meaningful talks
It hurts too much; my breaths have become shortened
I regret not having the courage to writing that email
My Dear Friend...

If I just pushed send
I know I could have shared stories about Milo and me
You wrote exactly this on my graduation photo frame:
"Excited to hear about all your guy's adventures"
I wanted to *my dear friend*, I wanted to write these exact moments
Our adventures, our silly pictures, moments Milo knew to help me
It was because of you
My Dear Friend…

For the two-and-a-half years that I got to spend with you
will forever be one among my most treasured
The walks at the park, funny stories we shared
Emotional hardships and struggles you got me through
I wanted to let you know,
If I just pushed send
My Dear Friend...

CHAPTER 23

becoming a mom

*I*t was weeks after September 11, 2001. I was stationed at Fort Carson, Colorado. This date will live in our souls forever. For weeks, Old Glory flew proudly all over. What better time to get married? Sigh. At lunch in our BDUs—I was 21. My first marriage started in one of our country's most pronounced states of sadness and confusion; they were unprecedented times. We were married within a few days after 9/11. At lunchtime, I picked up my boyfriend from his infantry unit. When I dropped him back off, he was my husband. We got married in our BDUs with another couple we knew very well. His wife traveled from Germany. We paid a hundred dollars and sat in front of a window and the ceremony began; we were glancing over at our friends like we were ordering movie tickets and, in reality, it was the start of a horror show. The echoing stamp of a notary was the sound of a lock and key in retrospect. Crazy, young, naïve life.

It all started six months before the week of 9/11 when I looked at the board where all of us from AIT (Advanced Infantry Training) school (after boot camp, a school to be trained for our job in the military) read where our first duty station was going to be. As my recruiter promised, it could be anywhere in the world (see foreign lands!). I should have known not to trust anything he said. I scanned down the list and it read: Pvt. Feenix, Fort Carson, Colorado. Ok, so not exactly a foreign land. My platoon, among whom I had developed some friendships, were all separated at that point. Everyone on their own journey all over the world. Never to be seen again. We said our goodbyes and wished each other luck. My bus ride was from Fort Lee, VA to Fort Carson, CO. I was nervous to be out of training and on my own. This time, there were no contacts, and I wore glasses. I did not want another pink eye catastrophe. There weren't going to be set times to meet for formations to class or chow. No yelling from the drill sergeants and cadre on how stupid we were. Wait a minute— FREEDOM!

This post was going to set the standard for my career. History has a way of pushing its dark past back to the present. This particular post had its rounds of negative events, including a movie based on facts from right inside the location. The 2018 movie, *BlacKkKlansman*, a true story, had my old unit patch worn by actors portraying soldiers shooting at off-post ranges. With the atmosphere of hate and prejudice, the patch flashed in scenes, and I thought, *of course*. During my enlistment at this post, there were monthly scheduled meetings telling us to not take pamphlets or go off to dinners without permission from our chain of command— specifically focused on not accompanying certain hatred groups. Another sad tragedy was the high-profile murder of Vanessa Guillén. The regiment I was in moved to another post by that time, but she and I shared the same unit patch. I was so disheartened by her murder. The power and control of individuals with rank in the military seems untouchable still. Will this "zero tolerance" of abuse ever change? Soldiers should have a sense of pride within each unit. I have been to many veterans' homes to see a wall of earned unit patches, plaques, and souvenirs of foreign lands. They are proud displays of service. Accolades, accomplishments. They should bring happy memories. This particular unit patch only brings up bad memories for me.

During my time and experience in my first duty station, it was the wild west. My platoon had so many intertwined relationships. One example was my squad leader, who had a wife in another state, a corporal in our squad as a girlfriend, then, on one known occasion, he paid another soldier for sex and she used the money to buy groceries. This squad leader was a pervert with all females in his squad and the harassment was so uncomfortable and inappropriate, I would scan the area to see if he was in my eyesight. I was picked on by the senior enlisted. Picked on for my brown skin, the way I ran (I have posture, no idea why this was wrong or a factor to get picked on—I ran track and cross country and did great with my natural glide, my back straight). On our long PT runs a senior enlisted—short, skinny man—would run at my side, me being very much taller than him. He would call me out and recite, "Look at me, I'm so great!" running with his back straight in a dramatic way. I had short hair and that constituted me being gay at that time. "Hey, you, what side are you on?" "Do you think I look good, or do you think she looks good?" A wild west attitude of showing their guns and no one doing a thing. We couldn't. There were no senior leaders to ask for advice or to be a mentor. Everyone was out for themselves. It was lonely to be left out of discussions, and to be harassed, emotionally and sexually. The patriarchy was strong. The environment outside of work was a free-for-all. Young soldiers in barracks, drinking 'till dawn. Most not of age and quickly learned to push their limits with drink. I also enjoyed the Red Cup Adventure Nights—my favorite pour was Hawaiian Punch and Captain Morgan rum. Glug, glug, glug. We had coed barracks, and doors opened and shut all through the night. One soldier, who lived across from me, had his civilian girlfriend living there. He would leave in the morning for PT. They would stand in the hallway and kiss each other like we lived in an apartment complex. She would clean their room, come and go as she pleased. I got used to her and would casually talk with her.

Nothing was regulated. A great example: I got handpicked to go to support a field problem one time. Two PFCs told me we were leaving in fifteen minutes, so I needed to go and pack for a few days. We were driven miles away from anything. It was in the back woods of the post. We drove up to a lifted-on-blocks parked trailer and the sergeant said he would be back to check on us; he threw us a box of MREs (Meal Ready To Eat) and a couple cases of water, then sped off. "Ok, so now what the fuck do we do?" and statements of such. We walked into the parked trailer and saw at least three boxes of batteries, a variety of boxes of chem lights, and random engine belts. We found out the company we were supporting was a tank company. So, some batteries were not going to support this mission at all. We set up a couple of cots, walked around, and noticed the males seemed to be confused on why we were there. So were we. A few random soldiers came by the trailer and asked if we had certain parts and all we could say was no. That sergeant did not check on us; we called the warehouse and were told we needed to stand fast. OMG. In total, we spent two weeks out in the middle of nowhere. No showers, just disposable wipe cloths, no running water, no flushing toilets. We had to figure out how to do our business since it was a half-mile walk to the all-male structure. We didn't feel safe going alone. We peed in an empty bucket under the trailer. At night, it was cold, scary, and animals were everywhere. There was a discussion of males having NVG (Night Vision Goggles), so that stopped us from going under the trailer at night. After almost two weeks of absolute boredom, no smart phones, no streaming services, (it was over twenty-one years ago) no radio, we cracked! If I played one more card game, I would have gone nuts. The night we hit our limit, we looked back at the supplies left. CHEM LIGHTS. We decided to shut the trailer doors, crack open the chem lights, swirl them around on a string and have a rave party. We danced around swinging the lights, sweeping and moving our arms all around. The different colored spray from the open chem lights was so awesome, and it was everywhere. All over the inside of the trailer, walls, clothes, floor. It was a bright, glowing masterpiece inside the dark trailer. So much fun. Then a knock at the trailer door. We both immediately stopped, the creak of the door opened slowly. "What the fuck are you guys doing?" We laughed and asked, "Did you need a chem light? 'Cuz we are out." He shut the door while mumbling and we just laughed. We destroyed our clothes, but it was definitely worth it. The two weeks were up, and the sergeant strolled in—we were on the journey back to civilization.

Originally, in my pre-non-knowledge of the military, I had no idea what to expect. There wasn't a class on what the differences of each branch were, the history. Not unless you had family who could tell you or your enlistment being a decision based on generations of enlisting. I had no clue. There was no screening of medical issues. Or past mental health. I did not want to jeopardize my chances of leaving my town, trying to avoid the abuse my parents gave me in the past. I needed a purpose; I was stuck working multiple jobs and had no chance at any college. The military, I thought, would be my chance. It was just an endless pounding, rabid environment.

I didn't know my existence on the post would be so strenuous and difficult. I had never been to Colorado, and I got to enjoy seeing so many different towns along the way. Finally, on the last push into Fort Carson, CO, the bus traveled to the welcome center. This is where all the new incoming soldiers completed all their paperwork, got issued cold weather gear, took classes on post regulations, and finally, on the last day, received orders for our new unit. During the in-processing, there were soldiers who came from all over the world. All had different jobs and were going to be split up after the week at the welcome center. Slowly, I gained friendships with a small group of soldiers. One, in particular, came from Fort Lewis, Washington. He was tall, dark, and handsome. Gabriel. His eyelashes could hit me from a talking distance; his dimples melted inwards as he talked and smiled. We soon became a group of two. He was so charming; it was hard not to blush when he had your attention. He was the life of the party. Enjoying meals, laughs, and spending more time together—I thought it was not going to be so bad after all. Our group went out on the weekends to clubs and lived it up. We could dance all night and drink in excess. I turned 21 that first week at my duty station. I had a hard initiation into the group, and when they found out it was my birthday, they yelled in excitement, "Let's party!" We didn't need an excuse to drink, but this gave us a great reason. We all went to a local restaurant for a "birthday glass" of straight liquor, which I downed. The glass was the size of a large beer stein shaped into a margarita glass, but only had straight, no ice, no juice or fillers, Southern Comfort. As I type, I am getting a bit queasy remembering that night. I remember the glass, the bathroom toilet, and not much else. Way too much, too fast, and no breaks. What a night! But Gabe was there to help me.

The time came to be picked up by our new unit. Gabe and I said goodbye and gave our new addresses to each other. It was a quick transition to the barracks building and I was by Gabe's side again. We spent every day at chow and hung out after our duty was done for the day. Inseparable. It was only six months before we got married. We lived in a house with one of his sergeants, in the family room on a roll-out bed. For a short period. It was affordable. My love was deep. I loved every minute with him. We partied and life was good. No stress.

Within the first few days of marriage, Gabe and I had discussions about having a family and that we should start soon. Soon it was. Within the first weeks of marriage, I found out I was pregnant in two memorable ways. Our dream life would take a drastic turn. First, I had a good friend who was in my platoon (she and her husband were avid substance abusers). Cocaine was one choice that I know of. She was so tiny in stature, and I would worry after a partying weekend her heart would give out during a long PT session. We would be running next to each other, and she would be amped, and in just a couple of minutes gave me a play-by-play action of her entire weekend. She would tell me they partied and had an eight-ball of cocaine with friends. I worried about her. She was such a sweet and true friend for the months we were stationed together before she left for Germany due to military orders. We called ourselves the Powerpuff girls. I was the brunette, Buttercup, and she was the blonde, Bubbles. Silly, but the names always made us laugh. She opened up to me with a dark story about her past. She explained when her husband went to a military school she felt so alone; she needed her husband to be by her side, she deeply missed him. So, knowing he would only be able to come back if there was an emergency, she got high and miscarried. Intentionally. Her husband was ordered to come home and take care of her. I felt an overwhelming pain for her. Her state of desperation at that time and not having the support or resources to help in her state of sadness.

One weekend, she called me in the middle of the night and was very excited to tell me I was pregnant. She said she "dreamed of a pink-sequined fish." I thought she was high and laughed, telling her to go to sleep. I was a bit delirious and put that call in the back of my mind. The second way I learned of my pregnancy was a battalion formation. We were ordered to wear full battle rattle. It was an hour listening to each officer tell us how well we are all doing. On and on. Speech after speech. Platoons of soldiers, all at parade rest. Listening to a faint voice from a distance. Words would come in clear from officers who could project their voice and the new butter bars would have a rhythmic tone and laugh occasionally. I started to see black and white spots swaying side to side. I passed out. Front row, and I fell sideways. When I woke up, they ordered me to go to the medics.

At this time, I had started smoking cigarettes, a military pastime and I was with Gabe, who also had the habit. A pack every few weeks, just to light up and puff every so often, which was the only way a soldier could take a break. I was smoking on my way to the medic's office. There was just me and another female who had checked in. We both sat quietly and nervously. We both took pregnancy tests. A few minutes of quiet passed and her name was called...she got up and they said the test was negative. She screamed, "YES!" I laughed a little bit, then it was my turn. I hadn't been married that long, so I hoped I wasn't sick or had any serious injury. My name was called, and they told me it was positive. I was pregnant. Woo! That was super quick! I got back in my car and immediately looked at the pack of cigarettes and threw them away. My friend was right; the pink-sequined fish came true. I had a girl. I don't remember how I told my new husband he was going to be a dad. I most likely just blurted it out.

As a growing family, we needed our privacy. Gabe and I moved into an apartment of our own—it had one bedroom, one bath. Our own home. We had adopted two cats. Being married, we had a housing allowance to pay eight-hundred dollars in rent. But our rank was still low, as I was an E-3, a PFC (private first class). Our monthly pay was cutting it close with bills and living expenses. We struggled and did not know of many resources for help. Our ranks and our income would be at the poverty level. We would often receive a meat locker from our command to supplement food— a bag of meat, cheese, spaghetti sauce, noodles, powdered potatoes. I learned quickly about Gabes' vices. His drinking increased and only got heavier as time passed. I soon figured out Gabe had a problem; soon, I experienced his whole charming demeanor changing for the worse. When we first dated, it was totally fine to blow through money going to clubs. At the end of the night, we had the barracks to go back to. Now married, young, groceries and rent to pay, the situation got very stressful. We found out pawn shops were a kind of savior. DVDs could be sold for five dollars each. Just enough for gas or snacks. Gabe could not stop drinking in excess. He spent money at the PX to overload my AAFES credit card, which we could not pay off, on his alcohol. He spent entire paychecks on alcohol. We had nothing.

Gabe would be gone a lot due to guard duty and field problems. The stress of a new family was wearing on him. There were times of great bliss with Gabe, then came the switch. As time went on, the pressure of being a specialist E-4 for Gabe and me being a PFC E-3 rank was overwhelming. The strain of working long hours and the amount of money we were making being spent so fast was overwhelming. He could have guard duty all through the night, long extended stays out in the field, being called into duty any hour. My duties should have been limited, but were shunned, and I still had to drive forklifts, transport supplies, lifting equipment, and work outdoors. Our arguing began to increase. The short period of the honeymoon stage quickly disappeared. I learned about his dark side and how to live while walking on eggshells. I couldn't even have imagined this just a few weeks before our marriage. He was my knight then—loving and fun. As soon as I was pregnant, as soon as we both decided to make a family, his feelings changed.

Being pregnant in the military was difficult. At the time, there wasn't a sense of senior leaders being happy for you, but there were restrictions to adhere to and limitations on some of the duties. The time came when I couldn't fit into my issued BDUs, which did not take long, since I did gain a total of seventy-five pounds. The Army-issued pregnancy BDUs were huge tablecloths of fabric with a head cut out. The top flowed with no shape or tapered back. And the pants were no better, with a large, stretchy waistband of fabric. Due to liability, and some sort of ridiculous protocol at the medic office, I got one ultrasound. Only one. The picture was of a small pea-sized figure, and that was my baby. They explained they could not give any other pictures from the ultrasound since it was too early to determine the baby's sex. I hope that regulations have changed. Knowing would definitely carry less stress in buying items and deciding names. I bought only green and yellow sleepers and onesies as a result. The only other prenatal exams were spread out: weight, blood pressure, and the fetal heart rate monitor. The Army had weekly and monthly breakdowns for regulations about pregnancy with physical limitations. It was not until later months that I could finally wear soft shoes or tennis shoes. There was a protocol that by a certain month, you are no longer allowed to march; they made me march until the very last day. It was not fun trying to keep in step, at a pace, wobbling. It was also hard during the snowy season trying not to slip during a march. My issued Gor-Tex jacket for the snow did not zip up any longer. I was just too big. So, I had to stand in many formations, belly out, snow falling on top.

I have told tales for both my daughters about their momma and her memorable moments. I love to now see the big smile they have. I just wanted to be a good mom. I was trying to not repeat my childhood. They always like to hear about my cravings and what they "made me eat." In fact, I really enjoyed eating for two; I was a champ. There was PT (physical training) every day, rain or shine, 6:30 a.m. formation. I could not participate any longer, being pregnant. But I still had to show up in formation and, on the way, I would get a breakfast sandwich. A bit of a morning snack after having nausea for four months straight—it tasted so good! Morning sickness hit hard for me in the beginning and the very smell of food cooking in the kitchen or the smell of the garbage was a kick to head to a bathroom and throw up. Gabe took over cooking and he made sure I had steak for our baby; he wanted our baby to grow big and have a lot of protein. My daughter is an adult now and is a connoisseur of meat-eating—my little carnivore. For me, I may have steak once every couple of years, if that. The look of steak makes me gag to this day. After the period of nausea though—hello food! If Gabe and I went to the movies, I could eat three large pickles, the ones that are left in a large jar. Disgusting to me now, but a delicacy then. There was a mall nearby and I would stop at a Great Baked Potato food kiosk. They had giant, cantaloupe-sized baked potatoes. I would get sour cream, butter, cheese, bacon, and broccoli. That was my favorite for sure. Sauerkraut was another golden item to inhale. It took me nineteen years to have it again and triggered memories of my being pregnant at that time. These foods and experiences have left a forever imprint—some good and some bad.

Gabe had a very good group of friends from his unit and one of the girlfriends put together a baby shower for me. She had all the typical games. We ate melted chocolate bars on a spoon, which looked like poop. We tried to drink a baby bottle as fast as we could as a contest. There was food, decorations, and friends. I had a great time, and Gabe was appreciative. That girlfriend gave us a large bin of diapers, towels, and onesies. Our friends were very giving, and we were set for our baby. I recently found an old tape that had the baby shower on it. My daughter got to see her mom young and pregnant with her. It was a special moment. A baby book couldn't give her the visual experience of her parents together and married.

The day came. I went into labor and got driven to the post's hospital. Sixteen hours of labor. The contractions were getting more consistent, and I had to bear through the overwhelming belly tightening and release. For hours with contractions, and it finally came down to the pushing. It was exhausting. Baby seemed stressed and I was so tired. It seemed she did not want to come out and I would have had to have had an epi-siotomy. Time was ticking and my baby needed to come out. There was a set of medical tools if I could not push hard enough. I pushed with everything I had. I didn't think the labor would ever stop. Gabe was there by my side; I gripped his hand and yelled in a low growl. I had a fever towards the end of the labor and was on an oxygen mask. The last push. The doctors and nurses said, "This is it!" They pulled my baby out. But there was no noise. I called out saying I didn't hear anything. I didn't have my glasses, but there was a quick rush of nurses and the strong feel-ing of something wrong. Alarms went off, beeping and chirping; doctors rushed out and into the room. I heard the nurse say, "It's a girl!" It was not a celebratory feeling, though, with the blanket of stress and worry overcoming the room. There were sounds of monitors with an alarming alert call; I was confused and no one had the time to explain things to me. The priority was my baby, and I didn't understand the severity of the situation. I would lift my oxygen mask and try to see where the nurses were going. Could I just see her? My baby was quiet, blue as I was told. I had no idea why at this moment of giving birth I could not hold her. Like in all the movies—the embrace and close shot of mom and baby, end scene. Not in this reality. I was cared for because of my fever and afterbirth procedures. I could not see her. No one was talking to me. I weakly asked, "Where is she? Why can't I hear her?" I just lay there help-less and crying. She was not breathing when she came out. Gabe told me they were with our baby. A nurse finally came in and said she was doing great. "She's a fighter." "A fighter?" I thought, "What happened?" After a short time, I heard a faint cry. I collapsed in the labor bed and sobbed.

Later, I understood she was so big and had so little room inside of me that she inhaled her first stool that's supposed to happen outside of the womb. They called it neonatal aspiration of meconium. She couldn't breathe. This condition, MAS, is one of the leading causes of death for babies during delivery. The meconium also infected my bloodstream and sent me into a dangerous fever (we have joked since, that "if she was going down, she had to take me down, too.") I got a quick look at her and managed to say that Natasha was her name. I had been trying to figure out between two names and when I finally got to see her, she was my Natasha. They rolled her out. I was given much attention after getting cleaned up and rolled into a long room divided by curtains. Not too long after, I got to see my baby. She was lying in an oxygen-filled tube. A full set of beautiful black curly-cues, caramel colored skin, tiny nails and long sized arms and legs; her body was still curled as in the womb and reluctantly stretched. Her light-colored eyes would slightly open and shut quicker. A faint and quick cry as her welcome into the world was a bit rough. I knew she was going to be a fighter and she wanted to be here. I accepted this challenge and we have been a pack since.

While checking on Natasha, I walked in and noticed a man standing there, glancing at his son and Natasha. She was beside a baby boy, born around the same time. His head went side to side. The man looked back at me, smiled, and said, "Woo, she is going to be tall!" I laughed quietly. The boy was measured at sixteen inches and Natasha at twenty-one inches. After I got released from the hospital, it seemed like it was only a few hours after giving birth. I couldn't rest and have a long-extended stay. As soon as Natasha could be weaned off the oxygen bubble, they sent us home. Long labor and quick recovery. Military-minded staff, it was a "push and squeeze" situation. It was time for me to be released, MAS be damned. Get back to work. Get on with it. My Tasha, she was mine, though. She was a fighter. She started thriving.

We were a family, the three of us. Along with some flowers, the car ride home was exciting. The hospital staff helped with the car seat after we failed to connect it the right way. I sat in the back of our two-door car with the car seat positioned between the two front seats. It was a tight fit. I just held my hand out for Natasha. She would distinctly grab and squeeze. I never babysat as a teen nor ever held a baby, but it was like a punch in the gut. I knew exactly what to do. The funniest moment was the first diaper I put on her. I got everything ready, laid the blanket down, got wipes and a diaper. I took the tape off both sides and opened the diaper and she let the cutest fart out. I couldn't contain myself and laughed for almost ten minutes until I cried. I have no clue why it got me so bad, maybe it was just unexpected—something so small like that, making a toot. Natasha laughs when I tell her of the infamous First Fart. I was in tune with her hungriness, even before she woke up, and I knew exactly what to do, even though my own daughter was the first baby I had ever held. In the past, I was so scared to drop a baby that I wouldn't hold one. But with Natasha, it was instinct. Since her birth, it has always been us. This mom, despite her own beginnings, is in absolute love with and is proud of her daughter—from what would become her profound sense of confidence, athletic capability, her charming senses, her easy-going mentality and approach to life. Gabe was attentive. He loved to lay Natasha on his forearm and have her lay on his chest while she napped. He made me feel special while proudly looking at us. That feeling would not last very long, but I do remember it being a happy time. It was a good beginning for the three of us.

CHAPTER 24

resilience

How can a person have, achieve, attain resilience?
Is it nature vs nurture?
Childhood trauma, events from your youth?
Struggles, learned behavior, survival mode?
The answer is not clear to me
There are many stories, books, movies on streaming services
There are annoying quotes on posters,
nicely framed and in your face
"Hang in there" or "whatever doesn't kill you makes you stronger"
The most cringe worthy of them all
After being abused and beaten
I don't ever think back at the poster
And thank the spirits that my ex-husband didn't kill me
Just his fists can make me stronger
Not my ideal form of motivation
Or when I was the fortunate convoy who missed being shot at
While a civilian contractor's family gets a tragic death call
Resilience is an odd word to me

My interpretation is…I have to, I must
Others have called me passionate, independent, feisty
Well, yes. That's me. I have been literally kicked, harassed and emotion-
ally torn down
So if I get a bit feisty it is to warn you
To stay back at a distance from me
Passionate, who doesn't get this way
I have been independent since my childhood
I figured out how to stay quiet, not be in the way
Always be on my best behavior
Just in case my undiagnosed bipolar mother
had me shipped back to my birthplace
Never wanted, called a bastard up to my thirties
My resilience was almost broken at seven
When I held a pair of scissors to my tiny wrist
I'm here to tell you that I lived through this experience
struggled 'till now
My interpretation…I have to, I must.

the one time I should have used my voice

From meeting at the welcome center to marrying and becoming pregnant within six months, the range of emotions from love to horror was like a carpet being rolled out as we walked down this aisle of our journey. Sadly, most of this horror story unraveled during my pregnancy. My marriage's foundation was unfortunately built around me being able to tread lightly over drunken emotions. It has been over 20 years since that marriage. My experience has damaged my thoughts of true bliss and now triggers pain. Gabe was my knight in shining armor. I loved him. He made me laugh and being with him was the last time I felt comfortable being myself. At this point in my life, I still struggle with the idea of the healthy characteristics of a partner. Obviously, trust is what a huge factor. All these distorted concepts are written throughout.

The very charm I fell in love with vanished as soon as I put on that ring. It was time for Jekyll and Hyde to shine. Gabe turned into an abusive monster who stopped hitting me only if he blood got on his hands. A bruise was nothing to his rage. I loved him, did everything I could to not make him get angry. I thought ahead and wanted to make his home life peaceful, but it was never enough. Once the liquor was poured, it was another battle.

There were endless events while I drove, especially—he would get mad, push, punch, slap me in the face, stomach, or legs, try to aggressively pull the car keys out of the ignition while we drove. Yelling at me. I had to continue to drive, crying and hoping it would stop. His temper would turn on and off in an instant. Disappointment took him to extreme places. If he got into trouble for his uniform or boots not being up to code, then he came home to teach me a lesson. I could never win this battle. The constant shoving and pushing around left me in a panic for my then unborn daughter. I would curl into a fetal position and try my best to move my belly away from the abuse. The poor baby must have had an emotional journey developing in a womb that was in distress. He kicked me and yelled at me. I had a busy schedule with my own unit and being a soldier. I began to enjoy the time apart from Gabe and feel safer not being in the same area as my beloved husband. Being with a small group of friends, I could simply laugh and smile again. My home life was not brought up. These female soldiers would talk about their marriages. None seemed to be experiencing what I was going through. I felt alone, confused.

When I drove to pick up Gabe every day, I would make a point to be overly empathetic and just listen to any of his problems. Not to dig too much but always sympathize. It was exhausting. I grew up in a fake household and found myself thrown right back into one. Most times, if he started to get on the path of rage, he would light a cigarette, knowing I was pregnant, and knowing that I hated him smoking around me. He would brush by me, shoulder check me, sit down in the middle of the couch, smacking his lips while glancing at me with disgust. He would put the cigarette to his mouth and light it up, blowing the smoke in my direction. Sundays during football season were the worst. I had heard of fans but not a super-fanatic, diehard lover of football. I would be in another room watching our 19-inch TV/VCR combo in the bedroom while he sat in the family room enjoying the large TV. I could hear him screaming and shouting. If his team lost, I would endure his anger of the loss and he would teach me how much he hurt physically—that, or he would lock himself in the bedroom for hours. I would sit quietly hoping he passed out from all the beer; it was the only time I could have any sort of peace. The crack of the bedroom door would make my heart pound. What personality of Gabe was coming toward me? To say the least, when I start to hear the trumpets of the football season anthem, even today, it brings up too many bad memories.

True crime genres of serial killers and sociopaths' stories are a pastime for people now, with the shows on streaming services and discussions on podcasts. Most of those close to these unfortunate people have a glimpse of what they will become during their childhood, with some abusing animals before turning their rage or desire for control onto people. Gabe, in turn, had certainly dimmed my spirit; even our cats weren't immune from his wrath. I was told only after the fact of marriage and being pregnant about Gabe's childhood. He unfortunately had a horrific accident at an early age, which left him in the hospital with brain swelling. The frontal lobe was altered, and at this most crucial age of development. The frontal lobe does, in fact, control emotions; his mother told me he was never the same again. Once a happy, thriving boy turned into a man of violent rampages. His switch to turn off high amounts of anger were altered. His brother told me that he would throw hamsters against the walls, just as a young boy should throw a baseball with his dad. Gabe showed no emotion to these hamsters. Stories of Gabe locking his brother in bathrooms, being aggressive with no switch. Gabe did not graduate high school and got a GED later from not being able to control his emotions and having erratic behavior. He would get into trouble with the law once, as I know it, by assaulting a police officer in his teens. His family feared him. My Gabe from the welcome center did not show an ounce of this side. I did not meet his mother until I was very pregnant, and she unleashed his past in private. His family knew Gabe too well and was always scared of his violent actions. I didn't have to share what he did to me with his mom; she already knew I was the victim of his wrath. His mom visited us once while I was pregnant for a very short stay. She and Gabe got into a huge argument, and he switched into a violent rage. He screamed at her and threatened her, his yelling in her face all too familiar. She left upset and crying. I only saw her one more time after I gave birth to Natasha, when we drove back to his hometown to meet his dad.

When we got married, we adopted two cats. They were my companions in the stress- filled environment of home. I loved coming home to their cuddles and leg swipes of their tails. But, just as I did, they felt the environment getting unstable when Gabe would start to yell. They would scatter in our apartment when his rage was present. On occasion, he would search for a cat, smirk in my direction while I'd cry "noooo" in a panic, then pick it up by its neck, let it dangle, and throw it against the shower wall. Not even the lightest touch of humanity or care. Just like those hamsters, his rage couldn't care less about these cats. They both would come to me if I was alone, when they would be able to scamper around the apartment. I noticed when Gabe came home, they stayed behind our large TV entertainment stand or behind the couch. Not trying to be a victim in Gabe's state of darkness. He once took one of the cats after an argument, grabbed its neck, and hung it over the third story balcony threatening to drop it. He screamed at me on the balcony that if I ever left him, he would kill the cats. He shook it a few times, while I was crying and begging him to stop. I told him I love him and would never leave him. He told me I loved them more than him. In the future, when I mentioned I wanted a divorce, his rage was so intense. On that occasion, he grabbed my 201 file (military records) and held his lighter to it and sinisterly yelled he would "burn it so I couldn't leave." All this happened while I was becoming a first-time mom. I was pregnant, hormones taking over, susceptible to stress, tired. My husband making me breakfast in bed, making me comfortable, foot massages, holding my belly. Living a Hallmark movie I was NOT!

So many incidences of abuse. It was a period of my life that I felt so alone, scared, and did not know where to turn. I remember our first Christmas together as a married couple was creeping up fast. I wanted to have a happy holiday and I saved up and got a couple of presents. One was a small box of three sports balls for our baby. We got into an argument about something insignificant but disastrous for Gabe and he went on another lovely alcohol infused binge. This ended with him yelling loudly, walking back and forth angrily, waving his arms. He scanned the Christmas tree and ripped open the few presents; I told him I didn't spend too much money on them. Our money from the military was spent on Gabe and Gabe only. Groceries were limited, bills were piling up. But alcohol was the priority. Once a month we could afford to go out to a restaurant, and we could splurge. What a small treat. I had multiple credit cards open in my name. We had a military Star card that we could use on gas and the shopping center. We would walk through the gas station on post and load up on snacks, putting it all on the credit card. Gabe had no credit and could not get any credit cards or anything in his name. I had gotten a car before we married; I paid for that, too. I explained that the present was for us. This was the only time he felt bad in our short-lived marriage.

After most of the abuse he would see blood and tell me he would never do that again, that he loved me—so, I stayed, believing him at his word. I could be the punching bag, him kicking me, pushing, hitting and all of a sudden he would stop and lightly touch the blood from my lip, his whole demeanor changed. I would still be frozen and in shock as Gabe would help me up, smile, and with his charm hold me. Show me the love I didn't know but deserved. He told me he loved me, and he was sorry. He just couldn't help it. He was going to change. But it would not be true. The cycle would continue. There wasn't any support in my life at that time. I hid the fact that I was completely scared of my newlywed husband.

Living off post was not any better. During our marriage there were too many parties with his infantry buddies whose lives were also a drunken mess. One friend, his drinking buddy, would be there to keep the party going. These nights of long, hard drinking and sharing stories. One party that didn't end so great; I was extremely tired, heavily pregnant. It was early in the morning, and I wanted to leave. Gabe got mad and started to be belligerent. Slurring his speech, throwing the beer can side to side, spilling it. There was no chance of having a civil conversation at this point of no return. I left the house; Gabe started to chase me. I started the car, and he jumped on the roof of the car. He was yelling at me; the other wives present were unfazed. This kind of scene is unfortunately too typical with military couples. Stress, money issues, all an emotional whirlwind defining the military lives of many. His buddies got him off the hood and calmed him down. Unfortunately, after a short time and another beer, they figured it would be ideal for him to just go home with me. That night was like any other drunken night. Loud screaming voices, violent aftermath.

This best friend, Johnny, was not someone who Gabe needed to hang out with. One night Johnny, after a drunken party, punched a glass door downtown, breaking his arm. He tried to commit suicide by taking pills and getting drunk. He drove at max speed down the wrong way on Main Street hitting a woman driving her car. She was in critical care, but survived. He left on a short leave to go home and came back with a wife. She, dealing with her own mental health struggles, wanted a divorce within six months. The emotions in their arguments were not handled appropriately. The immaturity of not understanding how to properly communicate turned into rageful arguments. Our stories were all intertwined. It was a fucking mess.

I lived in an absolute hell. After each violent collision with his fists and kicks, I would always be so afraid for my baby; I would hold my belly and make sure there was a kick or movement. If not, I would start to spiral emotionally. I would go and get a snack and wait for the sugar (glucose) in the bloodstream and...ok, there's a kick.

When I was close to my due date, there was a night that would change me forever. This night after yet another violent rage, he pushed me into a wall, kicked me in my side, and hit my mouth for whatever he got mad at me for that time. I remember wiping a finger along my mouth and noticing blood; I vowed it would be the last time I went through this. I finally had the courage to do something to protect myself. During this loud encounter, I tried to grab the landline to call the cops. He ripped the phone line out of the wall. I finally got to the door and wobbled down three floors to a courtyard. I called 911 on a pay phone. Gabe was immediately at my side; he stood with concerned eyes while switching right back into charm mode. I was on the phone crying and shaking with a dispatcher, who asked me where I was and what had happened. All the while Gabe was saying, "It's cold outside. Here, let me give you my jacket." Finally, an ambulance and two male cops showed up. I was put into the ambulance and checked for injuries. They photographed my face, hands, and side. They walked us both back up to our apartment. They wanted us to retrace our steps in the apartment separately. After this, one cop told me, "If I take your husband, he will get kicked out of the Army. He can't hold a weapon with a domestic violence charge." He stressed the consequences that would happen to my husband, not caring about what actually happened to me. What he was referring to was the Lautenberg Amendment, which makes it a felony for anyone convicted of a misdemeanor crime of domestic violence, such as an assault or attempted assault on a family member to ship, transport, possess, or receive firearms or ammunition.

At the very time, I was thinking about getting out of the Army, and Gabe had just recently re-enlisted. We had orders for Virginia. It was a predicament for this cop and Gabe's future. They were most likely former soldiers understanding Gabe's future if he were taken to jail. I then felt bad, took back my statement, and regretfully took the blame. I admitted to being the aggressor and I was arrested that night. They took me to jail.

I remember that night being unreal as we all walked back to the parking lot, and they asked me to turn around and then handcuffed me. The patrol car door was opened, and I was guided into the back seat. I could not speak a word and was in a bit of doubt and shock. The door closed and there was Gabe with his hand on the window, promising to get me out. Thanks Gabe, how kind of you. My knight in armor. The car ride was quiet and passing vehicles only glanced at my sad face in the back of a patrol car. After arriving, the processing time took 'till early morning. I was held with the population that got arrested that night. It seemed some were very comfortable in the holding cell, just stretching out, making a pillow with their jackets, or covering their faces while taking a snooze. Veterans of the facility. Others were pissed off and yelling at every correctional officer to "kiss their ass", "suck" whatever body part they thought of first, "fucking pigs." I was wide awake and didn't want to make friends but kept to myself and stayed away from the hostile ladies. Walking in my clothes at first, then getting issued jail attire; fingerprints, photographed, back to the holding area. This took hours. New ladies coming in looking like they got plucked from a working corner, mad, tired, the veterans who knew where to go when called. Finally, I was escorted back through dingy white concrete brick walls in the hallway where my final stop of the early morning was to be. At this point, I was so delirious and tired I was put in a bay of cots in a cold jail cell. I was placed in the middle of a large room surrounded by a second story of inmates in their rooms.

I was devastated— worried about the stress on my baby, being pregnant and in fucking jail for being abused. There were only a couple of hours of sleep to be had before the population of females would emerge. I couldn't see anything but the cots, emergency lights scattered around and not enough to get a full view. I could not get comfortable. My belly was so big, and my due date was so close. I was scared, senses were alert, and I just tossed around. Rolling side-to-side trying to get comfortable. That next morning, I was able to see clearly what was around me—the fluorescent lights crackled as they were turned on. Cold, industrial concrete with a light mint green faded stripe around the room. The second-floor cells were close together and seemed very tiny. Two staircases were at each end of the row of the cells, one full wall had a solid glass of protection for the correctional officers staring at our every movement. Cells opened and the other female inmates just scattered downstairs. Sounds of laughter and noise filled the circle room. I was all alone, sitting quietly on my cot.

Still in disbelief of what my decision was and where I was. For how long? Was Gabe doing anything? Only until I got a small pack of commissaries—paper, pencils, erasers, chips— was there any interest in my current situation. Suddenly, I was surrounded by a group of three females. They scanned me up and down, one at a time. A female asked, "Do you want that? You gonna use that? You won't need that." I was so delirious and hungry I gave up my pencils and paper without any thought. But those chips were kept close and covered by my hands. In my thoughts of delirium and doing what I thought was the best to keep peace in my new environment, I saw them as vultures descending. They needed it more than me. I didn't want to be there long enough to post a letter and receive one back.

Being an active-duty soldier who gets in this situation, my incarceration was printed out for my entire command to see. Everyone knew. Gabe had his chief/NCOIC bail me out. I was discharged after a day. The jail rushed the paperwork due to my pregnancy and not wanting any liability for me having a baby there. I was released and, once again, Gabe promised he would never do it again. What did I do? I went back to him. I was so tired from that experience. His chief supported Gabe as they walked to pick me up from the holding area. I didn't say much but Gabe sure did put on a kind show. He opened the car door for me. Got me comfortable and told me he loved me. I just wanted to go home and sleep. This was embarrassing for me. I had no idea what Gabe told his chief. Did he lie and say I was the aggressor, or did he tell the truth? Gabe should have been arrested. His chief looked sad for me. He was there for us constantly. He was our mediator. He never showed sides but was stern that we had a baby coming and needed to stop the arguing. Gabe got to go to his apartment when the arguments and the abuse of the night ended for more alcohol. So, there we were, driving back to our apartment, promises made. But the consequences were inevitable.

Chapter 26

stupid fern

Out of the blue, about five years ago, my daughters and I were walking around in a touristy spot and I stood in shock as I recognized an over 6'4" lanky guy. Holy moly—it was the chief! This was decades later, and he still looked the same.

My mouth dropped open. I approached him and asked, "Were you ever stationed at Fort Carson?"

He looked at me, a bit taken back, answering, "Yes, I was." I told him, "You may not remember me, but I was married to one of your former soldiers, Gabe, and this is our baby. Well, she's an adult now…" I said as I pointed to Natasha.

He stepped back a few steps, in disbelief. "Oh my god, yes! I remember! What a time that was." He mentioned it looked like we had been doing well and he was happy he got to see us again. We talked back and forth for a few minutes. I was still in shock to see him there. We said our goodbyes. What a nice yet emotional moment, seeing him.

After the arrest incident, as part of the judicial process, I was court-ordered to complete domestic violence group counseling. It was a misdemeanor charge for me. I walked into a small group of women; there was a licensed therapist there to oversee our curriculum. These women claimed to be the offenders with great pride. Their stories of why they were there were like any TV series showcasing the pissed off, deranged, cheated on—*Snapped*! "Yea, I stabbed that motherfucker," and, "He deserved what he got."

I sat in this group without having the need to hang out with my fellow classmates after class. I just needed to get through these mandated sessions. The result of this unfair fiasco was the police department ended up dropping all charges and later having my record expunged of the charge. They finally went through the evidence, statements from friends, witnesses of past abuse. Those two pieces of shit cops only protected Gabe, a fellow male. They knew what they were doing. In retrospect, they did not want his military career to end, and it didn't matter what he did to me.

So, as some time went by, the nightmare continued; we kept arguing. He would threaten me that if I left him, he'd call the cops and say I was the aggressor. After all, it had worked before. He kept my being formerly charged over my head as a deterrent. I was on probation at that time and could not be involved in another incident. I panicked that if I was again put in jail, I would be in there for quite some time and have my baby in jail. Gabe said he didn't "give a shit if that happened." History does repeat itself. As our marriage went on, one argument got bad, and he used the leverage he had to call the cops, telling me to "rot in jail."

He was going to tell them I hit him, he said. Make up a story. I told him I was done, and I was leaving. He started to push me around and knock me into the furniture. He laughed and said I had nowhere to go. It was the truth, but I had to leave. He wanted me to give birth in jail. I started to walk out of the apartment, and he dialed 911 and started to tell the operator that his wife...I didn't hear the rest; I slammed the door and did not stop wobbling out of the building and to my car. I was so scared, so desperate, and I drove to a nearby hotel. It was late at night. I had no money. I was visibly shaken and crying. I walked up slowly to the hotel desk and with tears filling my eyes, I tried to explain that I didn't have money. The hotel employee felt bad and told me to go and stay in a room. I told him I would pay him back when I got the money. He saw my belly, the pajamas, and my watery eyes and knew this was a special case. I was so grateful for his kindness. Since Gabe did call the cops, I had a warrant out for my arrest.

Which led me to the fretted call. After five years of not speaking with my adoptive parents, I called them. I explained everything. Everything. They decided to fly out to Colorado. They paid for the hotel room, and I stayed with them. They called attorneys. The attorney's office who communicated with the local police department let us know that in fact there was a warrant. I had to turn myself in, but just to do paperwork and be released. They knew of the past abuse. A day or two later, I had a police escort with my parents to my apartment to get the crib and baby items. I was due to be induced a couple of days later. The cops knocked on the door; Gabe answered and was yelling, asking, "Why isn't she in jail?!" He was smoking and the rage in his eyes was very present. He started to come closer. The cops saw the intensity of his anger; they told him to walk into the parking lot. The officers looked at me and told me I had five minutes to grab anything I could. We quickly grabbed clothes and all the baby items we could in the five allotted minutes. Gabe was so upset, but I left that evil place. Not forever, though. I will be a statistic living under the wrath of a domestic violence cycle.

I gave birth a day or two later. Being 22, I was lost. No adoring husband waiting for the both of us at home. Sixteen hours of labor. A fever, oxygen. What an experience. But I called Gabe to be there while I was at the hospital, against any better judgement, and my adoptive parents asked if that was the best decision. I wished I could slap me. Why did this abuser have so much pull on me? I was terrified of him, and I loved him—all intertwined. He was the father and I needed him, I thought. Our baby needed a father. I asked his LT (lieutenant) to be there just in case. So, they came. Gabe was present. I held his hand while I was in labor. Looking back, I should have asked. What are you doing? Why are you here? Kitchi be strong, you can do this journey on your own. These horrors will only continue.

My understanding of the cycle of domestic violence came decades too late—a common, ugly truth for the abused. Tension building, incident, reconciliation. Calm. A cycle which I lived and survived. I finally got it. This power and control wheel in the domestic abuse realm are tactics that the abusive partner will use to overwhelm the abused and keep their relationship together, by all means necessary. Some examples of the diagrammed wheel are: intimidation, physical violence, exclusion. Power is at the forefront of domestic abuse. Those who have been the victim will unfortunately have symptoms of low self-esteem, anxiety, depression and or not be able to trust people. It is a hard road to travel. I have struggled emotionally for decades with my own experience. I fell right into those categories. I wish I had been educated earlier in this. Maybe a class, some sort of support from the Army. At the time, I was too far deep into the chaos and was just focused on survival. However, the knowledge could have come to me, I wish it had been earlier.

Cycles are defined as, "a series of events that are regularly repeated in the same order." Or, "certain events or phenomena that repeat themselves in the same order and at the same intervals." Repeating, coming back. It has been my theme of life. I felt like a paddle ball in my childhood, cast out, then smack-dab right back to the "family." Nobody seemed to care about me. I was a nuisance. I kept running in my teens from any conflict or the feeling of being in the way. Then I cycled out to the world, and it brought me around to more temporary fixes, but always back to where I started. I'm still not quite sure how someone should love me as I deserve to be loved. I prepare myself for this person to control me, abuse me, and cement another layer that I am not worth it. I'm trying to get out of the cycles of my past. It isn't easy. I try to remind myself that I am worth it and that being happy is attainable.

With Gabe, the abuse did not stop. I was not strong enough to leave on my own and as a new mom, I thought Gabe was the only option. Try to be a family, I thought. Just a few weeks after having Natasha, the three of us made a PCS (Permanent Change of Station) to Virginia. We had to stay at the post's hotel since we were on the waiting list for housing. It was a long room, with two queen beds, a closet, bathroom, small fridge, a desk, chair, and TV. The furniture had not been updated for many years. I slept with Natasha in one bed and Gabe in the other. We had only the clothes that we could pack for the plane. Gabe went through the in-process steps at the new post. I was allowed to switch over to the Army Reserves at this point to still fulfill my enlistment, but to do so on a part-time basis. My career plans were changed for Gabe who wanted me to be home more. He didn't want Natasha to be left at daycare, so as my life unfolded in this marriage, I had no choice but to obey. Alleviating any further arguments, I did as he said.

Just a few days before another incident, I was so desperate to save our marriage that I called a psychic to ask what I could do. I scanned the local phone book and found her. This has to be legit, I thought. She listened to my concerns as I explained the struggles and the stress Gabe was in. I was so desperate to save this failing marriage. She mentioned changing the environment in the hotel room, recommending that I rearrange the furniture. She told me to buy plants, that it could give an uplifting out-look. Maybe with the stress Gabe was feeling, this could help, I thought, buying in. I proudly set down the fern on the desk and hoped it would give off positive affirmations, happy bohemian vibes, intergalactic heal-ing, while warding off evil spirits. Nope. Not at all. Never. A sociopath is a sociopath is a sociopath. Sadly, the houseplant did not change a thing. Stupid fern.

He had new company paperwork and updates on our home goods that were in transit. Our cats were in quarantine and stuck for an extra 30 days waiting for vaccines. The paddle ball was in effect and the game went on. It did not take long before Gabe once again started raging and was stressed out about the living situation; it didn't take much when alcohol was involved. There was an incident of abuse at the hotel when Gabe wouldn't let me leave the room after we began to argue. I tried to leave through the door, and he moved in, pushing me back. I paced with Natasha in my arms yelling and he moved away for just an instant. I made a rush to the window, opened it, and took off—escaping. I ran holding Natasha, crying, and made it to the lobby; the employees called the MPs (Military Police). Luckily, the curtain was pinched after he shut the window, showing evidence to the MPs that I did in fact escape through the window. Gabe told them I was previously arrested for domestic violence. He wanted me arrested. He demanded it. I had the courage this time to defend myself and tell them the entire story. The MPs escorted me back to the hotel room. Gabe was told to stay in the lobby with another officer. The MPs had someone from Gabe's unit come to pick him up. The MPs asked if I needed anything, and then they left.

We got assigned a home finally after a few weeks. It was two homes, split into four duplexes. We had the second story, a two-bedroom unit. This move was also disheartening due to my cats, my buddies who had been put in quarantine from our move, being left. The quarantine animal department would call to extend my cats' stay. They had to charge all the fees for medical care and boarding. Gabe found out how much it cost and refused to pick them up so he didn't have to pay. I had to leave them in quarantine and most likely, they were put up for adoption. It may have been for the best. Those poor cats were put through a lot of abuse.

This would be my final place with Gabe. I flew back to California on a few different occasions. I made the decision to take Natasha out of potential child abuse, thinking he would turn on her because of me, like he did the cats. I needed to leave. Natasha and I would fly back to California and stay with my adoptive parents. I left, multiple times, but didn't have the confidence I needed to make it by myself. I loved Gabe, and he showed me by his actions he could not love me back the way I deserved. Yet, I kept coming back. I had nowhere to go. It was debilitating and embarrassing to live with my parents again. Gabe would call. He would sound so charming, his voice imitating safety and making promises of never doing any of it again. How he loved me, needed me, all that shit. I went back. I WENT BACK. A cycle. Unless you have experienced the cycle of abuse, it's definitely hard to understand it. Natasha was only months old. I didn't want the abuse to eventually transfer to her. I needed to shield her somehow.

Inevitably, another argument arose, this one because he spent his pay on alcohol. He came home with six packs of beer. Started to drink them. We argued. He got livid and loud and started pacing in front of me. At this point, I knew he was beyond rage. He would give me a look of disgust and the stare would resemble a serial killer thinking of how to dismember his victim. He called his dad, complaining about the world and slurring words. He was yelling at him, "I'm tired of her, I can't do this!" The conversation did not seem to be going his way. He yelled back at his dad and hung up. He started to push me and get in my face. I grabbed Natasha and ran to another house. We were clothed for a summer day, and it was late fall in Virginia. I ran down the stairs of the duplex in the night. Natasha should have been in bed, sleeping the deep sleep of a child, but she had been born into an unstable household. I couldn't change that fact. All the houses looked exactly the same, so I wandered around trying to figure out which home was familiar. I gripped Natasha tightly and scanned all around me. I was petrified that Gabe would grab us. My adrenaline was kicking in, my eyes were filled with tears. It seemed I was the only one on earth walking along this cold path in the night. I remembered a couple we had met earlier; I just wanted to be safe and be near someone familiar. I'm unsure how I found the house, but it was a few blocks away. I knocked on the door and waited with a watchful eye, looking behind me. The wife opened the door, saw me crying, and let me in. I told her what had happened, and she told me not to leave. She walked me back to a vacant bedroom and told me I could stay the night. I had only met her through Gabe's company. I didn't feel safe still and was hesitant. I just wanted to run and get as far away as I could. It wasn't fifteen minutes before I knew I would not be able to settle down. I paced the room. Natasha was completely unfazed and was sleeping on the bed.

Then, like a scene in a thriller movie, there was a brief silence, then it was broken by the sudden ring of the phone. The wife handed it to me, saying, "It's Gabe." She looked concerned and fully involved, motioned for me to not accept the call. I reluctantly answered as he told me he was sorry and that he loved me. I was young, lost, vulnerable. I left the safety of that house. I told Gabe where I was. He drove up, with the music blaring, looking like someone possessed. Natasha and I got into the car. He said nothing. He turned the music up, started to light a cigarette, and a blank look covered his face. I knew at that instant it was not going to be a fairytale reconciliation. As soon as we got back to our place, the abuse started again. He was livid, ran around the unit in an uncontrollably dangerous manner. I tried to put Natasha back into her crib. He pushed me into the wall. I quickly got out of the room, still holding Natasha. We exchanged words and I said I wanted to leave. I tried to grab the phone; he ripped it out of the wall. I ran to the outside patio and screamed for help. I saw two males in the dark run up to the fence line. I was so desperate to get out. I asked them to catch Natasha. I was so desperate and scared I wanted to throw Natasha into their safe arms. I held her up and I screamed to help me. "Catch her! I'm scared! I need to get out of here!" They had no idea what was happening, and I did not have a lot of time. I heard Gabe in the background making a lot of back noise and objects being thrown. They ended up running away. I yelled for them to come back. I managed to go back into Natasha's room. I tried to place her in her crib. She was sleeping on and off, getting startled by the noise of yelling. I was yelling for him to leave me alone. As I placed Natasha down, Gabe ran into the room and pushed me into the wall, hitting my chin. I had my arms up to shield the force and he collided into my body. I was so scared. I wanted to get out of the house. But Gabe stood at the door. The glow of the MPs vehicle lights lit up our family room and the footsteps confirmed they were headed to our front door. I'm pretty sure those two guys who stood at the fence called them. My neighbors who always heard arguments stayed away from us at all costs. They would avoid eye contact with us and never introduced themselves. Gabe walked back and forth while the MPs positioned themselves with each of us. He started to pick at and scratch his nose, managing to scratch a small cut so that his nose dripped blood. He immediately told the MPs to arrest me since I had abused him. He yelled, "Look what she did to me!" Again, just like the night I was arrested, we were separated. Gabe was taken downstairs for his statement. I was completely overwhelmed, crying, holding Natasha in my arms. Natasha could sleep through anything. The poor girl had no clue what an environment she was born into. The MP officer told me to put her back inside the crib. I was hesitant not knowing if Gabe had convinced the MPs to arrest me, so I held Natasha as an anchor and felt safe with her in my arms. Nervously, I placed her in her crib, not knowing if I was going to be handcuffed and not able to see her again. As she fell asleep safely in her room, I explained to them what happened. Gabe was picked up by his sergeant and taken away. I was left to sit and reflect in the mess of all these incidences of abuse. I finally managed to sleep in the early hours of the morning.

Gabe was ordered not to come back. He had to be in the barracks. I finally made the decision that I would not be a full-time punching bag and I filed for divorce. I cut the string from that paddle; I needed to leave before Natasha was a victim. Not my baby. Natasha gave me the strength I needed to get out of the cycle. If I couldn't do it for myself, I needed to do it for her. At this time, I had no incoming money. I hadn't shown up to my Army unit because I had way too much going on in the short time since we moved to Virginia. Wavering on being put on an AWOL list, suffering those consequences also. I needed to leave. I had no choice but to involve Gabe's command and try and get resources since I was left with no means. They got involved only after I called crying, pleading that I could not afford any food, diapers. I needed help. This first sergeant listened, and I thought he would be able to help, but he just hung the phone up on me. He did not care about me and wanted to protect his violent and abusive soldier. I called the authorities from the military to deal with complaints. This department got involved. That first sergeant was ultimately relieved of his duties. The new first sergeant called me, introduced himself, and made a point to listen to me; I was able to ask for help. He was empathetic or scared to be relieved of his duty, too, but either way he made Gabe's sergeant come to the house and give me some money for living expenses. I was a complete mess to see Gabe again. He paced around the house; his sergeant managed to sit and not engage. I told them both I had no money. Gabe got mad and threw a $20 bill on the couch, grabbing it back when they both left.

Back to where I started from. No money. I had to open multiple credit cards to pay for everything. During this emotional period, I was asked to hold supervised visits for our daughter. I had called an attorney's office and they insisted on me not being confrontational and allowing the visits. I reluctantly agreed due to his abusive behavior. Gabe would have her in the barracks during the visit. When his sergeant drove her back, she was only months old. Her infant car seat would reek of second-hand smoke. Her clothes, her diaper bag. This father spent a couple of hours smoking around her and not caring about her health. These visits were the most painful times away from her. I couldn't wait until the visit ended and I could hold my baby again.

During the court process, I feared more abuse if Gabe just came back to the house. I finally got a restraining order that went into effect immediately. The fine print stated the order was for me and not for Natasha. I could leave Virginia but not with Natasha. The next step to be able to leave was a divorce. Since I could not afford a phone in case of an emergency or restraining order violation, I was given an emergency cell phone which only called 911. It was through a low income, family help crisis group. I met with the attorney a few times and she consoled me when I needed it, reminding me, sadly, that she had dealt with these matters more than a dozen times. The divorce decree was over forty pages filled with the abusive events I had recounted to my attorney. It was served after multiple attempts by a sheriff, which itself cost hundreds of dollars.

Finally, after all those months, it was the morning of the court hearing. I was so nervous and was placed in an area for restraining orders. Gabe was out in the hallway waiting for our case and appeared drunk or extremely hungover, sleeping heavily on the benches. My lawyer told me she had to wake him up to explain the process of the hearing and what to expect. With no hesitation, he signed his parental rights over. I'm not sure why it was so easy to sign over his rights. He could have felt grief and thought it was best to walk away. He could have just given up, felt at a loss. I was granted full custody of Natasha and we were finally able to leave Virginia.

There would be two court cases later on, initiated by Gabe on his behalf to decrease the already unpaid child support. At present, it totals over $55,000 balance. Since he lives out of state, he cannot be found, no valid address. The two involved state child support departments do not talk, do not take any legal action, and do not apologize for their system that fails way too many. He lives life being a dead-beat dad. I called a private detective, and his information did not help the matter. He told me that Gabe had listed ten different addresses in a month. The investigator mentioned to me that it is not unfamiliar that a party will make it hard to locate to pay any child support. That he is "all too familiar" with these circumstances. He also mentioned that these cases seem to be endless with no good results, but when this party, Gabe, tries to collect social security in his later years, the owed child support will be collected and dispersed. OK? So, in another twenty-five or thirty years. Great? That did not help when I was struggling as a single mom in the earlier years with Natasha. Gabe also had a warrant for his arrest, but no further information. Out of state cases are impossible to enforce if the other party cannot be located or doesn't have a valid address. I called my case manager for any updates over the decades, still no information.

Our divorce was finalized. I was living in California at my adoptive parents' house. I had a storage unit with all my home goods and no car. The car had to be left in Virginia; I could not afford the car payments and tried to sell it. Gabe saw my car for sale on the community board.

He had a friend call me and ask what I was selling it for. I responded, and heard Gabe laugh in the background while his friend repeated the asking price out loud. They hung up the phone. My "Car For Sale" posters were conveniently ripped down. I relinquished my car at a dealership.

Within seven months of moving back to California and trying to fulfill my Army enlistment at a local Reserve Center, I received my deployment orders. After that year-long deployment, I surprisingly got a call from Gabe's new baby momma. It was two years after our divorce, and it took me by surprise. We had a short conversation. I thought I had closed that chapter of my life. Left it, locked it up. She wanted to know if my marriage experience with him was similar to hers. She timidly asked me if Gabe would beat me during our marriage. I said, "Yes." We went back and forth comparing our traumatic events of domestic abuse. She and I had matching stories. Identical, unfortunately. She got pregnant. She said, "I didn't even want it." I could never say that about my Natasha, but different feelings for different people, I guess. She mentioned money issues, but this time it was a bit different. He would get mad at her and take her welfare checks and cash them. It was always about Gabe. Evil doesn't care. The phone conversation ended, and I never heard from her again. At the time, she told me she was no longer with him. But was she like me? I went back repeatedly. I know her son is just a few years younger than Natasha. In the future I will talk to Natasha about him. I didn't want to hide this fact, saying it could lead her to think that he stayed for him and not for her. It's a double-edged sword. What an unfortunate story we have.

It has been over twenty years since that marriage. The very thought of being in another relationship scares every cell in my being. I have not since had any sort of long-term relationship; a few months in, and if I sense any sort of red flag, any sticking point, I freeze and leave. Make an excuse or fight just to make it easier to get mad and leave. My experience in my first marriage damaged any belief in true love and triggered pain to never let myself go back into a possible bad situation. I feel I can't let myself be vulnerable or weak or I will succumb to more abuse and control. I want to feel safe. I would love to have a "Rip Wheeler" in my life, right out of *Yellowstone*. My ride-or-die, that guy that no matter the craziness around, would be there no matter what with only absolute love in his eyes.

I have no idea what a healthy partner should look like. Trust is lost forever. All these distorted concepts written throughout, the domestic violence cycle, and how my life became those statistics. I haven't discussed the details for more than a decade until now; I realize I am strong, and this will not be my end.

Chapter 27

"how do you tell a little girl?"

<u>How do you tell a little girl?</u>
How do you tell a little girl her father will never be there?
No father daughter dances, no daddy activities
An innocent little girl thinking she is no good
So sad is she to know that there will be no dad
Please don't be mad or upset
You are not in the way or a problem
You are so loved and cherished
There is only one to blame

But definitely not this little babe
It will be hard for you to hear why he had to leave
The truth will be a bit of a sting and may hurt too much
It will take some explaining of her father's dramatic past

This little girl didn't deserve a hurtful life
I had to make the choice to go
I didn't want his fist to come towards you
I am doing my best to shield you

In the future she will long to hear the truth with questions and concerns
Of why it's just a family of two, in the early years
It's best to shield these horrific times
This innocent girl can't know those times
A past too sad to remember the terrible times

A short snapshot of her dad is a lot to take in
Pregnant and in the womb
Stress has gotten the best of him
Kicking and hitting the unborn
A new dad doesn't want this title
Tried to get rid of *his* problem

So desperate his family left
Slurring his words from his demise
He was gone to no longer hurt us
How do you tell a little girl her father will never be there?

Will she want to know this man?
This brutal rageful man? And to call him Dad?
Who apparently does not care
Decades will pass with no communication
No calls on her birthday and Santa lists unknown
How can I tell her that this is the best for her?

She is not to blame but to be celebrated and praised
She is this beautiful strong little girl who is safe
No one to hurt her or live in fear
A new life with mommy and no traumatic woes
I will make sure to tell her it will be ok and all will be well

CHAPTER 28

fucked-up things

When my divorce was finalized, and Natasha and I left Virginia, I was very lost mentally and emotionally. I had a young baby to make my priority and the divorce left me homeless with no income. Can this shit called life get any better? I thought that a lot. The background life with my adoptive parents would wreak havoc once again on my psyche. Twenty-two, divorced, a single mom. One chapter ended and the new chapter began again in California with more winding roads and obstacles to overcome.

Once I gained my footing in California, I enrolled in an Army Reserve unit. I had to complete my last enlistment year obligation, and I had managed to get active-duty orders to establish some stability and pay. My in process was smooth. I was a Supply SPC in charge of the entire unit's supply room. This room ended up being my OCD nightmare. It had aisles of wall to wall, floor to ceiling, giant metal drawers, tiny barcodes, mixed matched bolts and nuts in random areas. My job was to reorganize. Each tiny drawer had hundreds of trinkets and bolts; washers, screws, and I had to make sure each had the correct size and matched the inventory list to the inventory number. I ultimately made a master supply list. This took weeks to do. So, I was busy to say the least. My initiation was typical. I was the FNG, fucking new guy. Just a few days before I was assigned to a platoon, they had a field training exercise. They used supplies and I had to recheck in, make sure things were washed, dry and organized. I was also asked to go to the secured armor room. a musty brick room, no windows, to separate the brass and ammo. An inglorious, time-consuming job. I started to open the ammo cans and soon noticed my eyes and nose were running. Damn it! The platoon activated CS gas and the remaining particles were caught in the sealed ammo cans. I scooped up the brass and all the movement picked up the particles—I had my very own gas chamber. This was the start to a not-so-great journey. I was always busy at this unit, but needed the work for the money and good attendance for the Reserve Unit. Fulfilling my enlistment. I had less than a year.

But my life couldn't just be smooth sailing. It had to get complicated. I don't welcome surprises and hardships are not wanted, but things do happen to pop up. I had been in the mindset of working hard, trying to better my daughter's life. My focus did not wander until one soldier, Danny, seemed to take an interest in me. He started to notice me, glancing at and following me around. Eventually, he walked up to me and casually asked questions. It was only a month after my divorce, and I was getting used to my new single mom life, never to be in the Gabe's grips again. It was after some time that hormones were sparking and I felt flattered. Was it a need to feel wanted? I have no clue. It would be another one of my classic mistakes. Danny turned out just like my first marriage—not a good match. He asked me out for a run. Then lunch. Then it moved to making plans to hang out all the time. If only I had consulted a magic eight ball and it had told me: outlook not so good.

Danny said all the right things. Making comments to take care of me and saying that no one should have ever treated me like Gabe had. I had told him what I went through because I thought opening up and being vulnerable was the right thing to do since Danny seemed to take an interest in my life. He was another charmer who swept me off my feet. I had his full attention at the beginning, and we spent almost every day together. I enjoyed this time, and if Danny drank, he did not become a monster like Gabe. This was a different feeling of being relaxed and not walking on eggshells. Danny was comfortable around Natasha which made our relationship easier. He did not seem to ignore her or shun her from activities. Time passed, and my adoptive parents started to voice their opinions, loudly, about my dating. They were very upset that I was seeing someone, and they mentioned this daily. The arguments sent me back to when I was a child—in fact, the arguing drove me closer to this guy. I firmly believe that if they had just let the sparks fly, they would have fizzled. My lovely, adoptive mom wanted to let me know that I was "trashy to drag Natasha around" while I was off dating. That I should "close my legs before there are two kids." I was barraged with comments. I felt trapped and knew it was only a matter of time before I needed to leave this house, and Danny's promises seemed like heaven.

After a grossly short amount of time, I ended up moving into Danny's house. I couldn't take any more stress from my adoptive parents, so I ran. Danny lived with his mom and two brothers. With me and Natasha added in, it was a packed house. His mom was not excited about me moving in and she, in turn, hated my guts. She would call me "flaca", or skinny. Not in an endearing way, but with disgust. Luckily, his brothers were very welcoming and loved to show Natasha the backyard with her toddler car and watch movies while eating snacks. This woman, however, still hates me to this very day. I stand at 5'10" and she is a full foot below me at 4'10" —she was threatened by the fact that I literally stood out and stood above her. Her pride and joy had brought home a tall, flaca woman with a young baby. If I walked into the kitchen, there would be groans of disgust. It was her domain, and I was invading her life. Danny was a momma's boy to the extreme. He never took my side. Danny started to look at me like I was the one with the problem, like what could possibly be wrong with his wonderful mom. As time passed, I felt trapped. With the relationship's honeymoon phase over, Danny started to become possessive and would often yell at me for wearing shorts above the knee, v-neck shirts, or open-toed shoes. I would get scolded for not eating his mother's menudo. I grew up with the bland palate of a potatoes and corned beef upbringing. I just wasn't used to many cultural foods. If I talked with any male— to Danny—well, I had to be sleeping with them. He got mad at me for trying to start college at the local university. He constantly picked and poked at me, lowering my already low self-esteem. But he had promised to take care of me.

At the time, I ended up getting a job at a grocery store during their strike. A scab, and proud of it. I needed a paycheck. Not liked by employees outside. The stares I got were a bit intimidating and the job I took for a temporary position; employees would look at me with disgust. I had to walk with shoulders high. I had prior experience working in a deli, so the store manager hired me as a deli manager. I loved this job and trained others in the world of sandwiches, fried food, salads, cleanliness and the notorious meat slicer. One employee that came to work with me could not grasp the fact to turn off the slicer immediately when not looking, using, or walking away. She was trained by the company and had hours of training, but still could not remember some vital rules. This was a huge safety concern.

My first introduction to the meat slicer had been back in the 90's with a deli trainer with eight and a half digits. He would show his hands and remind everyone to pay attention (later I asked what happened and he told me to keep it a secret, but he lost his fingers in a motorcycle accident, and it always scares new hires). Touché trainer, good one. I would find out just how important his rules were. I had received an order from a customer, and I grabbed her selected meat and placed it on the slicer. This customer told me she wanted it thinly sliced. So, I proceeded. Within a few strokes of the slicer, she yelled at me.

"Hey, excuse me, I asked it to be SHAVED."

I got startled, and turned my head, and the slicer cut me superficially, but enough to have a collective gasp.

I grabbed my finger and said with a cringy smile, "I will be right back."

I ran back to the sink and disinfected the cut and wrapped it up and stopped the bleeding. So, when the time came for me to train other employees in the deli department, my emphasis was the meat slicer. Unfortunately, that one employee who I kept telling to never leave eye contact with the slicer, never look away while the slicer is running, never quite caught on and I would consistently remind her. AHHH. Well, she ended up moving to a different store. Then I heard she chopped off one of her fingers! Gone. Shit. How many times can you tell a person how dangerous and important it is to turn off the slicer? It's unfortunate.

While working as a scab, I was making $23 per hour. This rate was definitely a help, being a single mom and all. At the same time, Danny was struggling at a local business, making minimum wage as a laborer. This did not sit well in Danny's eyes. His dominating machismo mindset did not appreciate a girlfriend making over twice what he was. He often told me I wasn't worth that pay, and he was not sure how I got that position, that I did not deserve a management position.

Another blow to our relationship was the fact we both got accepted to the Army's Primary Leadership Development Course. It should have brought us closer, but in fact it was a foreshadowing event. I only had a few months left in my enlistment, but to be promoted would be a great accomplishment. To end my enlistment as a sergeant. I had all the requirements and decided to accept this chance. There was a small group of us, and we flew to Ft. McCoy, WI. We were all happy to do this. We got bussed in from the airport to the post and were all ready to take this challenge.

Once we were all quickly rushed out of the bus we had to snap into training mode. After quickly in processing, we were led to our barracks and assigned bunks to drop off our gear and change over to PTs. There was no chance of seeing the grounds. This was not a vacation. We were hauled off to a huge field under a tent. It was wintertime and the temperature was crisp and soon the rain turned into snow. Hundreds of soldiers from all around the United States made multiple lines with our backs to the front. Shielding the testing soldier from view. Each of us wide-eyed, a bit scared and nervous. Jumping in place, stretching, swaying side by side. It was my turn to go through the PT test. Two minutes of sit-ups, check. Two minutes of push-ups? Easy! The adrenaline rush was intense; I was a bit shaky, but knew that I had to get this done. I passed. Then I noticed Danny doing his push-ups a few lines over. The cadre kept calling out the same number...3...3...3...3... Oh shit, I thought. He's not doing his push-ups correctly. He repeated his attempts, but they were not accepted, and it got worse when muscle failure happened. Danny did not pass the push-ups. They told him to get up and go see a few cadres in the back. He barely looked at me. Danny was sent home the first few hours of being there, along with two others who failed the PT test. I had to do this course by myself. I thought we could be each other's support system. I pondered the thought of leaving with Danny. I thought I needed him to be there and I was afraid that he may be mad at me for staying. There was a cadre who told me to stay, and that Danny would be at home cheering me on. I did stay and thrived in this environment. The course was long; the comradery of my class was strong. We supported and lifted each other's spirits during our training.

My class was just the motivating factor I needed to push myself. In a short amount of time, there were funny nicknames in the barracks and sarcasm flying around. Training days involved getting dropped off in the forest for land navigation. We went through a gas chamber— not fun— there was classroom instruction, twenty-four hours on duty followed by a field exercise to test our ability to stay awake and stay alive. I loved every damn moment! This was my calling. The group I arrived with flew home early, and I was the only soldier who ended up completing the course.

On the day of our final PT test, it snowed. We had on our full winter PT uniforms (beanie, jacket, t-shirt, gloves, shorts, pants) and right as we were instructed the two-mile run would start, we stripped down to summer PTs (shorts and t-shirt). The snow fell on all of us. I have never had a faster two-mile run! Snow was caught in our hair and eyebrows, snot was frozen dripping from our noses, and our skin was so cold! But I made it. I passed this course. We got a class picture and said our goodbyes, which was sad; all our new battle buddies signed the back of the picture. We wished each other the best of luck and were sent in groups back to the airport and flown home.

When I arrived home, I was excited to be promoted to sergeant. Unfortunately, there was one female—a future nemesis—who had not qualified for the same course and who I did not know liked Danny. She hated me for coming into the unit and acted like I stole her man! While dropping off our promotion packets to the battalion office, she slipped hers and Danny's in. Mine had some "missing" papers. Funny thing is, we all did our paperwork on a step-by-step process before we left for the course to make sure it was correct, and all paperwork was in order. Mine was sabotaged. Not knowing this, I was so excited to come back to the unit, assuming I was going to be promoted to sergeant. When I arrived home Danny was so enraged with jealousy, he practically stomped his feet and told me not to go to drill. He told me that taking off work was irresponsible. Shut your mouth with that bullshit! I left happily and went to the unit. I did not want to be controlled anymore. We arrived in separate cars, and I shunned his existence.

I had to painfully wait 'till the last thirty minutes 'till dismissal. I was amped the entire day and waited to hear there would be a formation. The first sergeant stood in front. Made a little speech about some of the soldiers' journeys. He was proud of those that went to the leadership course. He made a point to recall that those who did not pass would have another chance in the future. I just wanted to hear "Specialist Feenix, front and center!" He then called out...wtf?... Danny's name, along with the conniving female's name to get promoted. Holy shit! I was beyond livid. Out of the entire group in the unit, I was the one and only soldier who passed the leadership development course to become a sergeant. Yet, Danny and this girl got promoted. To make things even worse, Danny was so pumped, later he had the nerve to brag about it. He had failed, point blank, but he was sent home to be promoted? As soon as I heard, "Dismissed!" I was a raging bull and booked it over to this female. I screamed at her. We were both pushed into the LT's office.

He had no idea why I was so mad. I lunged at her, and the 1SG had to catch me. The LT's eyes were wide open. Our unit at this time was getting orders for Iraq and one by one, our Social Security numbers and names were given, and orders were for us to deploy. I did get orders soon and needed the deployment money, as a sergeant, for my daughter. And I passed the course; it had all but been erased. As I was pulled back from this female, I yelled, "You better make sure I don't see you during deployment! You better have an updated will for your daughter 'cuz it's going to be friendly fire!"

At the time, I was not messing around. I was kicked out of the office. My name and number came up in the following days for deployment. Karma does in fact work and I am a complete believer. As deployment months grew and grew, I was, in fact, separated from that unit and ran into some familiar soldiers who deployed with that newly promoted sergeant. They told me she got demoted to specialist for drunk driving. I never saw her again.

A week after the unit's deployment orders came, another great decision of mine. I thought, what does one do in a war time situation? You get married. Ugh. Danny and I were married at a county recorder's office. Natasha was running around the room as our witness. The room was cold, undecorated, a couple of chairs and a small table. The recorder was not of any religious affiliation. Just like my first marriage, the "wedding" felt institutional and lacked good vibes—a bad aura. What could go wrong? Everything. Everything can go wrong. And it did.

bon voyage

M y last night before deployment was one I will never forget. This incident only cemented how I had always believed I was perceived in my adoptive parents' eyes. I invited them to a popular chain restaurant. I did not get through the dinner, though. I sat with my daughter, who was in a highchair at the end of the booth. I was looking at my parents. I pulled out my updated will, ID cards, and power of attorney papers and I told them it all was for them. I explained the next steps. I gave them phone numbers of doctors, everything that they may need for Natasha's care during my deployment. They seemed nonchalant about the whole deal. Cold and indifferent. I explained my orders were up to eighteen months, we were all getting moved to an out of state post to train, and this was in addition to the eighteen months. Before I could get anything more out, my adoptive "mom" looked me straight in the eyes and said, icily, "I don't care if you get shot in the face—you signed up!" I'm giving you my child. I will be gone for a year and a half at least, and this is what you want to tell me? It wasn't a typical bon voyage. I didn't spend it laughing with friends and sharing loving hugs with them telling me, "I'm proud of you." I couldn't believe that this was our goodbye. So, I did the only thing I could do—I yelled at them, pushing my paperwork toward them. I stood up, gave my daughter a kiss. Then I left. The hardest thing was to just leave. I glanced back at Natasha sitting in the highchair, clueless about the situation. I wish it could have been a happy family dinner, but that last kiss is the only thing I had to push myself through another year-and-a-half.

Danny and I had orders for separate units. At the time, this was sad. I wanted to be with my husband then. But as fate and all the gods knew, this was going to be for the best. He, in turn, made the first month of training in Texas horrific. He would demand time with me and follow me like a shadow if I was in his presence. It got to be very suffocating and not endearing. I had to spend time with everyone, including males, and this sent Danny into an emotional spiral. I was trying to concentrate on gaining new friendships within a company I did not know and with whom I would soon be solely dependent on with boots on the ground. We were training and needed no distractions. Unfortunately, my past events would not make things easier when they resurfaced. The one time I should have used my voice came back to haunt me. My arrest was not completely expunged at the time. Paperwork must have been delayed or yet to be confirmed and submitted. My new unit got word through my security clearance that I was arrested with a domestic violence misdemeanor. My NCOIC came to me and said I may have to be left behind due to the past arrest. I had to explain everything, which was not something I wanted to do since I had just been assigned to this platoon. I ended up contacting the Colorado Springs Police Department to get the updated file. This took hours, since I was constantly pushed over to one department after another, then to a case worker and a detective. Finally, I had the correct paperwork and had the papers faxed to Texas. Having my specific job in logistics, I needed high security clearance due to transporting highly sensitive items. It was all eventually, thankfully, cleared.

All the while Danny was causing so much extra tension, he found himself in a rage of jealousy. He found ways to find me. I did not like this sort of strange and obsessive behavior. If I was training somewhere...

somehow, he would be there just watching. I couldn't train without the stress of his eyes watching. He was not in my battalion and should have been training in a whole other area, but he found me. He would sneak back and duck in and out visually. It was so overwhelming, embarrassing, and those with whom I discussed the issue were getting weirded out. He was so irritating! I did not want to be around him. When he would call my name to come to him like a dog, I started to avoid him and would scatter when he showed up. I needed to get rid of Danny; he was causing too much stress. I had to ignore him for all the strange things he did.

Time passed and we left the training camp and headed out to start our deployment. When we all landed in Baghdad and set up our camp, it was then I could get a break from Danny. He was gladly with his battalion who was far away from me and could not just show up unexpectedly at any time of the day. I was mentally done with him but legally stuck with him in the marriage. All the while, Danny held the rank of sergeant and flaunted his stripes. My packet was eventually corrected, and the "missing paper" was again submitted. I was promoted a couple months later, being in country. The original date was backed up a few months to account for the missing compensation, which I didn't mind at all. I had so many responsibilities and other things to worry about, and not Danny calling me and harassing me. He would call at all hours demanding to know what I was doing at that moment. Who I was talking to. Expressing that he was upset. I started this whole situation as a wife in the beginning and reassured him that I loved him and wanted him only. It was getting to the point where I just wanted to answer the phone and say, "Fuck off!" One incident that happened while on deployment was when he broke into my email and noticed I ordered underwear from Old Navy. Mind you, females were not in large numbers in Iraq. The PX (Post Exchange) trailers, which were truck trailers that had been turned into mini shops, had one way in and one way out. It had on both sides food, clothing, extra items which were convenient and fast. It rarely carried female personal items, basic items like underwear, and if it had sizes, they were not one-size-fits-all. So, I had to order them online. This particular order was for granny-style panties. I was in a war zone. I wasn't thinking about buying lacy, skimpy panties, high cut, or G-string. But that is what Danny thought I did buy. We had too many phone conversations screaming at each other. I was so pissed that he hacked into my email, looked at my order, and assumed I was starting a brothel. I hit my limit from all the arguments over the months and finally screamed for a divorce. "I'm fucking done! It's over."

He panicked. He was the religious type that thought I would never reject him and expected me to be a devout wife and obey, no matter what. He went into a convulsion of emotions and grew desperate. He demanded a meeting with his battalion's chaplain. Not a good choice for me and my strong feelings that had already turned toward what a huge mistake I had made marrying him in the first place. I got word about the chaplain meeting and there was no way to get out of it. I was so angry. I had to drag a whole convoy and put soldiers in harm's way to journey through Iraq for a meeting that I did not want to attend. Hours of driving through the heat and my insides were getting more and more enraged. I thought of every scenario and how the meeting could possibly go. I imagined a long, painful, devotional speech from the chaplain and my quick possible responses ending in a hurtful conversation. Bless these pour souls because I was about to go animalistic on their asses! I walked into the building and followed the chaplain signs, knocked on the door. Danny was sitting down with this chaplain, looking innocent. I know I made this young chaplain think twice about his job. I dug into both of their souls. I yelled at everyone and told him to kiss my ass. I wasn't religious, I wasn't praying, I was done with this. As I searched for my platoon, I felt lighter and knew that I had made myself very clear. I wanted a divorce and no verse of scripture could save this marriage. I made the way back to camp and I threw my wedding band from the Humvee on the journey back to camp. Done. Unfortunately, some more phone calls came, but I didn't answer. I threatened him that whoever went home first for their R&R (rest and relaxation) would file for divorce. It was him. We were officially divorced a few months later.

When the time came for my rest and relaxation (R&R) I was so excited to see Natasha after close to a year. The journey was long and tiring, the airports were busy, and the surroundings were different and fast-paced. I was a bit on edge to see huge groups of people and walked very fast by them. One stop when I got to go and have a quick bite, I was in my uniform, and a couple paid for my lunch. That was so appreciated! I sat in the airport not having my full gear, with a sweaty, sandy face, flies circling around my food, weapon on my person—it was nice. A small bit of freedom of not being in country. As I started to make my way through the airport, I heard over the intercom that my flight had changed terminals. I freaked and looked at a map and saw it was clear across the other side of the airport and in another building. I started to hustle over to the new terminal and gate. The waiting line to go to separate gates was getting longer. I made it to the last line before getting into the terminal and TSA at its best had flagged me for a security check. I was in full DCUs. I was told to strip down, and I looked at them and asked, "Are you kidding me? Can't you see I'm on your side?" But I still had to strip off my jacket, unbelt, and unlace my boots, which took time. The surrounding travelers were so disgusted at them. I remember a few saying, "You have got to be kidding me! She went to war!" and, "What are you doing? She's in uniform!" All trying to "show some respect." The TSA just shook their heads. One TSA employee waved her wand over me and told me to hurry up and get dressed. Maybe the overwhelming support of everyone helped. So, I was trying to hurry up and get dressed while running and being escorted to my flight. I almost missed it. The pilot was flagged also, and I was on my way home.

Smooth flying back home. I tried to picture how much Natasha had changed since I was not given much information or updates in the form of emails or physical letters. One package was sent to me when I was gone for close to a year-and-a-half, with my favorite bags of chips and handprint art from Natasha. It read: Happy Mother's Day. I still have it and cherished it as it hung on a wooden temporary barrier between the lineup of bunks in the tent. 'Till then, I only had a few moments on the phone and her running around. I started to get nervous to see Natasha. I borrowed a camera for the trip home, ready to capture sweet moments between us so I could have something to look back on. After landing, I walked out to the car and sat in the back with Natasha strapped in her car seat. My adoptive dad drove so we could bond again. Natasha sat with an inquisitive glance while she was busy with her books and mumbling to herself in a playful manner. After a short while, and after I repeated, "I'm your momma, I love you, Tasha," she was silent. No response. Crickets. My heart sank. It was hard to not let her see me crying or be upset; she didn't remember me, and it would take a while. So, I just played with her, and we went through the colors in her book. "What color is this, Tash?" I asked her. Natasha replied very happily and confidently, "Geen," very excited at her knowledge. I couldn't correct this young prodigy. It was only one letter. I just smiled. "What color is this?" I continued. She said, even more excitedly, "Wellow." Ok, too cute to even handle. Over the next week of my visit, it was very surreal to be with Natasha. We spent every minute together and I was so happy to be with her. The hard part was going back to the sandbox after having such a great time. But it would be only another five months before we would be together every day.

CHAPTER 30

round 2

I did not see Danny for a few years after our divorce. I settled into a house where Natasha and I were living our lives. I was trying to find my purpose again and identity after leaving the military. I struggled as a single mom with minimal support, low-income jobs, and a young daughter whose needs grew. I wanted to provide everything she needed. Most times, bills were set aside to afford groceries. I learned to build some confidence that was taken from my past and pushed and shoved myself to try and succeed.

Then out of the blue, Danny reached out to me. I got a text and it seemed important. With the history we had, I felt like I shouldn't. I thought I would be strong enough not to reopen that wound. Danny hoped I was doing well and seemed genuinely interested in my life. He sparked conversation after our being divorced for years already. He made small chat with me just like how we had started our relationship years prior. Chatting, coffee, dinner. During this short amount of time, he told me he still loved me and that he was sorry for how he acted. He would ask to take me out and I accepted. He showed attention and care. Danny explained that we were newly married and that being separated got to be too much. That was it. He wanted to do things right and better. I just swallowed all this up just like Gabe had promised in my first marriage.

Danny again made the commitment to take care of me. He drove Natasha and I around to look at model homes with the promise of buying a new house for us to live in. It was all surreal, but I thought it felt right. He missed me. Danny sure laid it on thick, buttering me up with hope and wishes. I found out later that, not coincidentally, this was the exact time he needed some stellar references for a federal job. At the time, I was unaware of any ulterior motives and was suckered into helping him. I signed this job application form with a statement that he was a great guy, that even in our divorce we had kept a good friendship and was not abusive physically or emotionally. All written from a template he had given to me. Danny had made these attempts to get me on his good side, including the promises of a future together, and a house to build a better future for our family. It was all a lie. I was naive and had been put on a pedestal so fast my fall ended up being swift and hard, leaving me feeling used. In his field, a glowing reference from an ex-wife would make a great impression on his application process. Again, just like Gabe, I thought I was doing the right thing for him by helping his career.

The promises were kept alive for just a bit longer. My birthday came around and Danny took me out. It was at a casual dining restaurant and we both got drunk. I was still in the mindset of us trying to make things work as friends and maybe one day more; since he was pushing for us, it could be more. We left the restaurant with Danny driving; I was too drunk. I was a bit out of it, and I stumbled into the house. I think we kissed. I had a staircase a few steps away from the front door and I tried to make it up to my room to sleep the drunkenness off. Danny's hands were all over me at this point and I told him to please leave, but he had different plans. He kept touching me as I tried to make it up the stairs. I could not stand by this time and sat on the steps and repeated that he needed to leave. He was adamant. "Bye! Leave now!" I shouted. But he pushed me further onto the stairs. He tried to kiss me and said, "Just wait," grabbing my clothing and starting to pull off my shorts. I told him,

"No, no!" I was so drunk and had no strength to push. He didn't listen. He took off my shorts. I pushed and pushed. He pulled down his pants and pushed himself into me. I had to stay there until he stopped. He held me close and would not let me move. I felt frozen to remember the other times men would push themselves onto me and use me. I said "no" repeatedly. After he was done, I yelled painfully at him to leave. I gathered myself and locked the door as soon as he left.

That event consummated the existence of my sweet, innocent, angelic daughter. She is my heart. The situation was not ideal. We talked for just a couple more weeks after I found out I was pregnant. No plans were made for the better future. No knight to show me what castle we could live in. No further attention given. Silence. I did make an unfortunate call to Planned Parenthood asking to make an abortion appointment. I could barely form the word and was crying uncontrollably. There was an appointment made and I my heart dropped as I felt an overwhelming amount of sadness and anger. I immediately called the office back and cancelled it. I felt so ashamed and hurt as an adopted child myself. What if my mom did that to me? I would never have had the chance to bring Natasha and now a new baby into the world. It wasn't a hard decision to cancel the appointment, but I completely understand the overwhelming effect of that decision on anyone. It is different for everyone. Circumstances. Your story, your choice. I made the best decision for me and grew this baby inside of me with a thousand percent love. I do not love her less, nor take the situation out on her. Mina was meant to be in my life. I cherish her and would do anything for her. To the moon and back.

For the on-again, off-again final two weeks of our countdown to not communicating, Danny's controlling ways and tantrums were amped. He started to be busy, and I was there accepting his apologies. The friendship was very strained. My babies were my only priority. Not the broken promises of Danny. I was surprised one day that Danny called to come over to my place. But this night would be the breaking point. He came to my house. I was sitting on the couch with a large sliding door next to me connecting the backyard. He said he was hungry and went into the kitchen. He clicked on the gas stove and paced around the kitchen. I was watching TV, so I didn't stalk every move. I did pay attention to the pacing and looking around; I just heard noises and saw with my peripheral vision, slightly. Next, he immediately said he was going to leave just for a bit. He walked over to the sliding door and shut it, announcing, "I will be right back. Bye." After a couple minutes, I thought about what had just happened and my senses screamed. What the fuck was that about? I immediately got up, opened my sliding door, and walked into the kitchen, seeing that the gas stove was on. I called his phone and told him if he was done with the stove to turn it off. He said "OK" and within minutes he came back.

Did he purposely leave the gas stove on? Why did he shut the only open door as he left? My gut said something was off. I did not trust Danny any longer. Before this incident we were chatting and talking about shows we liked. Danny mentioned, "I have been watching A Thousand Ways to Die." I responded with, "Ok?" storing this information in my subconscious.

Danny's life was going to change forever with a baby. With the wine and dine for a shining work reference to becoming a dad, Danny must have felt desperate and possibly thought about a way to fix his problem. Danny was living with his brothers at the time. I rented a house with Natasha. After I found out I was pregnant, I was not ready to just move in while it started to become distant with Danny. That same night after the stove incident, he wanted to stay over. We were in bed, watching TV. I asked him to get me water. He reluctantly went downstairs to the kitchen. This journey took an extra-long time. I heard so many noises from downstairs— cabinets clanging and shutting. I was a bit confused about what was happening. The hairs on the back of my neck crawled. He finally came up. He pushed the glass towards my face and told me to, "Drink it. Drink it all. Come on." In a normal setting, someone would just hand over the glass or leave it near the other person, but he persisted and demanded I drink it all quickly. I looked at him. I took the glass and slowly pushed it to my lips. "Sip. Here," he urged, pushing the glass with his hand to make sure I drank it all. One thing about the kitchen cabinets was that above the stove cabinet was where I put all my prescriptions with a variety of medicine: Nyquil, Dayquil, child medication, Benadryl, etc. I put all my medicine, pills, there. It was a perfect place since it was too high for my daughter to reach. There was no reason that it took a godawful amount of time, and the cabinets were being opened and slammed. I had a water jug in the corner of the kitchen, and he was already holding the water glass. I did not like this feeling. So, I took the glass and threw the water at him. I told him I was done with him. He left angrily. I walked him downstairs and locked the door. He texted me to, "Take care," and I didn't hear from him until I emailed him a few months after the birth of his baby.

The duration of my pregnancy was so peaceful, the exact opposite of Natasha's. I didn't have to worry about being hit or curling up to protect my growing belly against angry blows. My oldest daughter remembers this pregnancy. She often reminds me of funny stories including when I tried to exercise during the pregnancy using an exercise DVD. I would get so out of breath so fast, I had to sit down quickly. I was a very athletic person who had high endurance and loved to work out, but during the last tri-semester it was a struggle to even get up from the couch without it being an ordeal. I had happily gained another seventy-five pounds, just like with Natasha. Food was my friend. Food cravings were a bit different this time. I had four months of morning sickness with Natasha, and with Mina I had zero days. I craved bread and chicken with Mina. Natasha had been a great beneficiary to my cravings. We frequented the local wings shop. My favorite was a three-piece strip meal with two breadsticks and a side of veggies. Extra bread sticks were added. We went to that shop an embarrassing number of times and with my growing belly, I had to shift the table away from myself to fit in the booths. Natasha remembers the table being pushed into her tightly, but she didn't mind since she got the reward of the meal. Natasha was such a big helper; when I couldn't put my shoes on or lift certain items, she helped. It was such a happy pregnancy. I received monthly ultrasounds and saw Mina start to take shape and develop. This time I was in a civilian medical office, and I was told the sex of my baby as soon as they could tell, unlike the Army. It was a different experience during checkups and exams. If I had any concerns, my doctor was there to reassure me and take the information seriously. I did schedule a C-section this time. I was traumatized still from Natasha's birth experience, and I wanted this time to be quick and safe. During the final weeks before the due date, I started to do the natural nesting. I bought a crib, a swing, a breast pump, clothes, and got the nursery ready. I laid the new teddy bears strategically around the room. I was so excited to see my baby, ready to hold her in my arms.

I went into labor late at night and started having contractions. It was only hours from my original C-section date; I waited until the contractions were five minutes apart as I was told. This went on into the early hours of the next morning. I was exhausted at this point. I called the hospital and told them my contractions were five minutes apart and I was on the way to the hospital. Natasha and I got a ride to the hospital from a neighbor. The procedure seemed really quick—I was completely numb and there was a medical-grade sheet to block my view from the lower half of my body. I could only move my arms and head. After I heard Mina cry, and the doctor telling me, "Here she is!", Mina was lifted into my view. I was relieved and so tired at that point. The hospital had called my adoptive parents, since they were my emergency contacts, and they were waiting with Natasha in the waiting room. Natasha was the first person to hold her sister. I cherish that picture of the girls. It would be just the three of us, on our new journey as a family. I was excited for the future and new memories we would have. Mina was such a beautiful baby with a full head of straight black hair. Her skin was a light touch of caramel, and she had big brown eyes.

I stayed at the hospital for the full five days. I got to have Mina right next to me in a hospital crib on wheels. We slept side by side. I would just stare at her and hold her tiny little fingers as she gripped my finger tightly. Her long legs would be curled then straight as she got used to more room, not being in my belly. My recovery from the C-section was intense at first. I could not sit up very comfortably or walk around for the first few days. When I was escorted from my bed to the bathroom it was an ordeal—I couldn't stand straight up and was bent over slightly at the waist from the stitches. At this time, my adoptive parents kept Natasha while I was recovering in the maternity area. I got a call from them telling me that Natasha had a cold and that they didn't want to take her to the hospital and get me sick. I'm still not sure if that was the case. There were two beds in the room I was in. There were two other moms that rotated through. Their families brought flowers, celebrated the birth. It was a joyous occasion. The hospital noticed the lack of family support and they sent in a social worker to talk to me. They raised the question of no visitors, asked about any depression symptoms, and asked if I needed help. I told them I was so happy, that I had a strained relationship with family. But I'm fine. They gave me a spa kit with a robe and lotion. I later found out from a nurse it was a gift given to "special cases."

After coming home, I started the painful recovery from my C-section. I had just had major abdominal surgery and was expected to manage it, would have to heal, all on my own. I couldn't walk up my stairs without wincing in pain. Both of my pregnancies were very different. There were challenges with each. I had no choice but to ask my adoptive mom to come to my house to help. I couldn't walk easily and couldn't go up the stairs unassisted. I slept downstairs with Mina. But the help came swiftly, with negative recourse. At this point I could not bear to be in my adoptive mom's presence for more than five minutes. All my childhood trauma would rise up and the hate ensued. We both really tried to bring our relationship close for a few days with pressured subtle niceness. I was concentrating on healing, Natasha's needs, and Mina. But that period was short-lived, and stress kept escalating. The fake smiles disappeared, and the trauma resurfaced. She commented on me bringing another child into this world. Just as I was told in my childhood about being a bastard and never being wanted. She turned the conversation towards Mina. I was told again I was a horrible person. Just a few days into "helping", and there was an incident of her drinking vodka I had in the pantry and shouting at me—it was the final straw to get her out of the house. Natasha was on her way to school walking away from that horrific fight. She went on and on, slurring her speech, ranting about there being "two more brown bastards in the world." Once she would start to drink, the words of hate poured out of her. No reason for any of this. Screaming at me, walking around the house being disgusted about me. I tried to stay out of her way while she dramatically stomped around the house. She started upstairs in my room while I was downstairs. Mina was upstairs in her crib, sound asleep. The alcohol must have hit her hard and her vengeance was completely uncalled for. I heard her heavy footsteps and her ranting in the upstairs hallway near Mina's room. I walked over to the stairs and looked up. What was this crazy lady talking about now? There she was, slamming the extra storage cabinets in the hallway for no reason. "Your mom was a whore, and you are a whore!" slowly and loudly making her way down the stairs, "Two ugly brown bastards now, disgusting." She told me I "needed to close my legs and get a vibrator." She went on and on about how it was my father's idea to get me. She never wanted me. The same script that she screamed at me since I was a baby. The same disgust. Thirty years, and she still hated me.

She came down the stairs being belligerent and started to slam the kitchen cabinets. I firmly told her to stop slamming shit because Mina was trying to sleep. I called my adoptive dad to come and get her. When he arrived, she was a bit calmer, just grunting and making disapproving sounds. I yelled at him to, "Get her out of here!" He had no idea what he had walked into. Of course, just like my childhood, this woman's actions were ignored. He stood in the doorway while his wife just mumbled and gasped, yelling as though she was a victim and I was the aggressor. She walked out of the house yelling, "I'm done, I can't, I'm done!" It felt like I was back in the '80s. Unwanted. Ignored.

Chapter 31

court appointed vs. reality

A few months later after my recovery, things were getting settled in. I decided to email Danny some pictures and tell him he had a daughter, Mina. I felt I had to out of some sort of obligation. He came to the house a few times, and we discussed his financial obligation for Mina. We agreed on a small amount of child support. I really wanted to keep our co-parenting out of the court system and be mature enough to work together. That did not happen. Danny became controlling again and was dating someone with very high materialistic needs, someone who was unhappy Danny was paying the agreed-upon child support, upset, even, that he had a daughter.

It put a strain on my attempts to keep the peace. I asked him to meet me at a local park for him to visit. I would bring Natasha, and we could kick around a soccer ball while Danny got to spend time with Mina. Mina was only months old; I was breastfeeding at the time and needed to be close to her. This worked out for exactly one time. On the second visit, I drove into the parking lot. I started to glance over to Danny's car and noticed he got out of the passenger side. I got out and called out to him, "Are you the only one here?" Danny responded, "Yes, I just crawled out from the other side." He said this with such confidence. I shook my head, "Well, who is in the car?" Danny responded that his girlfriend was there. We had not agreed to this, and him being only a couple of visits in, pushing a random girlfriend who demanded to see my Mina? Nope. I told him the visit was over and to come without her next time. This incident was just the start to years of painful fighting and custody hearings. It only took one court hearing for the materialistic girlfriend to flee after a child support order was officially ordered and the back child support was enforced.

We both got attorneys and would be on a long path to settle things—the opposite of what I'd wanted for Mina. He wanted me to see Mina every other Monday. Period. That's it. He wanted Mina to be in the care of his mother full-time. I had to read every word of this request, and I was fuming. He served the paperwork on my birthday, just months after the park incident. His attorney had asked what dirt he could dig up from my past, and Danny knew the perfect story. The declaration wrote that Danny feared for Mina's life since I was convicted and arrested on domestic violence charges. I discussed the same incident with him years prior and the violent abuse I went through. Knowing the entire time that I had taken the blame for my first husband, Danny used the information I had shared with him in the past to slap me in the face.

Thankfully, I got to somewhat explain this particular case, and the judge ignored the attempts at undermining me. The judge frowned on these actions and chuckled over how Danny wanted Mina to be immediately taken from me and to live with his mom. The judge asked, "While you work full-time, you want your mom to raise your child? You want to rip your daughter from her mom's arms, who has been her full-time caregiver and who has taken full responsibility for your daughter, and you just recently came into her life?" Eventually I learned that Danny had taken paternity leave from his work during Mina's birth, taking his full salary and leave for Mina being born even though Danny did not see Mina until she was nearly a year old!

Years passed and issues arose. Attorney's fees increased. The situation got hard to handle. Many women would come in and out of Danny's life throughout the years. Some tried to push their way into our custody arrangements and start conversations that would in turn make him angry toward me. The power of persuasion for them was high. I was adhering to the custody schedule. I did not like it, but since Danny took me to court, the schedule was written. The process for Danny was a court-ordered gradual step-up plan to slowly increase his time with Mina. Danny eventually could take Mina for home visits for an hour. This was extremely difficult, and my heart sank; I cried the entire time. The handoff was emotional. I was holding Mina close to me while I walked toward the door and handed over her diaper bag to Danny. I tried to unlatch Mina from me; she tightly held on, and I had to piece-by-piece peel her legs and arms off me and hand her over to Danny. He just stood there not talking or reassuring Mina. This did not help, and only made the situation more traumatic. Mina would cry and scream, "Noooooo!" I could only shut the door as soon as he turned around and heard poor Mina screaming all the way out of the block.

As time went on, the exchanges became a bit easier. Communication was little to none, which worked very well. Unfortunately, Danny could not pull it together and took his frustration out on my dear Mina. She, too, was a victim of his abuse; she would have literal marks on her little body. The court system was well aware of our particular case, all too familiar with our battle over many years. Mina was so young during the first recorded case of abuse that it was extremely difficult to prove. The court mentioned that I would have to take her to a doctor immediately if I saw any marks again and to let them know of the abuse and what happened so that everything could be recorded. A parent's word is not final proof.

Once Mina was old enough to talk, I had to hear about her visits. By this time the custody schedule had been every other weekend. She would be very upset, crying and telling me she did not want to go back. At this point, I could not just say "no" to Danny. Mina relayed to me that she was hungry during her visits, and I would pack a huge snack bag for her to eat when she could. She would get little to no attention. The rotating girlfriends would make fun of Mina if she was crying. Why couldn't Danny stop this behavior? His actions weren't any better. Mina let me know he would scream in her face, and he would push her down. I couldn't say anything without a huge fight. I needed to protect Mina.

The last physical abuse was too traumatic. Mina was at an age where she could call me and let me know what was happening. During one visit, she let me know that Danny had hit her on the head. I was getting ready to come pick her up, so I told her to wait in her room until I got there. I went to the house calmly, as if nothing were happening, and walked back to her room and told her it was Mommy. Mina came out of the room all packed and waiting to get out of there. We walked to my car and Mina let out her feelings. She said her head hurt and Danny hit her. I immediately went to her doctor's office as I'd been instructed and in order to record the abuse. Mina alone told the doctor what had happened. Social workers confirmed there was something going on after they spoke with her. They did not feel comfortable with the situation and were trying to be advocates for Mina. Thankfully, after all these incidents, Mina was finally heard. Danny's visits could only happen supervised. Thankfully, the judge did not decide on just Danny's attorney's words, but on the advice of the mandated social workers. Even those supervised visits were stopped, too, by the appointed supervisor, who noticed the negative effects the visits had on Mina. The stress has since been lifted, but Mina suffered a lot and has had to deal with her own PTSD and anxiety from the abuse she experienced. She is now thriving and is a beautiful, independent, and creative young lady.

Chapter 32

"two sisters"

Two Sisters
Two sisters so in love
One giggles, one laughs
One cries, the other denies
It's never the older one's fault
It's not perfect, but it works

I love to see the two playing together
Chasing each other and loving one another
So warmly and never ceasing
Their energy like a waterfall
Everlasting and continuous

Two are side by side as soon as the day starts
The younger one follows her sis every step of the way
Wanting more love and big sissy's hugs
Boo boos on her knee made better by a kiss
Always ready to play

Two sisters so in love
Every picture that is taken shows the chemistry
A life together in sisterhood
Some tantrums or pouts are only natural
But never long term, it's hard to remember
Who's at fault

A new game is played, no rules are spoken
Whatever it is, their interpretation
Childhood imagination and sisterly love
Princesses or zombies the two can play
Never forgetting their love
Or ignoring the other's wants so unselfishly

Two sisters go hand in hand
Everywhere bringing delight
It is so nice to see a bond so tight
Remember, you two, I won't always be there
Make momma proud of you
Always look back at the memories you shared
Sisters are forever and never forget to love one another
In the future years

CHAPTER 33

moving forward

*L*ooking back at my life's hurdles and obstacles, I'm grateful I'm the one who's typing these words and not one of my daughters who's telling my tale— having the burden of retelling their mom's story or pleading for social or legal changes in a memorial speech. This is not my finale. I'm turning my pages slowly. I wrote in the beginning, "These funny little letters swirling in the universe have brought me into a better place." Those exact letters that swirled have allowed me to unravel these events. I am grateful that after twenty years I can finally speak of these injustices. I am slowly working on gaining confidence and growing comfortable acknowledging that I am not to blame and should not be ashamed. I'm pushing to pay attention to my triumphs. Accepting my past as what it is. Moving past the indoctrination that told me I was worthless, unlovable, and would always be abandoned.

Having the courage to share my story has not been easy. The abuse I received was not my fault, and it still hurts how extremely unfair it all was. This trauma will take a lot of work to not think I deserved it, or think I was a curse; I will need to gain trust back, working to calm my anxiety with self-care. Knowing that I am important. I do matter. I have been there, done that, and got the merch.

If I could go back in time and tell myself, "Oh, I know this all looks like a burning trash can of shit. It's going to be all hurricane category fives. The overwhelming feelings of 'just end it all' are strong and will be ongoing. Do not listen— return your focus to your true motivators. Your girls. Keep the fight going— those fantastic, beautiful souls will give you so many blissful memories and those will keep you going."

Be stubborn, be strong. I am a firm believer that all things happen for a reason. I have my two girls for a reason. They are my heart and soul. I will do anything for them. Their journey into the world could have been a bit more fairy tale-ish but, gratefully, they were both put into my world. I love them dearly. I hope one day their own world will be absolved of the harshness of patriarchy, injustices, and abuses of power. That my girls will be able to live in a society that wholeheartedly loves and accepts them. A society where their own daughters will be accepted as exceptional, not weak-minded.

I have learned that anytime someone asks, "How are you?" and I start to tear up and emotionally breakdown, it's time to gather my words and talk with someone. There is always a way to connect when these feelings emerge. I have learned to put it down on a page, like here, for example. I have become an avid marketer for writing as part of the healing process. I have a few close acquaintances who tell me, "Nah, I'm not a writer, it's no good, I don't have a story." My response is, "Yes, you do. Were you just put on this Earth as an adult? Where did your story begin?" I share, "Get it down, brick by brick; it will eventually lead you down a path."

My conclusion is that I don't have a conclusion. Life is messy and rough. There are no participation awards. I'm still on the ongoing road to recovery. I'm making myself a priority. Life does not ignore pain and wrap the positives in a red bow. But constant treading will eventually give you the endurance to keep moving your arms and legs, keeping your head above water. Survival. I have found my way of treading is to stay close to what I love. I have surrounded myself with the love my daughters give me each day. That is the most important factor I have realized to stay afloat myself. When I have risen from the deepest of despair, they are there to grab my hand and walk with me. To guide me to the light. The moments I share with them are filled with so much love.

To my daughters: you are both loved "equally", and your mom is so proud of all your accomplishments! I brag to everyone whenever I can. Your heads on my shoulders and our shared moments of laughter make my heart continue to grow. You are both in my life for a reason. Our silliness together makes me laugh so much! I love you both to the moon... and back.

Acknowledgments

*O*ver the years I felt so alone. My mind was in chaos. I did not have any tools or skills to help me deal with my past. It was not until I realized how to release emotions in a positive way. Writing. I slowly developed a love of writing. Words started to flow, and I could make it how I wanted. I climbed into that world and made it mine. As I got a bit more confident, I started to work on short essays of my experiences. I gathered all my essays, arranged years of my work. Which eventually turned into *Discarded*. Many thanks to the art of writing.

I would like to give some gratitude to a family; parents L & R and their son, along with caring and perfect match daughter and husband, whose love and support gave me the push to go to the next steps. From the very start they welcomed me into their family. They encouraged me to keep writing. You are all cherished. To R & S and family, whose kindness and support started from day one. A talk of legacy was mentioned; this legacy is your genuine smile, strength, and making those around you feel at ease. It's been a pleasure to get to know you. I appreciate you. To JL and the years of free therapeutic vent sessions with calm and supportive tones that helped me navigate back to keeping my head above water. Thank you for being there at a moment's notice.

Having a drive to continue writing. Releasing the pain. I joined a veteran's writing group. Their support gave me the courage to continue writing. This group was just the motivation I needed. At times, the group invites guest speakers to share about the publishing process, and authors' experience. One guest speaker had knowledge, inside information, and passion. I was fortunate to be a part of a workshop by Susie Schaefer of Finish the Book Publishing. She was the motivation I needed to inspire me to publish my memoir. At the time, I didn't have the confidence to take the next step. Susie reassured me that I am worthy and to tell my story. I appreciated her early recognition of a "yes, you can do this" attitude. She kindly and patiently guided me through the process, and quickly responded to questions. Her gentle guidance is what cleared away any negative roadblocks. Thank you, Susie, for your care and support.

With Susie's help and her having a broad network of professionals in the writing world, I was introduced to a variety of editors. I was instantly connected to one editor; Lisa Shrewsberry, with Fine Lines, LLC. Lisa made a kind note after reading through *Discarded* that committed to preserving my voice. I was reassured that the goal was not to change my style of writing and flow. Lisa was the empathetic shoulder I could lean on. I felt I was given a one-on-one feeling of importance and could rely on a quick response to put my mind at ease. No matter my moments of overwhelm during the process and feelings of anxiety, Lisa helped to relieve any negativity I was feeling. Over the phases of editing, I got to deep dive into her world and felt in control of my style of writing. Faint sarcasm and bluntness were not shut down; but given freedom to express my story, without constraint. I could not have finished my manuscript without the help of Lisa and her kind presence and patience. She was an absolute professional and I owe so much gratitude to her. Thank you!

Moving on from the final edit. I was introduced to a talented proofreader. Madison McMillion, an editor herself, whose keen eye for small details improved structure and formatting issues. Her knowledge of editing was a perfect match to give my work a positive lift and catch any errors. She delicately cared for the manuscript and put her full attention towards the corrections and comments. I greatly appreciate the hard work and the long hours of proofreading. A huge thank you to Madison who brilliantly performed with dedication to help me clearly tell my story. Having one of the first exclusive looks at *Discarded*, being immersed in my world, Madison was gracious enough to write an advance praise review. She beautifully wrote a glowing reflection within this testimonial. With much appreciation to you, Madison.

After the final adjustments were made, *Discarded* was excitedly ready to move on to the next steps. I worked through the process of finding a professional to write a foreword. In the back of my mind, this process needed to be someone who could relate to or was involved in the veteran community; a source expanding on the reality of the struggles with PTSD, MST and other VA qualifications from service-connected injuries. I was guided towards Sydney Shrewsberry MSW, LGSW. Sydney knows first-hand of the devastating effects and had a clear insight into the struggles that this community faces. She breathed in my manuscript and devoted her time to writing a beautifully crafted foreword. Her professional words hit me like a brick after reading her kind words. I couldn't help but to well up and cry happy tears with the validation of my feelings. She understood with great empathy and laid out the challenges in such a straightforward way. She cemented the idea that invisible wounds are also a devastating factor to one's mental well-being and to give empathy, not discriminating against one's pain. My hope is that those who read the foreword have a sense of hope; we can thrive, pushing to tell our story. Respecting the first-hand experience with clear insight by a devoted professional to the veteran community. I can't say enough about how much I appreciate your words, Sydney. In overwhelming recognition to you, I thank you.

Having a close, tight group of trusted female professionals is powering. Each of my next contacts are positive powerhouses. Rosa-La Pastora, a retired Army veteran, came to mind. A business owner, mother, and advocate for female veterans alike is just the tip of the iceberg. We met in a women veterans' group. She instantly was welcoming and had such a happy and positive vibe that being in a new unknown environment made me at ease. She has an infectious smile and laugh that kept the group engaged and we began to bond very quickly. She was very supportive and understanding about different challenges each group member experienced. I knew she would be a perfect fit for an honest response to *Discarded*.

Another outstanding reviewer is a person who has worked in the mental health field. ML, a therapist (BS, CTRS) who has a contagious smile and a heartwarming, happy disposition; who greets and welcomes everyone in her surroundings. I was honored to be a part of her group and learn valuable lessons to help cope with day-to-day stress and know that I had met someone who I could trust. She is just the shoulder to lean on if I had a bad day, she knows exactly when to console those who need it. Her support means so much to me. Thank you.

To my girls.... I cannot say enough about how much I deeply love you both. Each of you has brought your own kind of sugar and spice into my world. Individually your talents have amazed me. Every moment seeing you grow into young ladies has been a beautiful experience and so satisfying. You both are my world. Your laughter gives me so much joy and the sweet moments shared make my heart grow bigger. I love to brag, uncomfortably I have been told...but it's all pure love and I want to yell to the world...I'm so proud. I love you both.

About the Author

*K*itchi Feenix grew up in Northern California; a once spirited self, whose love of team sports and social settings helped provide an outlet for a challenging household. Adopted after being abandoned at birth, then repeatedly reminded of not being wanted from those who should have protected her, Kitchi learned from an early age to shut down, lose her light, and struggle to find a purpose; asking *Why, and who am I?*

After being employed in various jobs in her young adulthood, Kitchi wanted more. She enlisted in the U.S. Army and spent the next six years in logistics, then ending her fulfillment as a Sergeant. She experienced one deployment for Operation Iraqi Freedom (OIF) and the military seemed to take more than advertised; the hidden secrets and avoidance of protecting victims, Kitchi was ultimately in this cycle of abuse. Instead, she chose to leave the military, reluctantly ending her dream of retiring within the ranks.

Yet, this did not break her. Years passed and her joy was wrapped into raising two young daughters, whom she loves resoundingly. Kitchi experienced the meaning of unconditional love through them, and cherishes be able to see them grow into beautiful young ladies. They have been Kitchi's anchor through the challenges and unfortunate circumstances, while Kitchi continued to pave a path towards a better future for herself and the lives of her daughters.

Kitchi is passionate, caring, and a great listener who deeply cares about those close to her. She used her "hard work" ethic and earned her Bachelor's Degree in Science, with a focus on Psychology. While in college, Kitch was introduced to a poetry class and it became a creative process that had never been explored. This opened up a world where she could express the incidents of her past, free of judgement. It was just what Kitchi needed. Writing became a safe, therapeutic way to let out memories and exhale the negative.

A deeply soulful person, Kitchi has learned that the experiences of her life have been the catalyst for her to help others heal their past. She wrote *Discarded* to tell her story, but that's only one part of *the why.*

Her hope is to comfort those in pain by letting them know... *You are special, you are wanted and needed. If you find that niche that can make you smile, stay curious, be interested, and have an emotional release...hold on to that...you are worth it. Let your heart shine in the warmth of healing.*